"Don't Touch Me"

ASTA
PUBLICATIONS

"Don't Touch Me" Copyright © 2012 by Arteria Stevens

Library of Congress Cataloging-in Publication Data
Stevens, Arteria "Don't Touch Me"/ Arteria Stevens

Includes references and index

ISBN: 13: 978-1-934947-71-5
LCCN: 2012916316

First Asta Publications, LLC trade paperback edition

1. Memoir-Non-Fiction. 2. Self-realization-Non-Fiction. 3. Child-Sexual Abuse Non-Fiction I. Title

Editor: Mary Jane Escobar-Collins
Proofreaders: Emily Brishler, Sarah Kasman, and Stephanie Sabeerin

Printed in the United States of America.

"Don't Touch Me"

By Arteria Stevens

ACKNOWLEDGEMENTS

First and foremost, I want to give thanks to God for inspiring me and for giving me the strength and courage to tell my story to the world. My purpose is to take all of the wisdom and knowledge that you have spoken into me and share it with the world. It's only there because you gave it to me God, and I thank you for all of your wisdom. I want to commend every author out there who has opened up their life filled with painful memories to the world, because it takes a lot of courage to face your pain. Pain is a necessary part of the process through life and it's something everyone faces at many different levels, but as long as you don't run away from it, you will get past it every time.

I want to thank my wonderful husband Michael Stevens, who has been my rock and who loves me through my pain. Thank you most of all for loving me unconditionally! Thank you, hubby, for allowing me to open up our lives to the world. I could not have done this without your permission and support. Thank you for working right beside me. I want to thank my twin daughter, Shanta Self, for constantly encouraging me to stick with my goal of writing my memoirs. Thank you for allowing me to be transparent about our lives and thank you for believing that my stories are significant and can have an impact on a world full of hurting people. You are my angel and I love you and I thank the most high for blessing me with you. To my mom, Barbara Tate, thank you for raising me in love and thank you for being a loving mom still, today and showing me love. Thank you for raising me to be a strong woman. To my sister, Tonita Anderson and brother, I love you always. To my son-in-law, Mayes Self, thanks for keeping me laughing. I love you. To my nephews, Jeremiah and Miles, you are the best! I love you always. To my stepdaughter, Amanda, and her two beautiful children, Ariana and Austin, who are a huge part of my heart, I love you. I love you my beautiful Niyana and Maijah. I will never stop loving my HOGHOP family. You know who you are. Our bonds are forever.

Big thanks to the team of people who helped to make everything possible. Thanks to my photographer/videographer, Jene High. You are awesome. Thanks to Assuanta Howard, and Asta Publications for working so diligently with me and for all of your guidance and support and thanks to the editing team at Asta Publications. You all are awesome!

God, it all begins and ends with you, so thank you again, God, for where I have been, where I am now, and where I am going. I know that everything is working for my good and I trust you and I trust all that you have spoken over my life.

TABLE OF CONTENTS

INTRODUCTION

I was just sitting and pondering over my life and it dawned on me: I am the mother, wife, and woman that I am; divergent from the child I was raised to be.

Growing up in the projects in Atlanta, Georgia, I am the child who smiled in the mirror again and again, but never saw the face of beauty staring back at me. Brought up in a black holiness church, I am the child who couldn't comprehend molestation at the age of nine when it happened to me. I am the girl who longed so deeply for my father to just be Daddy all the time and never evolve into the stranger he became at night during my eighth grade school year. That transfigured the way I saw him forever. I am the anguishing child who faced distressing hindrances again and again. I am the child who got married at seventeen bolstering along all my baggage of the past. I am the child who gave birth to a child.

I am the demoralized child who grew up to be the depressed adult. I am the child gravid with low self esteem dragging it along into my adult life. I am the emotionally mutilated adult.

I am the child who can tell it all now because of all the lessons I learned growing up as that child.

As an adult, I needed to understand why things happened to me. I'm forty-two now and finally healing. In the end, everyone will know how I finally stumbled on to my healing roads.

I don't need to pretend I'm perfect. I don't need to be afraid to reveal intimate details of my life. Life is a lesson and there's nothing embarrassing about life's lessons.

CHAPTER ONE

"GRANDADDY"

In 1971, when we moved to Taliaferro Street on the west side of Atlanta, I thought Eagan Homes Projects was a delightful place to live. I was starting pre-school that year. Despite what I am about to reveal, we had an array of blitheful days in our childhood. I spent a lot of time outside playing with friends. I spent just as much time uproaring indoors with my family. I had a brother eleven months older than me, a baby sister, and of course there was Mama and Daddy.

In 1976 we started attending church with Daddy's cousin who was also his best friend. His best friend was now a transformed man having found God. He was no longer drinking and hanging out. As time went on, the more we went to church, the more we began to evolve. Daddy stopped drinking, smoking and hanging out at night. I still hung around my friends when I was home but our beliefs were changing so much.

Before Daddy joined the church, he didn't go around his own daddy because for some reason he was angry with him. He learned to forgive over time, and one day we all went over to visit Granddaddy and my step grandmamma. They were amusing and very affectionate. They overindulged us with goodies and made us laugh all the time. We enjoyed going to their house to see all the chickens and hens they had in their back yard. They let us help feed them. They also had lots of dogs in the backyard as well. Granddaddy had a wooden leg and he walked with a limp. I never knew what happened to his real leg. Granddaddy and Grandmamma always gave us money and goodies whenever we visited them. I was glad Uncle Lynn, who we refer to now as Pastor Nichols, talked Daddy into making amends with his father. Daddy had often referred to his daddy as low down and dirty. I never knew why and as a child, I never asked Daddy questions about Granddaddy. Daddy and Granddaddy were finally behaving like a father and son.

I liked listening to Granddaddy and Grandmamma talk. They were both hilarious. I wondered if this was why Daddy was so comical. Granddaddy was always picking me up and sitting me in his lap, giving me the tightest squeezes and kissing me smack on the lips. Daddy and Mama kissed us on the lips every night at bedtime followed by "I love you" and "Say your Prayers." No wonder Daddy was so affectionate; his whole family was like him, I thought while reflecting back on Granddaddy.

Granddaddy asked for more hugs and kisses than anybody I'd ever seen. I guessed he was making up for lost time with his grandchildren. He was always so elated.

As I sat on Granddaddy's lap he shared funny adventures and spoiled us with Coca Cola and candy. Instead of sitting my brother Scootie in his lap, he gave him tight hugs. Scootie was ten and my little sister Sonia was five.

For the first time, Daddy and Mama left us to spend the day with Granddaddy early one Sunday morning. He cooked us breakfast consisting of lumpy grits, runny eggs, and toast, which I didn't like. Instead, I settled for a glass of Coca Cola in exchange for helping him clean the dishes and fixing Grandmamma's medicine. Grandmamma, who had been sick all week, was too sick to get out of the bed. I took her a tray of soup with crackers. She didn't seem interested in eating anything but she thanked me for being her big girl and taking care of her. She didn't sound anything like the jovial voice I found so intriguing. She seemed frail as she coughed up every word she spoke. I rushed over to her with a glass of water. She took two small sips before passing the glass back to me and collapsing back on the pillow in a feeble state. She didn't answer me anymore when I asked her if she was okay. Granddaddy came in and assured me she'd be fine once she got a couple days of rest. He said Grandmamma had pneumonia, but he assured me that she would be alright. He closed her door tightly so she wouldn't be disturbed before we walked back to the front of the house in the living room.

Scootie and Sonia were sitting on the floor playing with all the toys Granddaddy had surprised us with earlier. Granddaddy pulled out a new coloring book and crayons for me as he sat me on his lap, and helped me color. He kept shifting me on his lap stating that his leg was falling asleep. I compliantly continued to color and allow him to shift me around on his lap.

Granddaddy sat patiently answering all of our questions and entertaining us with funny stories for a couple of hours while holding me on his lap. I was surprised Sonia didn't climb up on his lap. She wouldn't have let me sit on Daddy's lap for long. She made a big fuss about being Daddy's baby. Daddy told me I was his big girl, so I didn't mind letting her be his baby.

Eventually, Sonia tired of all the toys and climbed up on Granddaddy's lap as well. I started climbing down, but Granddaddy announced he could hold both of his grandbabies. Sonia and I laughed, and then Granddaddy asked her to color him a pretty picture like the one I colored so he could hang it up on his wall. Sonia wanted him to help her the way he helped me. I ended up standing innocently between Granddaddy's legs so he could use both of his hands to help Sonia hold the coloring book. I even joined in and helped Sonia with her picture while telling her how pretty it looked.

Once we were finished we asked Granddaddy if we could go feed the chickens in the backyard. Granddaddy said yes. He rarely said no to us about anything. We were running out the door to go around to the backyard. I was the last to head out the door. Granddaddy beckoned me back in the house before I could catch up with my siblings.

We hadn't seen Grandmamma up all day because she was still in bed sick and running a high fever.

"Tweety, you want a green apple?" Granddaddy discreetly whispered in my ear. I nodded yes.

He put his hand up to his mouth to indicate I had to be quiet. "You can't tell Scootie or Sonia because I don't have but one apple," he whispered.

It never occurred to me why he was giving *me* the apple. Maybe he wanted to be nice to me since I helped him fix Grandmamma's medicine and serve her food earlier. I helped him wash the dishes as well.

I figured I could eat the apple real fast before going outside to help Scootie and Sonia feed the chickens. I loved green apples. Granddaddy knew they were one of my favorite foods.

Granddaddy peered out the door. As I was looking towards the kitchen, he locked the screen door. I walked in the kitchen expecting to get my apple. Granddaddy came into the kitchen and sat in a chair. I turned to look at him wondering why he wasn't giving me the apple.

"Where's my apple Granddaddy?" I asked impatiently.

Granddaddy smiled holding out his arms toward me.

"Well, come here and give Granddaddy a hug first!" he said.

Granddaddy must have been about to thank me for helping him today. I smiled proudly walking over to hug him. Granddaddy squeezed me real tight pulling me close. He looked at me smiling.

"Now give yo ole granddaddy a kiss." I smiled as I leaned forward to kiss Granddaddy thinking he must've been real proud of how much I helped him out.

Granddaddy grabbed a tighter hold on me when I leaned forward to kiss him. He had his legs spread. He pulled me between his legs. I didn't panic because I didn't have any inappropriate thoughts about Granddaddy in my nine year old innocent mind.

Granddaddy was kissing me too long. When I started to back away in an attempt to break the kiss, he leaned forward and kept kissing me. He drew me even closer. I felt him pressing me up against his body parts. I felt his tongue trying to force its way into my mouth. My eyes were wide open. I couldn't move my arms. They were pinned to my sides. I started struggling against Granddaddy's mouth.

All at once, Granddaddy was squeezing my backside and sliding my dress up, pressing and gyrating my body against his. I felt as if he was swallowing me up. I felt smothered. He kissed me so hard till I could taste blood on my lips. The more I fought the harder Granddaddy pressed me against him. He held me even tighter. Something between his legs was pressing up against me, hurting me. I wanted to get away from whatever was causing me pain. I was having a hard time trying to get away from Granddaddy. I reached down attempting to move his hands off my backside. Finally, I was able to break away from his mouth. I was out of breath.

"Granddaddy! What you doin? Let me go!" I gasped for air at the same time I talked.

Granddaddy was breathing hard as well. He looked at me panting. "Awe now, Granddaddy just want a lil sugar!" he uttered with a deceitful look. Granddaddy was chuckling while trying to calm me down. He still had his hands on my backside. I struggled trying to remove his hands without any success. Granddaddy was leaning hard into my body continuing to press my body up against what felt like a bone rubbing hard against me. Before I could say anything else, Granddaddy jerked my head back quickly to his mouth even though I was tilting my head trying to stop him. With his hands gripping my buttocks, he gyrated my body against him roughly. At first I wondered if it was something sticking out in his wooden leg causing me so much discomfort.

His tongue was licking around the outside of my lips as he tried to force his tongue in my mouth.

He muttered quickly, "Open your mouth."

I was determined he wasn't getting my mouth open to stick his nasty tongue inside it. As a child I never heard of such a thing. I felt his wet tongue licking me and it felt so disgusting. Eeew, his nasty spit was wetting my face! If I opened my mouth to speak, he would be able to stick his yucky tongue in. I kept my lips tightly sealed while he continued to thrust his tongue forcefully. I was able to turn my head to the side, but I still couldn't get his hands to budge from me. Eeew! He was even licking my cheeks.

I wanted to wash his licks off my spit-smelling face as I felt the air drying all the damp areas. *Why was he licking on me like he was some kind of dog?* I needed soap to wash my face, lips and the inside of my mouth just in case something got in my mouth.

I caught my breath from the struggle. He continued to grip me tighter while licking my cheek. He started rolling down my panties from the back causing me to panic even more. He was breathing funny and squeezing my bottom hard with both of his hands.

"Granddaddy no! My mama told me not to let nobody touch me like this! Granddaddy!" I shouted.

Granddaddy was ignoring me. He was starting to reach at his pants trying to unfasten them while holding me tightly with his other hand. He couldn't keep as tight a grip on me with just one hand though. This gave me a chance to break free backing out of his reach. I didn't bother to pull my panties back up. I just pulled my dress down and moved away.

I didn't know what to do next. I stood still feeling a painful throb from whatever had been pressing hard against me. I realized just how much Granddaddy was hurting me at that moment. Granddaddy looked at me in a duplicitous manner.

"You don't wanna give Granddaddy no sugar?" he asked.

I took two more steps back. I wanted to distract him.

"Can I have my apple now?" I said hesitantly.

Granddaddy started laughing. I looked at him hoping he would head over to the refrigerator to get the apple. I planned to call out to Scootie and Sonia to come share the apple with me as soon as he walked towards the refrigerator. I wanted to be near my brother and sister.

Granddaddy sat there patting the round lumps between his legs as I looked curiously trying to see what was hurting me so bad. He had his pants unbuttoned but still zipped. I couldn't help but wonder what all that stuff bulging from his pants was. He ran his hands up and down his pants. I stood frozen wondering what he was doing. He again reached over his huge belly down towards the round lumps in his pants smiling.

"How 'bout *them* apples? Huh? You like them apples don't you? Huh? Come on back over here and sample these apples," he said impishly.

Granddaddy broke out in a half nervous laugh. I started slowly backing away from Granddaddy's smiling face. I wanted to be as far out of his reach as possible. I was filled with confusion while slowly backing closer to the door. *Why was he doing this to me? What was he talking about anyway?* My gut feeling told me to just run outside. I could out run him with his wooden leg.

Granddaddy was watching me inch towards the door. His smile faded more and more the further away I got. He was still breathing hard trying to anticipate his next move. He kept touching his bulge as if he was trying to adjust something. He wanted me to come back to him. He seemed to think I liked what I saw. *Did he think I was going to come over and touch what was in his nasty pants, talking about 'them apples' like I was crazy or something?* Mama said it was bad to do that. It was nasty to touch someone down there.

Just then, Sonia was knocking at the door. Sonia was looking anxious. Granddaddy locked the door earlier so Sonia started knocking on the door.

"Tweety, come on outside with me and help me feed the chickens! Tweety!" Sonia yelled.

"Okay," I was quick to respond.

I wanted to ask Granddaddy why he lied about the apple and why he put his hands on me in a nasty way. I didn't know how to stand up to grown folk. I was always taught to do whatever Granddaddy and Grandmamma said. I would never disobey them.

As an adult, I wondered if Granddaddy ever hurt Daddy when he was a child and if this was why Daddy stopped seeing him for many years.

Leading up to this day, we had begun going over to Granddaddy's house every other weekend. Granddaddy would compliment me on my weight picking up more and more every week as I continued to fill out into early maturity.

Most of my elementary school years I was called "boney" all the time. Mama would threaten to take me to the hospital to have me "tube fed" just to get me to eat half of my dinner plate. Once I started my fourth grade school year, I would hear the neighbors yelling out to Mama saying that I was finally trying to get some hip bones. My aunts would say that I was finally getting a little "meat" on my bones or that I was finally getting a few curves in my hips and backside.

"Bout time you finally starting to fill out a little bit. Gull I ain't think you was gone ever gain any weight!" Grandma Lola Mae said one day.

When the women in my neighborhood argued, they would turn around, poke their backside out and slap it before shouting out, "Kiss my ass." As kids, we picked up on this gesture of patting our backsides after being called a name or picked on. Of course, this was done behind our parents' backs when we got angry with one another. We didn't say any of the words, but the message was the same. I only patted my backside if someone did it to me first. All of a sudden, I had something worth patting when my backside seemed to suddenly poke out. Before I gained weight, I used to hear, "That's why you ain't got nothing worth patting, now, wit yo *boney* self." When I finally started forming a few curves here and there, I proudly chanted a rhyme with my friends.

Now put your hands on your hips
and let your backbone slip
shake it to the left
shake it to the right
shake it to the very one that you love the best!

After struggling to break away from Granddaddy, on this warm sunny day as Scootie and Sonia played outside, I tried to reach the latch to unlock the door. Sonia was waiting patiently outside the door after she called me to come join them feeding the chickens. It was too high. I looked at Granddaddy without saying anything. Granddaddy unlocked the latch while whispering something in my ear.

"Come back in when they ain't looking and I got something for you, okay?" he said.

I was speechless. He was too close to me. I was screaming silently, *"Don't touch me!"* I went outside to join Scootie and Sonia while mumbling to myself.

"He must be crazy! I ain't going back in there with him! He must think I'm stupid or something, putting his hands on me!" I muttered under my breath.

I was very angry about what Granddaddy did. I wanted to go wash my mouth. As soon as I got around the side of the house I fixed my panties, which were off my backside. I wiped my mouth and rubbed my face as hard as I could but I still didn't feel clean enough. I used my dress top to try to wipe some more. I didn't want to go back inside. I knew Granddaddy didn't have any right to put his hands on me in a sexual way.

Grandmamma was in the bedroom towards the back part of the house sound asleep. She didn't hear anything.

Granddaddy kept trying to get me to himself. He called me, but I had Sonia come with me every time he called me to do something for him. Every time I stood near him I silently screamed the words, *Don't touch me!* Something inside of me kept telling me he couldn't get me alone again. I sensed I'd be hurt bad if I let him get me alone again.

Granddaddy called all three of us in the house. He came up with a chore for each of us. He told Sonia and Scootie they were going to wash his truck for him. Scootie was excited because he would get to use the water hose and play in the water some. It was hot outside, so this was refreshing. The thought of the water hose made me wish I could rinse off my face. I would rather have been outside in the water with them. Sonia felt like a big girl as well. They both liked their assignment.

"Tweety, I have a different chore for you. You can help with something in the kitchen. You Granddaddy's *super* helper so um gon have to do somethin *extra* special for you," Granddaddy said sinfully.

I wasn't stupid! I knew exactly what he was doing. I could feel it deep in my gut. Something very bad would happen if I let him trick me this time. I had to think of a way out fast. Sonia and Scootie ran outside with Granddaddy and he got them started.

I went to the bathroom to look out the window at them. At that moment, I envied my brother and sister. They seemed so carefree while I felt so trapped. I quickly washed my face and mouth with bitter tasting soap before stepping back on the toilet lid to look out the window. I listened as Granddaddy instructed Scootie and

Sonia to get started while he and I got started with something else. I stepped down off the toilet and ran in the bedroom with Grandmamma. I climbed in the bed next to her. I felt resentment towards Granddaddy for all his plotting, trying to get to me.

"Putting his damn hands on me!" I was so furious over the thought of Granddaddy touching me that I used profanity for the first time in my life.

Grandmamma stirred to see who was in the room with her. She looked very frail. She *sounded* weak as well. Her voice was very hoarse. I didn't mean to wake her up.

"Who is this in here with me?" Grandmamma said feebly.

I tried to sound sick too. "It's me Grandmamma. I don't feel good. I wanna stay in here wit you," I said.

Grandmamma turned around slowly. "Child, what's the matter with you?" she asked faintly.

I put on my best act. "I don't know Grandmamma. My *stomach* hurts. I just wanna lay here with you, okay?" I answered.

Grandmamma felt my forehead. By this time, Granddaddy sent Sonia to see what I was doing and to tell me to come here. Grandmamma spoke up for me even in her incapacitated state.

"Sonia, you go tell your Granddaddy this child is in here sick and he is to leave her alone! She doesn't feel good," she said before collapsing into a frantic cough.

Sonia came over to me while I was patting Grandmamma's back. "Tweety, what's wrong?" she asked inquisitively.

I wanted to cry because of everything I was going through just to keep Granddaddy away from me. My eyes watered up because I wanted to tell Sonia why I was so upset. I stuck to the story all the while tasting bitter soap in my mouth.

"My stomach aches Sonia," I said tearfully.

Sonia was so caring all the time. She came over to hug me. I wanted to cry even more. After she left, I let a few tears fall. It was around twelve o'clock in the afternoon.

I didn't know what time Mama and Daddy would come pick us up, but I was determined I was going to stay right up under Grandmamma until they came to pick us up. I just hoped it was much sooner rather than later.

An hour passed, then I fell asleep. I didn't know how long I'd been asleep. Sonia came in the room sounding all anxious.

"Tweety! Granddaddy said he was going to take us to get a Split Dog and then we're going to the store and he's going to buy us whatever we want! You better come on so you can get what you want!" Sonia said excitedly.

I was wise to Granddaddy. I was not moving away from Grandmamma. He wanted to hurt me desperately. I sat up. "Bring me back whatever y'all get," I said not knowing what else to do.

Sonia looked surprised. "Tweety, you don't want to go pick out your own stuff?" she said, noticing my unusual disinterest in going with them.

I shook my head no.

I lay back down and turned my head. Sonia said okay as she left the room. Granddaddy was still trying to get me. Sonia dawdled back into the room.

"Tweety, Granddaddy said if you want something to eat, you have to come with us and get it yourself."

My stomach was growling. I was hungry, but I would rather starve than be around him where he could get me to himself again. I kept thinking about all his nasty spit on my mouth and how he hurt me when he was squashing me up against his huge body. I thought long and hard. I knew Granddaddy was trying to see if I was faking. If I didn't come, he would have to believe I was really sick. He would have to feel sorry for me. He probably would have to just go on and let Sonia buy me something. He couldn't let me just lay there and not feed me, I surmised to myself.

"I don't wanna go," I finally concluded.

Sonia looked concerned. "Tweety, Granddaddy said he wasn't going to buy you anything if you didn't come. You're gonna be hungry," she said apprehensively.

Sonia spoke in mostly proper words. She used more proper words than I did. I tried to look really sick so she could tell Granddaddy how sick I was.

"I don't feel good. I can't go because my stomach hurts too

much," I lied.

Sonia kissed me. "I hope you feel better Tweety. I love you," she said before turning away.

I was quick to respond before I choked up. "I love you too."

Sonia left the room. Granddaddy sent Scootie in the room next. Scootie ran into the room immediately calling out my name.

"Tweety! Granddaddy said we can buy anything we want from the store. I'm gonna buy me *two* Split Dogs and *two whole big bags* of chips and I'll probably get me *three* Snickers bars! Naw, I'll probably get *five* Snickers bars so I can eat one every day after school and then I'm gonna get some strawberry cookies and a grape drink *and* a Coca-Cola. Tweety, you better come on and go so you can see what you wanna get for yourself! Granddaddy said you can pick out *whatever* you want and he'll buy *all* of it! Man, you're *crazy* if you stay here!" he spoke convincingly.

I contemplated what I might buy if I went, which made my stomach growl even more. I didn't want to pay the price I'd have to pay when we came back to the house with Granddaddy. He'd make me complete my little chore. I had a pretty good idea what his chore for me consisted of. I wasn't stupid, not one bit.

"I don't feel good. Just bring me something back okay?" I said matter of factly.

Scootie stared at me for a second. "You sure you don't wanna come Tweety?" he persuasively asked again.

I nodded no. Scootie sighed and sounded regretful.

"Okay then. Well, we're getting ready to go so, bye. I hope you feel better," he said before finally giving up and walking out.

I heard Granddaddy asking Scootie what I said when they were standing right ouside the door. He told Granddaddy he tried to get me to come, but I said I wasn't feeling good. Granddaddy mumbled something inaudibly as they headed down the hallway.

"I told her we were getting ready to leave Granddaddy. She still didn't want to come. Her stomach hurts or something," Scootie responded loudly.

I sighed when I heard Granddaddy's truck crank up to pull off. I didn't expect much back from the store, but I'd at least get a Split

Dog I figured.

I lay there determined to be brave. I couldn't feel sorry for myself. I was going to tell Daddy and Mama what Granddaddy did to me. I just didn't want to say anything to Grandmamma because I didn't know if she would believe me. I knew Granddaddy would say I was lying. Even if she did believe me, I didn't want to make her sad. I'd just cause everyone to be unhappy. I couldn't bear the thought of causing people I loved to be sad.

What if the police got involved? What if Grandmamma and Granddaddy got into a fight causing one of them to get hurt? It would be better if I just kept my mouth shut. *What if Granddaddy told Daddy and Mama I was lying? What if they believed him? What if they got mad at me?* They'd probably never believe me again. They'd think I was a bad child. They might even believe I was crazy! Grown folks would never believe a child over an adult and I knew for *sure* Granddaddy was going to lie. Grownups are not supposed to lie, but he would.

The entire time these thoughts were going through my head, I heard the truck pulling back up again. I was hungry, so I didn't care what they brought me as long as I had something to eat.

"Healing Roads Journal"

It was necessary for me to go back through this memory and pull out the defining purpose. Its purpose is intended to help other people in various ways. I celebrate this memory now simply because I have learned how to face my fears. And, I am wiser today for having faced it. I have forgiven and released the pain. I'm at peace with this memory because of the greater good it can mean to someone else struggling with their own pain. For me, I've turned my tragedy into triumph.

CHAPTER TWO

"STUBBORN"

Sonia came straight to Grandmamma's room. "Tweety! Look what I got!" she exclaimed while appearing very adrenalized.

I sat up in anticipation. Sonia had a bag full of goodies. I saw large chip bags, several packs of cookies, candy, pickles, and juices. She couldn't pull everything out of the bag because it was so full of things. I longed for a Split Dog in spite of all the junk food she had with her. She'd already eaten half of her Split Dog. I looked for something else.

"Where's *my* sandwich?" I asked.

Sonia's expression indicated that she neglected to get me anything.

"Granddaddy said that you were too sick to eat so he didn't get you anything. You're hungry?" she asked.

My eyes watered up. I nodded yes. I couldn't believe Granddaddy didn't get me anything to eat. I hadn't really eaten all day. I picked over breakfast because I didn't want lumpy grits and eggs. Sonia held out her tiny piece of left over Split Dog, which was a fried sausage link.

"Do you wanna bite?" she asked pitifully.

I took a bite. Tears were running down my face. Sonia thought I was crying because I didn't feel well. Just then, Granddaddy called Sonia. She ran out to see what he wanted. She came back in the room without her food.

"Tweety, Granddaddy said if you're hungry, he'll take you to get something to eat. He won't let me share my food with you 'cause he said that you need to go and get your own stuff."

I absolutely refused to ride in the truck alone with Granddaddy. I was never going to let him put his nasty hands on me again. He would only punish me worse for making him try so hard to have me to himself. He'd be even rougher. The thought of him touching me made me cringe.

Sonia sat on the bed. She had a bottle of orange juice in her hand.

"Do you want to taste some juice?" she asked feeling sorry for me.

I nodded yes again. Sonia handed me her juice bottle. I was thirsty enough to drink all of it. I took a few gulps passing the bottle back to her. She felt empathetic.

"You want some more? You can have some more because I bought two," she said consolingly.

I drank some more.

"How come you won't let Granddaddy take you to the store so he can buy you something, Tweety?" she finally asked.

I couldn't hold back my tears. I sniffed while wiping my eyes. "I don't feel good. I already told you that," I answered.

I wiped away the tears, but more kept coming. Sonia was patting me. My nose was starting to run.

"Can you go get me some tissue?" I asked.

Sonia scurried to grab some tissue and came back. Grandmamma slept through everything. I knew she must have been pretty sick to sleep so soundly.

Sonia felt sorry for me as she watched me cry. "Tweety, you want me to go ask Granddaddy to take me back to the store to get you something so you can feel better?" she asked sympathetically.

I nodded yes. She asked me what I wanted.

"I just want a Split Dog and some chips and some juice and some cookies or something." I know they had way more than I asked for.

Sonia left to go ask Granddaddy. Scootie came in the room.

"Tweety, Granddaddy said come on and he'll take you right quick. He said you can come right back and lay down. He won't let us come back in here no more. He told us to stay up there with all that food so we don't make a mess."

I wanted to scream out and tell on Granddaddy. I was absolutely sure he wanted to squeeze and hurt me some more. He didn't even care that he was hurting me. He had to know how hard he was squeezing my body up against him. He was a cruel man. He was not nice. He was a fake. I saw right through him. He didn't care about me at all. I couldn't believe he wouldn't feed me. I would starve before I let him lick on my face and hurt me again. The thought of him was repulsive.

"I'm sleepy. I wanna go to sleep," I said quickly.

I turned my head. Scootie walked off. I lay in bed crying. The noise woke Grandmamma.

"What's wrong child?" Grandmamma reached and put her weakened arms around me.

"I don't feel good." I had to say something.

Grandmamma was patting my back. She felt hot and was perspiring. In her ill state, she fell back to sleep. I moved away because she felt so hot. I also fell off to sleep again. When I woke up it was starting to get dark.

Mama and Daddy were taking forever to come pick us up. I stared up at the ceiling. I tossed and turned. My stomach growled continuously. Anger built up in me more and more. I kept thinking about Granddaddy. I silently echoed, *"Don't touch me!"* Similar thoughts raced through my head over and over. I couldn't believe he was making me starve just because I wouldn't let him kiss me and do nasty things to me. He had to know he was being a bad person. He shouldn't think I'd want him doing those things to me. *Why was he being mean to me for not letting him harm me?* What he said about apples in his pants bothered me too. He made me look at him. Mama said we're not supposed to ever look at grown men's private parts, not even Daddy. He even acted like he wanted me to touch him. He crushed my body real hard against him and he hurt me. I don't want his nasty body touching me ever again.

I cried myself to sleep again. Mama and Daddy finally came at about nine o'clock at night. To me, it seemed like an eternity of torture. I lay there watching the hands on the clock slowly change from one minute to the next and the next. I forced myself to go off to sleep again and again. Mama woke me up.

"Tweety, baby what's wrong? You sick?" Mama asked tenderly.

I stirred then I stared at Mama wanting to make sure it was really her. I was happy to finally see Mama. I could finally be rescued from Granddaddy. I wanted to get as far away from Granddaddy as I could. Granddaddy was standing in the room. I couldn't say anything. I looked at Mama.

"Are we getting ready to go home?" I asked

Mama smiled while feeling my head to see if I had a fever. I started to wonder if I was sick for real this time because I felt weak.

"You ready to go Tweety?" Mama asked.

I tried not to cry again.

"Yes ma'am," I whispered.

I was having a hard time keeping myself from crying again. I sighed when Mama put her arms around me. Mama looked at me tenderheartedly.

"Your daddy's waiting in the car, so Mama can take you straight home okay?" Mama said consolingly.

I nodded yes as a single tear ran down my face. Granddaddy suddenly spoke. "You don't have to take them off so fast. They can spend the night if you want them too."

Mama smiled before answering. "No, I better take Tweety home since she's not feeling good."

When we got to the car, Mama let me sit in the front with her and Daddy. I hugged Daddy trying to smile. I even felt drained from walking to the car. Sonia and Scootie had a lot of energy. They talked about how much fun they had. They showed Mama and Daddy all the treats they bought.

Daddy looked down at me with no goodies. He asked me how I was feeling. I said I was feeling fine. Daddy asked me about my stomach.

"Your stomach still hurtin Tweety?"

I nodded no. Daddy seemed relieved.

"That's good," he replied.

Sonia told Mama I stayed in bed all day long. I wanted to tell Daddy what happened but I decided to wait until we were far away so Granddaddy couldn't accuse me of lying. I wanted us to be as far away as possible so that Daddy would not be able to turn around and go back. I waited until we were just about home even though I was feeling faint from being hungry and thirsty. I couldn't hold back my frustrations. I burst out crying. Daddy almost had an accident.

"What in the world is wrong with you Tweety?" Daddy shouted.

I didn't know how to say it.

"Does yo stomach hurt again?" Daddy asked.

"No, that's not it!" I exclaimed.

Mama looked concerned as she spoke. "Tweety, what's wrong baby?"

I was sobbing so hard till it was difficult to understand my words. I blurted everything out. "Granddaddy got *mad* at me 'cause I wouldn't let him pull my panties down and I *told* him *you* told me not to *do* that and he was licking my face with *spit* and stuff and, and, and, he didn't feed me all day long!"

Mama couldn't make out what I was saying. Daddy and Mama both told me to slow down and speak clearly. I repeated myself still crying.

"Granddaddy was trying to *touch* me and do something bad with me and I wouldn't let him touch me anymore and he was *slobbing* and spitting all over my *mouth* and stuff and trying to *do* something *nasty* wit me!" I cried.

I had to take a deep breath and inhale because I was crying so hard. I gulped, and then I cried even harder while explaining.

"And he didn't feed me all day!"

By this time Daddy had pulled over. He and Mama were looking at each other and then at me. Daddy was the first to speak. The whole car was quiet. Daddy looked at Mama with a shocked look.

"Did...did, now, did uh, did she just say what I *thought* she said?" he asked in disbelief.

You could tell Daddy was upset because he started stuttering.

Daddy looked like somebody just died or something. Mama began to speak calmly.

"Tweety, your Granddaddy was putting his hands on you in a bad way?"

"Yes ma'am. He was putting his tongue on me and everything with his nasty *spit* on my face and, and, and he was touching my backside and trying to pull my panties down and do nasty things and everything. I told him my mama told me not to *let* nobody do that to me, but he still kept on." I wiped the continuous flow of tears from my eyes as I talked.

Daddy listened silently taking a few deep breaths. Mama spoke next.

"Did he pull your panties down?"

I told Mama how I got loose from him after he pulled my panties down and then she assured me I could tell her and Daddy everything and they weren't going to let anybody hurt me again. After I answered all their questions, Mama asked Scootie and Sonia a couple of questions as well. Scootie responded first.

"I didn't know what Granddaddy was trying to do to Tweety, but he did call her in the house when me and Sonia was feeding the chickens and I *do* remember her being in there for a while. OOH! I didn't even *know* he was trying to do something to Tweety. I would've beat him up for touching my sister!"

Sonia suddenly broke out in explanations as well. "I thought Tweety was sick for *real* Mama. I didn't know Granddaddy was touching her either. I would have told our Grandmamma on him!"

Sonia asked me why I didn't tell Grandmamma. I looked at Mama.

"I didn't want to tell Grandmamma 'cause I thought I was gonna get in trouble," I explained wiping tears from my eyes.

Daddy was boiling with anger. Daddy turned to me as he spoke.

"It's not yo fault baby. Yo Granddaddy knew...knew *exactly* what he was doing!" he said.

Daddy started backing the car up.

"Ranch, what you doin?" Mama looked scared as she questioned Daddy.

Daddy had a determined look on his face.

"Um gon...gon go...go blow *that* bastard's head wide open!" he said.

Daddy had a gun in the dashboard. Mama called out to him.

"Ranch, No!"

"He... he... h... he gon die tonight! He done lost his mind, touchin... touchin *my* child!" Daddy snapped.

Daddy drove away from the projects we lived in. I started sobbing.

"No! Daddy, I don't wanna go back! I just wanna go home! Daddy please!" I screamed.

Daddy still had a determined look on his face. "It's gon be alright baby," he said.

Mama reached for Daddy's arm before speaking. "Ranch, don't go back. Let's just go home. You upsetting Tweety! Ranch, all you gon do is end up in jail."

"Um...um...um just gon have to go jail tonight baby, but he ain't, he ain't *gittin* away wit... wit this mess right here!" Daddy said.

Daddy was holding the gun he took out the dashboard.

"Ranch, I'm begging you, don't go! We just won't let them go over there no more Ranch! These children *need* they daddy Ranch! Listen to me. Tweety *said* he didn't get a chance to do nothing so let's just leave it at that and let God take care of him," Mama said.

"Mookie, h... h... he don't put his hand on one of mines *period*, and... and... and get away with it!" he said.

Sonia started crying as well. "I don't want you to go to jail Daddy," she sobbed.

Scootie was looking fearful but he sat quietly. Mama knew she had to calm Daddy down. She began to speak.

"Okay, Ranch, so what you gon do? You gon go over there and shoot yo daddy and then what? Let the police come and take you off to jail and leave me and the children behind? And then what me and the children suppose to do Ranch? Huh? Answer me!" Mama yelled.

Daddy slowed up, but he continued to drive as he explained.

"Mookie, you don't understand. He done put his hands on...on *my* child now, and he made the biggest mistake of his life 'cause he *sho'* touched the wrong somebody's child! Now...now somebody's gotta teach him. He mighta *thought* ... he was crazy all these years, but um gon *show* him who... who... who the crazy one is *this* time an... an... an I... an I... I guarantee you he ain't gon...gon act crazy no mo! Not after *I* get done w...w...wit 'em," Daddy said angrily.

"Ranch, that ain't yo job. God'll git him. That's God's job. Yo job is to be these children's *daddy* and to be *my* husband. He ain't gon ruin *our* lives. Now Ranch, you'll be letting him *win* if you go back over there 'cause yo family gon *lose* you. We don't have to go back over there ever again. Tweety said he didn't get a chance to really do anything, so we still got a chance to make sure nothing else happens from this point on," Mama explained rationally.

It was silent for a minute.

"Ranch, *please* just turn around. Give me the gun," Mama said.

Daddy finally gave her the gun.

"I'm still gon go over there and beat the *crap* out of him! I guarantee you, he...he...he gon know not to put his hands on one of *mines* again!"

Mama looked frustrated still as she continued to talk to Daddy. "Ranch, I'm telling you, don't go! We won't go over there no mo and we won't take the children anywhere near him again. Just drop it before you end up doin mo harm. Look Ranch, Tweety's hungry! Go get yo child something to eat."

I shouldn't have opened my mouth. It was going to be my fault if anything bad happened. Daddy saw tears running down my face.

"You want Daddy to go get you something to eat Tweety?" he asked.

I started wiping my eyes. "Yes sir," I said.

Daddy's heart dropped looking down at me.

"Okay baby. Daddy's gon go git you something to eat, o...okay?" he said.

Daddy pulled into the Gulf Gas Station to turn around. Mama gave a big sigh of relief. She was wiping tears from her eyes as well.

"Now...now Tweety, if you want Daddy to go over there and beat him up, I'll go beat him up. But if you don't want me to go, then I, I won't go," Daddy said.

"I don't wanna go back over there ever again Daddy!" I cried.

"Yeah Daddy, we just won't go back over there. I don't care how much candy and stuff he got." Scootie spoke up as well.

"Me neither Daddy!" Sonia joined in.

Daddy asked us all for a hug. We all gave him a hug and kiss. Daddy told each of us he loved us. Then it was Mama's turn.

"Give me some sugar Mookie." Daddy said to Mama.

Mama gave him a kiss and Daddy asked me if I wanted Burger King. I eagerly nodded yes. I was so relieved. Mama gave me a hug and kissed my forehead.

Daddy let me order whatever I wanted. I was so hungry that I ordered two Whoppers with cheese, a large fry, a chocolate shake, and an apple pie. I couldn't finish one whopper. Daddy ate the other whopper and everything else I couldn't eat. Scootie and Sonia each got a cheeseburger and a small fry. That's all Daddy would let them get because they had already eaten. Daddy took me to the store and let me buy some junk food like Scootie and Sonia as well.

"Healing Roads Journal"

My brother and sister have no detailed memory of this event occurring. Therapy helped me understand that it wasn't significant enough for them to retain in their memory. It was my pain and my trauma, so I've never forgotten. Mama says she remembers. Some of my relatives who Mama told about it still remember this happening as well. About three years ago, at the time I was writing this, it was important for me to feel validated by someone else who confirmed their memory of what happened to me. When my Aunt Nikki told me she knew all about what Granddaddy had done to me, it confirmed the importance of the event to me. What happened to me mattered enough to someone else, which made "me" matter. I finally felt like I had rights; rights to be angry, rights to talk about it without feeling ashamed, and rights to confront the pain without fear. At this time, my brother and sister were accusing me of inventing lies. Now I recognize we only retain memories relevant to our own defining purpose in life.

CHAPTER THREE

"BRAVE AND GOOD"

I was anxious to go to church after what happened at Granddaddy's house. No one said anything else about what happened ever again. We didn't go visit Granddaddy anymore. I wondered if I should have felt guilty about this. If it weren't for me telling, Daddy and Granddaddy might still act like a family and maybe Scootie and Sonia wouldn't have to miss Granddaddy and Grandmamma. Grandmamma didn't do anything bad, but now all because of me she couldn't enjoy her grandchildren anymore.

Church was a welcomed site for me. I needed to feel close to God. I sat in church eager to learn more about God. I paid just as much attention as the adults because I was hoping God could fill all the empty spaces in my heart.

Everything went back to its regular routine. School had been in session for a while. It was a new year in 1977 and I was feeling like a big girl, all grown up and almost ready to graduate from the fifth grade. The only thing that changed was us not seeing Granddaddy or Grandmamma anymore. We didn't even call them anymore.

Back in school one Friday, I had to walk home early in order to go to the doctor with Mama for a routine check up. Mama gave me a long speech before heading to school about not stopping to talk to strangers along the way. She told me to come straight home and not to stop anywhere. It was the longest speech I ever had. This would be my first time walking home by myself. I convinced Mama I was a big girl now and that I was almost ready to graduate from fifth grade.

On the way home, I walked around the front of the first apartment building instead of the back facing the woods like Mama instructed.

I climbed up on the short brick wall and walked along the edge as I often did when I took this route home with my friends. This time I tripped and fell causing a deep scrape along the front of my leg. There was also a deep gash with blood oozing. I immediately experienced extreme pain. I looked down and saw white meaty flesh from where the skin was scraped off into a rolled up knotted ball. Blood started pouring down over the white flesh rushing onto my new white baby doll socks and black, shiney, patent leather dress shoes. My first thought was to be brave. Big girls don't cry.

I looked around, but no one was in sight. I was unable to move. I was hit with immense pain every time I moved an inch. Mama said don't talk to strangers, so I couldn't cry out for help. I needed to be brave and get up and walk. As soon as I stood up, more blood gushed down and the deep gash felt painful. I fell back to the ground unable to hold back my tears. I started to cry wondering how I was going to get home. My leg and sock were covered with blood.

"Oh no!" I cried out.

I rocked back and forth holding my leg just above the bad scrape trying to stop the throbbing pain.

A young man looking in his late teens to early twenties stuck his head out his window.

"Oh no, lil girl, you alright?" he asked

I continued to rock back and forth crying, too afraid to answer.

"Hey, lil girl don't cry. I'll be down in just a minute okay? It's gon be alright," he said.

I didn't know if I should be more concerned about the pain I was in or the stranger Mama said not to talk to.

"Oooh! Hey lil girl, that's a bad scrape. I know it hurts. Can you stand up?" he asked.

I shook my head no, not wanting him to try to move me and cause more discomfort.

"Okay, well just wait right there a minute pretty girl. I'm gon get something and clean you up. I'll be right back. It's gon be okay, don't cry," he said.

He went inside his apartment and came back outside empty handed.

"I'm wetting a towel in warm water so I can help you. We need to get you up off this ground okay? If I help you stand up will you try and walk a little?" he asked.

I nodded yes then he grabbed me around my waist and lifted me. As soon as I stood up I began to hop and limp from the pain and the tears began to pour down again. I couldn't stand so the man picked me up.

"Hey, awe, hey don't cry now. It's gon be alright. Come on. I'm gon help you okay? Where you live?" he asked.

I thought about Mama telling me not to talk to strangers and feared I'd be in trouble if Mama saw this man holding me. Mama said under no circumstances was I to talk to anyone. *Men* especially. The man had on jogging pants but no shirt.

"Hey, let me just get you cleaned up and put on a shirt so I can get you home okay?" he said.

I didn't answer. The man carried me into his apartment and sat me in a chair. He went into the kitchen and came back out with a warm wet towel. As he inched closer to my bloody leg I held up my hands to stop him.

"It's gon hurt!" I shouted.

"Awe, come on now pretty girl. I wouldn't hurt you. I promise. I'll blow it, but we gotta get all that blood off you and we gotta stop the bleeding okay? You gon be a big girl for me?" he asked.

I nodded yes and closed my eyes tightly. He began to blow before he placed the towel on the scrape. I felt a huge sting and jumped, but I tried to be brave and not cry anymore. I huffed and puffed until the stinging stopped while he continued to blow. He went in the kitchen and got another warm towel to clean all around the scrape and down my leg where the blood ran down.

"See there. Now let me kiss all around it," he said.

He started kissing my leg, but it didn't feel proper; especially when he kissed up towards my thigh where I wasn't hurting.

"I told you I wouldn't hurt you, didn't I? So, what's yo name?" he asked.

"Katerina," I replied.

"Katerina? That's pretty. A pretty name for a pretty girl," he said.

He cleaned up as much as he could and took the bloody towels back in the kitchen. The pain eased tremendously afterwards. I knew I had to get home. I slowly eased up to see if I could stand. It hurt but I could limp home. The man looked up and saw me standing and began to speak.

"Oh, hey pretty girl, sit down. Don't stand up on that leg yet. You can sit there for as long as you want to, okay? You don't have to rush, okay? You want some cookies?"

I nodded no remembering Mama said to never accept candy or cookies from strangers.

"Well, let me look at yo leg one more time," he said.

He knelt down to look at my leg. I noticed he was staring at more than my leg. He was staring at my panties. I closed my legs and continued to watch him nervously as the smile faded off his face. He started touching my other leg pretending to examine it as well. He was nice like Granddaddy was, offering me sweets and petting me. As he hovered over me, the bulge in his pants reminded me of Granddaddy. I was suddenly very frightened.

"You got some pretty lil legs. You know that?" he said.

He started rubbing his hands further up my thighs. I tensed up knowing he wasn't supposed to be touching my upper legs. I closed my legs tighter to keep him from going any further. The man stood up and walked around my chair and began to message my shoulders and back telling me everything was going to be alright.

"Does this feel good, pretty girl?" he asked.

I became more and more uncomfortable. I looked towards the front door and noticed it was closed shut and locked. I knew I was in a world of trouble. Mama told me not to talk to strangers. It was all my fault. Grandaddy didn't get me, but this man might have me cornered. I felt something eerie inside of me warning me he was bad. He was pretending to be good, but he was not fooling me one bit. My chest was beating fast telling me something was wrong with this nice man.

"You sho is a pretty lil thang. You sure you don't want any cookies?" he asked again.

I nodded no again.

"I gotta go home," I said.

"Well just wait here one minute okay? I promise I'm gon get you home okay? Hey, I know what. You can lay down on the sofa if you want to. You wanna lay on the sofa so you can feel more comfortable?" he said.

I nodded no.

"Why not? You scared of me?"

I nodded no again.

"Well then, just go over there and lay on the sofa for a minute so you can be more comfortable. I'm not gon hurt you pretty girl, okay?" he said.

I looked down at my leg and thought of an excuse.

"I can't move. I need some Band Aids," I said.

"Okay, well just hold on one minute okay? I'll be right back. Just sit right there for just a minute and I'm gon go upstairs and find some Band Aids for you okay?"

I nodded okay before he kissed my cheek.

"There you go you lil sweet thang. Don't move pretty girl okay? Just sit right there and I'll be right back."

He winked his eye at me before heading up the stairs. As soon as he hit the first couple of steps I dashed to the door and unlocked it and took off running as soon as I stepped outside. I didn't look back. I cut across the street and up the steps dodging between more buildings instead of going straight home. I went all the way around through back buildings to make sure the man never caught me. I didn't stop to look at my leg, I just kept running. I had to cut back through more buildings in order for Mama to think I came home the normal route. As soon as I saw my building I finally felt safe enough to stop and focus on the sharp pain. My leg was throbbing and covered with blood again. I leaned down to grab my leg and cried, both out of relief from my escape from the weird man and the pain in my leg.

Mama was standing in the door. She called my name and rushed towards me.

"Tweety! How in the world you do all this? Lord, I tell you the truth! If it ain't one thing, it's another. You done messed up yo pretty legs. Oooh! You may as well git ready 'cause it's definitely gon sting 'cause I gotta clean it wit alcohol and peroxide."

"Mama no!" I yelled.

"Well Tweety, you gon have to grin and bear it, that's all I can tell you," Mama said.

Mama cleaned my leg and put peroxide and Campho-Phenique on it before calling a cab to take me to the doctor. At first, we were going to take the long walk to the clinic, but my leg was too bad to walk.

I never talked about the stranger, fearing I would be in trouble. The doctor wrapped my leg and gave Mama some smelly ointment to put on it everyday until it healed. It pussed up for a few days before it started healing. Mama kept grunting about the permanent scars she feared would be left from the injury. I didn't care much about the scars. All I know is that it healed and I was back outside being a "Tomboy." It wasn't very noticeable to me.

After the experience with the man and me looking at his bulge and thinking about Granddaddy again, I didn't want to play much with the boys at home.

At church, a boy named J Bug would watch me like a hawk. I was not in the mood to be bothered. The first day I came to church and saw him, I thought he looked like some cute boy right out of a dream date magazine with his light skin, thick curly afro, and perfect smile. He looked half caucasion and half black. He shook my hand and introduced himself after service that first day I went to church. Immediately my short lived crush began. As time went on, one day he touched my backside inappropriately resulting in me socking him and telling him to keep his hands to himself. That didn't seem to deter him from attempting to touch me inappropriately on other occasions. It always resulted in a hard punch and a warning to him to keep his hands off me.

After the incident with Granddaddy, I sat on the mostly adult side of church next to Mama. I became clingier. I felt safe next to Mama.

J Bug's cousin Curly was very friendly. She wanted me to come over to sit on the children's side of church. Curly waved me over to the children's side again. I didn't want to go because I was still feeling shy about approaching all the other children. But I got up slowly to walk around. As I walked through the dimly lit room linked to the children's side again, there were some babies asleep. J Bug was walking in the opposite direction heading to the bathroom in the hallway just outside the dark room. I didn't think anything about him because I already let him have it before about touching me. He should have known better by now.

I felt J Bug's hand grip my backside really aggressively when he passed me in the dark room. Here we go again. Apparently he didn't learn his lesson. I reacted by knocking him flat on the floor. He was surprised at my strength. Dissatisfied, I walked over to him sitting on the floor and punched him a couple of times in his upper back. I told him to keep his hands off me.

"I don't even like you no mo!" I shouted.

He got up real fast putting his hand to his mouth shushing and trying to calm me down before somebody heard me.

"Okay, Okay, baby. Shhhh. I'm sorry. For real though."

He came towards me reaching for my shoulder. I jerked away before he could touch my shoulder.

"Don't touch me!" I snapped.

He dropped his hand real quick. "Okay, look, I'm sorry sugar pie. You accept my apology, baby?"

I walked off silently. His endearing words agitated me more. As I walked away I heard him mumble as he grabbed his throbbing shoulder.

"Shoot! Baby you strong!"

J Bug slipped in a few more aggressive touches every now and then. I punched him every time he put his hands on me. He made vulgar comments about what he wanted to do to me when he would seize an opportunity to whisper in my ear. Any time he could get me by myself, outside after church or even in church when no one was looking, he was all over me.

It was bad to be a "tattle tell" so I never told any adults. Plus I knew he'd get the skin beat off him if I told on him. I didn't want to be blamed for causing him to get in any serious trouble. Besides, if Granddaddy didn't really do anything much, what J Bug was doing couldn't be *that* serious enough to get him in trouble with his parents. J Bug's daddy was quick to discipline him and Mother Jordon came to his rescue on occasion.

J Bug became more aggressive by touching my vagina as I was sitting alone on the church porch outside one night cooling off from the heat inside the church. I tried to knock the fire out of him.

"You old nasty thing! Keep your hands off me! I'm not playing with yo old *nasty* butt!" I talked loud on purpose.

I was surprised he would even *try* touching me because I hit him hard every time. After a while I started talking loudly to him in front of my cousins to get him to back off. I was glad it worked because he was getting out of hand. I was tired of having to look over my shoulders or sit with my ears covered just to keep him from walking up to me and whispering nasty stuff in my ear. I decided J Bug was just a good looking jerk and I lost all interest in him.

Every time J Bug came near me, I reminded him not to touch me. Curly asked me why I was upset with her cousin. I was too embarrassed to say why.

"He play too much," I answered.

J Bug started acting like he had some sense after a while because my cousins were quick to come to my defense whenever I seemed irritated about anything. I spilled the beans to my cousins who boldy told him to keep his hands off their cousin if he didn't want them to break his hands into several pieces. I made them promise not to tell Scootie out of fear he'd tell Mama or Daddy. They would have probably punished me by making me sit with the adults from then on.

I felt sorry for J Bug sometimes because I knew he got severe beatings. His daddy was a minister in the church and was really strict about stressing obedience by not sparing the rod. The adults whispered about an incident when his daddy approached him and out of fear, he wet his pants.

As time went on, we adapted to our church family more and more. The church beliefs were strictly by the Bible. Everything in the Bible was given a literal interpretation just as it was written and lived in the Bible days. Saturday was the Sabbath and we ate according to Moses' laws. We didn't eat pork or fish without fins and scales, including shrimp and lobster or animals with webbed feet like ducks or animals with split hooves. Of course we had to grow into a lot of these changes.

It took Daddy a minute to give up chitterlings and pork chops. We couldn't cook on Friday nights or Saturdays. We couldn't do any kind of work or go to the store on Sabbath days. Mama had to wear her head covered. She started wearing all white every where, even when she came to our school. The children questioned us.

"Why yo mama always look like she goin to a wedding or something?" children would ask all the time.

Mama's head coverings looked just like long sheer wedding veils hanging down her back. I was thankful Mama didn't need to come to school very often since we were growing older. We never had discipline problems and we made mostly straight A's. As for our neighbors, they'd gotten used to Mama in her white even though it got really quiet sometimes when she walked past. My friends always stared at her. Sometimes they sang "Here Comes the Bride" once she was out of sight. Mama's friend, Ms. Beth didn't come over much now. She boldly joked with Mama about being too "holy."

CHAPTER FOUR

"THE LAKE OF FIRE"

Our family started singing gospel as a family at church in 1978. It was the summer before starting my sixth grade school year. The church was on "Whites Mill Avenue" in a large brick home in a residential neighborhood. As the church began to grow in membership, cars were parked along the street because the church yard was full.

We were called "The James Family." I sang alto, Sonia sang soprano, and Mama and Scootie sang tenor. Daddy was the lead singer who switched from lead to alto on the occasions when I had to take the lead. Sonia was too shy to lead even though she had a beautiful voice. She wouldn't sing loud enough to take the lead. We practiced at home while the neighbors crowded around our porch to listen.

I adapted to singing in front of a crowd in spite of my natural shyness. Daddy taught me how to take the focus away from the crowd when singing. If I felt nervous, I fixed my eyes on a specific object straight ahead or I closed my eyes while focusing on the words.

We were at church all day on Saturdays. We were at home on Sundays playing with our friends. We usually skipped church on Sunday nights. Daddy was getting ready to go back to work on Monday mornings. We also went to church many days throughout the week.

We had Children's Bible Study early on Saturday morning followed by choir rehearsal. We had lots of fun. We learned how to sing all the books of the Bible, along with the biblical months.

We learned how to quote the entire Exodus 20 word for word. We were taught to read strictly from the Original King James Version Bible.

We were being taught more and more every day. I heard a lot of interesting testimonies among the pastors and ministers. Pastor Nichols had a compelling testimony about how he was prayed over and anointed with oil by Mother Jordon resulting in him being healed from a terminal illness. Pastor Nichols testified about how the doctors gave him six months to live, but when he went back to the doctor, there was not a trace of his illness found anywhere. He'd been a true believer ever since, committed to giving his life totally to God.

Mother Jordon had the greatest testimony of everyone. She testified about being pronounced dead. After many minutes, of being prayed over by a minister who prophesied to her, she was revived. In her testimony she dedicated her life to God realizing God raised her from the dead to give her another chance to serve him.

Mother Jordon was the center of the church. She stood before the congregation and addressed everyone.

"Peace to the household of faith," she always said whenever she stood before the congregation.

The congregation responded in unison.

"Peace!"

"All is well?" she asked.

The church again responded in unison.

"All is well!"

After service the ministers all addressed one another the same way.

"Peace Sister Nichols," someone would say.

"Peace," she responded.

The children even addressed the adults the same way instead of saying hello.

Mother Jordon was the founder of the church. She first began teaching and instructing a handful of people. She set expectations for us as Christians, as well as put the teachings in writing for everyone to learn the ways of God. Everyone went to her to clear up confusion regarding the scriptures and the beliefs instilled into us.

There were a lot of strict teachings. No matter how confusing people may have been in the beginning, Mother worked patiently with the Holy Bible in her hand, reading scripture after scripture to back up her teachings. She was very knowledgeable of the Bible scriptures from Genesis to Revelation.

Mother was full of wisdom. She embraced everyone with love. She welcomed alcoholics, prostitutes and drug abusers with open arms. Many were healed through her diligent prayers. Most of the congregation had a testimony of deliverance from addictions or unacceptable lifestyles. Mother had cast demons out through laying hands on people while praying for them. She was a powerful woman of God.

I looked confused after joking with Curly one day after service.

"I said I was just playing," I said.

"Girl, don't you know that *all* liars shall have their part in the Lake of Fire, which burneth with fire and brimstone?" Curly exclaimed.

"The what?" I asked. I had no idea what she just said.

"The Lake of Fire, which burneth with fire and brimstone!" she repeated.

"What in the heck is The Lake of Fire!" I asked. I couldn't even remember the rest of what she had said.

"Girl! You don't know what The Lake of Fire is?" she asked.

"No," I said.

"Girl, that's where people who lie and sin gonna end up. And there ain't gon be no water or nothing and they gon be thirsty. They just gon burn forever and ever and they ain't gon die. They gon *wanna* die, but they ain't gonna be able to commit suicide or nothing. Worms and *everything* is gon be coming out of them and they gon be *smellin* bad. They gon be *begging* for mercy, but ain't no body gon be able to even help 'em. Not even God!" Curly said.

This was a scary thing to me. I was about to react, but there couldn't be such a thing.

"Good one! Curly, girl you almost got me with that one. That's a real good one!" I said.

Curly stepped back. "You don't believe me?" she said.

"*Sure* I do!" I was sarcastic in my response.

Curly called her cousin J Bug and my cousins over and then she called a boy named Mikey over as well.

Mikey and his sister Nae Nae were the smartest children in the church when it came to bible study, quoting scriptures, and answering questions. They could tell you where to find scriptures for almost everything we were being taught. All the children and adults spoke very highly of both Mikey and Nae Nae.

By the time all the children were gathered around me, Curly asked them a question.

"Okay, ya'll just answer this one question for Tweety okay? Is there such a thing as The Lake of Fire?" she asked.

"Yeah!" They all said at once.

J Bug looked at me surprised. "Tweety, you don't know about The Lake of Fire?" he asked.

"Well, Curly just told me," I said, still looking surprised.

"You big dummy! It's in the Bible plain as day," Mikey opened up his smart mouth.

Everybody started laughing because he made it sound funny. He also made me look stupid. I stood there squinting my eyes at Mikey.

"Shut up! Ain't nobody talking to *you*," I replied.

"Well I was talking to you! Don't get mad 'cause you dumb. Can you say R-e- v-e- l- a- t- i-o- n? That's a book in the Bible *you* need to read. I can tell you don't read the Bible. You know what? You *so* dumb to be so smart," Mikey said.

Everybody started laughing again although they tried not to.

My cousin Weiner came to my defense. "Well, if she didn't know, she just didn't know man. We all had to learn," he said.

J Bug agreed. "Yeah, that's right. Hey, don't worry 'bout it baby. You gon be alright. That's what we all here for, to learn," he said with a wink.

J Bug placed his hand on my shoulder and massaged it briefly as he shined his cute smile at me. He had not tried to touch me in a long time now. I wondered if he might have been finally growing out of his mannish behavior.

"Darn! Here you go baby! Take *my* bible then!" Mikey continued to be smart.

I rolled my eyes at Mikey. "Shut up talking to me with your black butt!" I retorted.

"Oh, I guess that mean you light skinned like Curly then!" he responded back.

I wanted to slap him. They all laughed every time Mikey opened his mouth. I couldn't do anything else but roll my eyes. I swung my hips around and turned my back to Mikey. I turned to face Curly.

"Ain't nobody studying his butt! Can we move away from butt head over there?" I said.

Curly started leading the way while still trying to keep from laughing. She looked sympathetic.

"Tweety, don't worry about him. Come on," she said.

As I walked off, Mikey was still being smart. "Don't forget yo Bible! Lord knows you gon need it! It's free!"

Mikey burst out laughing. I couldn't stand him.

In the mean time, J Bug must've said something about me.

"You like that bald headed girl man? Well *I* don't!" Mikey responded to whatever J Bug was saying to him.

Other than Mikey, I was received very well by every other boy in the church, which was totally different from how I felt about boys at my school. I took on a different attitude about myself when I was at church. I felt more confident about myself around my new church friends. I felt comfortable being myself.

<u>"Healing Roads Journal"</u>

Not only was church making a great impression on me, it was changing my entire family's beliefs and embedding in us the fear of God. The voice of God was represented through the words of Mother Jordon and Pastor Nichols. Whenever they said God said it, we believed it just like everyone else. The congregation feared, so we feared. They had faith, so we had faith. There were many testimonies and witnesses to the power of God's presence over our leaders in church. Most of the children in church had more of the fear of God in them than the adults. These were my peers who I followed in many ways.

CHAPTER FIVE

"Shon"

We visited Daddy's mama, Grandma Lola Mae over the weekend. My cousins Neecy and Yolanda along with their brothers, PJ and Sam, were there. I was excited to see the girls, and their brothers were excited to see Scootie. Another favorite cousin of mine named Jan was also over at Grandma's house as well.

I listened as Neecy and Jan told me all about their boyfriends. We sat in a corner whispering and laughing. I got picked on for never having a boyfriend before. I tried to convince them I didn't really want any boyfriends. They accused me of being scared.

"I'm not scared. I don't want no stupid boyfriends, now," I said.

"Girl, you don't know what you missing," Yolanda responded as she held out her hand for Jan to slap her five then she slapped her back five.

They swapped kissing tales while I frowned at the thought. Neecy's boyfriend ate half her bubble gum out her mouth.

Neecy and Yolanda had to leave, but Jan and I continued to talk. We were upstairs along with some other younger cousins. All the adults were downstairs talking loudly and laughing. There were always lots of people over at Grandma Lola Mae's house.

Jan and I weren't really paying the younger children any attention. My Aunt Minnie's brother, Shon, was also at Grandma's house.

Shon came upstairs where we were. He was telling jokes, making us laugh at him. He wore shades while acting real cool, bragging about all his girlfriends. He talked about how they fought over him. He looked like a man, but he still acted like a teenager, so I assumed he was still a teenager. He was arrogant. He bragged too much about his good looks and he kept rubbing his chin. Shon was dressed sharp from head to toe. He showed off his expensive shoes and silk shirt.

He had on loud cologne. He was sitting back chewing gum, smiling.

Jan asked Shon for some money. He pulled out a roll of money as if he was going to pass it around. He told me and Jan to come here. We went towards him thinking we were about to get some money. He asked us if we wanted to make five dollars.

"What we gots to do?" Jan said.

Jan was eager to earn some money.

Shon sized up Jan, who was the same age as me. I was going to the sixth grade but she had been held back a year. She was still much faster than me. After Shon looked Jan up and down, he sized me up and motioned me over to him.

"Yo, *she* gotta do it."

"Who, me?" I asked.

Shon nodded.

"Yeah, you," he said.

I asked right out, "What do I have to do?"

"You ain't really gotta do nothin. Just sit in my lap," he said.

I responded to him real fast. "No," I said.

I walked away. Jan was still standing there.

"I'll do it!" she said.

Shon shook his head no turning to me.

"Tweety gotta do it," he said.

I went on the far side of the room with the little kids and acted interested in what they were doing. After Granddaddy, I wasn't about to sit on his lap. I knew what he wanted to do.

Jan came over telling me I was crazy. I shook my head.

"I don't want to," I said.

Shon called me, but I ignored him.

"Yo, Tweety, okay, look! I ain't gon bother you no mo. Just come here and look. Lemme show you somethin real quick," he said.

Shon took more money out of his roll of money. Jan was pulling me towards him when she saw all the money.

"Come on girl! He gon give us some *money*. Shoot!" she said.

I let her pull me over to Shon who was holding up twenty dollars.

"You want this twenty dollars?" he asked.

Jan grabbed my hand and held it out for the money.

"Yeah, give it to her! She gon split it wit me, shoot," she replied.

Shon was playing games. I reached for the money, but he held on to it. He grabbed my hand pulling me closer. I wasn't scared because Jan was standing right there as well. I was real calm.

"Let me go boy," I said.

"Boy? Who you callin boy? Oh, I look like a *boy* to you?" he said.

I treated him like I would have treated one of the teenagers in my neighborhood. Shon shined his big wide smile at me while rambling on about nothing.

"Tweety, Tweety. How old you is?" he asked.

"Why?" I said.

Shon started laughing.

"Oh, you thank you smart don't you?" he said.

Shon started tickling me. I started to laugh, but I was trying to stop him. I grabbed at his hand. Jan jumped in helping me break free. She tried to make it seem like a fun game or something. She wanted Shon to grab her and tickle her too. She jumped in front of me laughing.

"Hey, watch out now! Move girl. I'm talking to Tweety for a minute," he said, ignoring Jan.

I was growing impatient with his games. He caught my hand again.

"Let me go!" I shouted.

"Do you want the twenty dollars or not?" he asked.

I put my free hand on my hip.

"I already said to give it here," I said.

Shon burst out laughing.

"Naw, see you gotta do what I asked first. Just sit in my lap for five minutes and that's it. The whole twenty is yours," he said.

"What about me, man?" Jan interrupted.

"I got a twenty dollar bill for you too, if Tweety do what I asked," he said.

"Well, what do you want me to sit in your lap for?" I asked.

"Nothin. I just want you to sit here five minutes. Yo, ain't nobody gon *hurt* you. Look at you, all scared and stuff. I just want you to sit here for ten minutes and that's all."

"Naw, see, at first you said five minutes and now you're saying ten. Uh uh. I might do it for one minute," I said.

"Naw, you gotta sit here for at least til I count to twenty. Just til I count to twenty and that's it. Come on now," he urged.

I looked at Shon's lap and I couldn't help but to notice the bulge in the middle of his pants. He was touching himself anxiously and his legs were spread apart making it obvious he wanted me to sit on his bulge. He was stroking my hand softly begging me to just sit on him for a few minutes. Memories of Granddaddy flashed through my head. I didn't want Shon touching me. I relaxed my hand so he could relax his grip, then I snatched away and backed off.

"My mama told me not to be sitting in folks' laps," I snapped.

Shon whipped out another ten dollar bill.

"Look Tweety. You know you want this money. You can have all this. Look at all this money. You want it, come and get it," he said trying to cover his bulge with his hand.

I didn't like how desperate he was behaving. I didn't like how he was grabbing himself and trying to cover up his bulge at the same time. He caught me looking and smiled.

"Tweety, so what you know 'bout this?" he said with a big smile on his face.

"What?" I said looking away embarrassed.

"You know what I'm talkin 'bout," he said.

He patted himself before rubbing himself.

"You like that right there?" he asked looking more serious.

"Wait a minute, I'll be back," I quickly said.

I ran downstairs. I didn't tell on him but I didn't go back upstairs. I didn't want Daddy to get angry like he did when he found out about Granddaddy. He could end up hurting Shon and going to jail. Aunt Minnie would stop liking me if Daddy hurt her brother.

Jan came running downstairs trying to get me to come back upstairs. I squeezed in a spot on the floor between Mama who was sitting on a sofa. I wasn't budging.

I told Jan I wanted to stay downstairs because it was too hot upstairs. Every time I pictured Shon rubbing his pants and shining his sly smile my way, I got angry. I thought to myself, *"Don't touch me!"* I was becoming more and more repulsed by men's bulges. They weren't nice because they could cause you pain. I would have never touched a guy's bulge knowing what I knew.

Jan sat on the floor next to me. We stayed right there until Mama and Daddy were ready to leave.

A few months later, Shon was killed in a gambling argument. He was shot in the head. Shon was twenty one years old. I never told anyone about Shon trying to pay me to sit on his lap.

"Healing Roads Journal"

This is my first time ever talking about this incident since it occurred. In fact many other events are revealed here for the first time ever. It feels great being transparent.

CHAPTER SIX

"MY CREW"

By sixth grade, I had developed physically a lot more. A lot of boys *and* men were noticing me more and referencing towards my rear end. I didn't like grown men looking at me. I could tolerate boys I hung around or went to school or church with as well as the next girl, but I was bothered by the adult men. In the sixth grade, in 1978, people were always telling me I looked very mature for my age. They often told me I could easily pass for a high school girl.

I had a best friend named JC in my neighborhood, who had a larger fanny than me and boys constantly hit on her, too. We both vowed we were going to be the smart girls in the neighborhood by keeping boys in their place.

JC had a darker complexion than me. Her hips weren't as wide as mine. Both our hair was average length, not too long and not too short. I mostly wore my hair in flips. She wore her hair curled under in a bob. JC lived with her grandmother. Her mother was absent from her life for some reason, and her father lived out of town.

My brother had two best friends in our neighborhood, Mark and this other boy named Vance. I heard Vance bragging to some boys about having his way with JC. I told JC what he said, expecting shock and disdain along with denial, but when she smiled, I questioned her flat out.

"Did you do something with Vance or not?" I asked.

"Well girl, I ain't gon lie to you, I sho did! I couldn't *help* myself girl. He so fine!"

"JC! We promised each other we weren't going to be stupid like the other girls around here!" I said surprised.

JC started laughing, but I was really hurt. I took it personal and wanted to cry. I felt betrayed. It seemed as if all the other girls were disrespecting themselves with boys and JC was the one girl who would stand by my side and demand respect from boys. She went behind my back and turned on me for some stupid boy. I wanted us to be best friends forever. I couldn't be best friends with someone who had a bad reputation. Boys would start to think I was promiscuous like her. It was hard enough making boys respect me. After Granddaddy, it was of grave importance no one else disrespected my body. JC was the only friend who seemed to understand and agreed with me on this issue.

JC also had sex with one of the older boys who we both had a crush on named Antonio. Antonio was four or five grades ahead of us. Even though I had a crush on him, I would never have slept with him. JC got completely wild with boys and built up a bad reputation. I walked around to her apartment and knocked on the door and I could see through the cracked door, and she had some boy lying on top of her on the sofa.

"Tweety, come back later, I can't talk right now!" she muttered.

The next day I was sitting all alone on the Community Porch and I caught her sneaking out of Antonio's house. She smiled as she walked past me.

"JC, I *know* what you've been doing! How could you sleep with all those boys like that?" I asked contemptuously.

"Honey child, all I can say is, one day you gon have to find out for yo self. *Damn* Antonio is fine and his dick is..." I interrupted JC before she finished her sentence.

"I don't wanna hear about his *thang*! Yucky! That's gross! You mean to tell me you *like* letting these boys take advantage of you? I can't believe you're so stupid!" I yelled.

"Honey please! You just don't know gull, shit. It's fun. You oughtta try it one day. I gotta go clean up fore Granny git home. See you later alligator," she said with a big smile.

I stopped speaking to her. She was so busy going over to boys' houses she didn't even notice that I stopped speaking to her. She eventually moved away to live with her father out of town. Her grandmother couldn't handle her any longer.

In my crowded neighborhood in the projects, there were a lot of people outside. Men and boys commented on my backside all the time. I gained all my weight in my butt and hips. I had to smack boys in my neighborhood about touching me. Boys were always trying to touch on the girls, not just me. I punched anybody who grabbed at me. Some of the girls didn't mind it at all. Some of the girls turned this into a chasing game. I got angry.

As I grew up, Daddy taught me how to set standards for myself. Daddy would observe my friends outside and call me over to hear his observations. He saw a boy hit one of the girls on her bottom while he ran and laughed at her, she basically did nothing but laugh in a silly way and chased him while showing all her pearly whites.

"Tweety come 'ere right quick baby," Daddy called me from the Community Porch.

"Now Tweety, you see how he put his hands on her?" he asked.

"Yes sir," I responded.

"Well, Tweety, you not gon let no boy touch you like that 'cause you gon let them know right from the jump start that you ain't like none of them other girls out there. They not gon just put they hands on you 'cause *yo* body ain't *none* of they play toy. Ain't that's right baby?" Daddy said.

"Yes sir," I replied.

Daddy put his hand on my head ruffling my hair as I nodded.

"If any one of 'em put they hands on you, you take and knock the living day lights out of 'em! If they try and hit you back, just pick up a brick or big stick or something and let'em have it! You hear?" he said.

"Yes sir," I replied again.

Daddy affirmed me. "That's Daddy's smart girl! You ain't gon be stupid like some of these other girls out here... you gon be smart. Ain't that's right baby?" he said.

I nodded as Daddy gave me a kiss ruffling my hair again in his loving way. I walked outside with my head up, smiling. I felt proud about being different. I felt special. Besides, after Granddaddy, boys' private parts were yucky to me. I didn't ever want to see or touch any boy in a sexual way and I didn't want them touching me. I frowned when boys groped themselves in playful ways and made comments to girls about their stupid body parts.

When Daddy saw girls outside kissing their boyfriends and letting them lean all close up on them, he called me inside for another lesson.

"You see how they just let them boys do whatever they want to in public Tweety?" he asked.

"Yes sir," I said.

"When those boys get through using them and disrespecting them, they gon be looking for somebody respectful like you 'cause you not gon be used goods like some of these girls out here. Ain't that's right Tweety?" he asked.

Daddy always put an "s" on "that's" when he asked "Ain't that's right?"

I always agreed and got Daddy's firm approval. I felt validated for being different and keeping my self respect. He was always telling me who I was and asking me questions all the time. It was through my daddy's words and questions that I learned to set higher standards for myself where boys were concerned.

Daddy even talked to me about picking intelligent guys or guys who didn't smoke or drink and disrespect girls.

"Now Tweety, when you see any boy out there disrespecting any girls, they'll do the same thing to you. If they disrespect one, they'll disrespect another. Ain't that's right, baby?" Daddy said.

I was quick to turn my nose up at ignorant boys.

When Daddy wasn't telling me things, Mama had a way of captivating me with stories about her childhood. She'd catch me in the house watching "The Brady Bunch" all alone and come sit down with me and engage in her stories.

"How come you not outside wit yo friends, Tweety?" she asked.

"I wanna finish watching The Brady Bunch. Their all out there being fast with their boyfriends anyway, especially Paulina. She be just letting her boyfriend feel all on her in front of everybody like that's something cute, and they be slobbing all over each other's mouth and stuff and I think it's gross. I'm not *ever* letting any boys touch *me* like that 'cause *that's* disrespectful to me. And her boyfriend be talking about her to all his friends. 'Cause I be *hearing* those boys just talking about all those stupid girls who let them touch on them like that," I said.

"You know, I remember I had this friend named Blinky, and she was my best friend, and she reminds me a lot of Paulina," Mama said.

"What happened to Blinky?" I asked.

"She ended up getting pregnant, miscarrying and losing the baby after the boy beat her and stomped her all in her stomach 'cause she found out he was cheating on her," she said.

"Oh no! What happened to him? He didn't feel sorry or nothing?" I asked.

"Well, *he* got his in the end. Lisa, his other girlfriend had older brothers, and he ended up gittin her pregnant too, but when he tried to walk out on her, he got his butt beat, and I mean they tore his red butt up too!" she said.

"Good! That's what he get!" I said.

"Mmm hmm, well he sho got it. But just like Paulina out there letting that boy disrespect her in public, you just mark my words, when he git done wit her, he gone talk about her too. She ain't doin nothing but giving herself a bad reputation. Just like Blinky," she said.

"Well, whatever happened to Blinky?" I asked.

"She ended up wit a real bad reputation and boys never respected her ever since then. She got wild and I had to stop being her friend 'cause I said, she ain't gon ruin *my* reputation, 'cause I had a good reputation and boys respected me," she said.

"That's just like JC, Mama! I couldn't be her friend anymore either 'cause of *her* bad reputation," I said.

This was the first of many more of Mama's stories to come all throughout the years and I never got bored or lost interest. I learned many lessons. Mama kept our relationship strong as mother and daughter. I would spend hours sometimes listening to her childhood stories about growing up in a place called Summer Hill.

As I grew up in my neighborhood, I was very observant but I began to form a friendship with a particular group of friends who I saw everyday. Antonio's sister, Paulina, who was two years older than me, another girl named Anita, who was my age, and Lanette, who was a year ahead of me. They were all a part of my neighborhood crew. Of course, Paulina tried to be the boss of us all since she was the oldest. I didn't consider her too fast because she hadn't slept with anybody. She and her boyfriend just kissed all the time.

Anita had two brothers named John and Ralph. Paulina also had another brother named Gregory. Antonio was the oldest brother of the two. Murphy lived next door to Anita across the street. He hung out with both Paulina's and Anita's brothers. Murphy was constantly imitating Michael Jackson every time you saw him. He was entertaining so we liked him a lot.

Murphy's mother, Ms. Rae Rae, straightened and curled my hair from time to time. We all hung out over Paulina's house a lot. Her mama was real cool. Ms. Janice was a Christian lady, but she wasn't overbearing. She was funny. Mama and Daddy liked her so they trusted her around me. We thought she was cool because all her children called her Janice instead of Mama, and she didn't mind. I knew if I ever called either of my parents by their first names, I would have gotten slapped dead in my mouth.

Since most of the boys hung around with us girls, Scootie and his friends didn't hang with the other boys much. Scootie made a big deal about not wanting his sister around him all the time. We spent enough time bonding together whenever we were in the house. When we were outside, Scootie wanted freedom away from me.

When I hung out on the Community Porch with my crew, music was always playing. Neighbors played their stereos so loud till it sounded as if the music was playing just for us. We even yelled for them to play certain records and they gladly played requested records for us to clown around, singing. Sometimes someone would bring their Boom Box and play it if no neighbor was playing music.

I never knew all the words to many new songs now, because we didn't play "blues" in our house since starting church. We were only allowed to listen to gospel music. Occasionally we snuck and turned the radio on when Mama and Daddy weren't home. Since the stereo was downstairs in the living room, it was hard not to get caught. We didn't hang out in the living room downstairs much anyway. We'd rather watch TV upstairs or hang out in our rooms.

I couldn't figure out how all my friends knew all the words to every song. I felt real dumb when we sang along to the radio. I was the only one who only knew the hook and the bridge. I knew just bits and pieces of the verses. I knew all Daddy's old songs though.

Because we had been in church for some years now and not listening to blues, I had no idea about the difference between black and white radio stations or AM/FM. Whenever I turned on the radio, I just scanned through the AM stations since the radio was always on AM. I was becoming very eclectic as I listened to a variety of music when I could find a station. I didn't have much time to listen to the radio before Mama or Daddy came home since I was busier watching TV or hanging outside.

Music was a constant pastime outside. From dance songs like "Dance To The Music" by Sly & the Family Stone, to James Brown's "Say it Loud, I'm Black and I'm Proud." Then, fun songs, like, Aretha Franklin's "Respect," Isley Brother's "It's Your Thing," Kool & The Gang's "Jungle Boogie," Sledge Sister's "We are Family," and Jean Knight's "Mr. Big Stuff." Of course there were the slow songs, like, The Temptations', "Just My Imagination," The Jackson Five's "I'll Be There," Aretha Franklin's "Do Right Man, Do Right Woman," and The Chi Lites', "Have You Seen Her."

We still listened to old songs, but the new songs never stopped coming. Everytime I looked up, there was another new song.

I was still extremely self-conscious about boys making comments about my big butt. I couldn't fathom the thought of doing anything sexual with boys and their comments made me feel uncomfortable and ashamed, the way I had felt when Granddaddy touched me. It killed me to be felt on and I cringed at every touch. It was nasty and I didn't like any of it. It didn't bother me to see other girls with boys; I just didn't want them to touch *me* that way.

Cliques just kind of evolved in our neighborhood. Everyone had their own crews to hang around. I liked my crew very much, just like I liked my church family. Scootie and his friends were into band and school. They had their own clique.

When it came to sports, all the guys in the neighborhood were friends. They came together to play any kind of ball games. Everybody participated when we played neighborhood games. If you could play the games, then it didn't matter about your age.

This was a time when the older teenagers played with the younger children, and brothers and sisters played together. When we played "Dodge Ball" or "O.U.T.," of course the younger children got out first because they were the easiest to get hit with the ball.

When my brother wasn't around, he and his friends were at band practice at school. They hung out at each other's homes to practice together. They also liked to hang around the gym at school playing basketball or down the street at our neighborhood basketball court. Sometimes they hung out on the little field in front of our door shooting marbles, wrestling, or playing catch football.

I was the only girl who liked playing football with the boys. I could catch and throw pretty well. I constantly competed with Scootie to prove I was as strong as he was. I always had a problem with Scootie thinking he could rule over me.

Whenever I played football outside with the other boys and Scootie wasn't around, I had to make the rules clear before starting a game every time.

"Don't try to feel on me or I'm quitting!" I said.

Sometimes they tried me anyway. I wouldn't hesitate to throw the football down and walk off the field in the middle of a game. Depending on who it was and how obvious the touch was, sometimes I would accept an apology and play again. Sometimes Scootie was around and he told me to just leave and let the boys play.

"Why don't you go do girl things? Go on and hang out with the other girls. Darn!" he said.

He was just being protective by keeping the boys eyes and hands off me without fighting. He heard comments and didn't like boys disrespecting me. He instantly spoke up. I didn't want him fighting so I constantly argued I could handle the boys on my own.

"Fine then! Be stupid if you want to!" he said.

"Who said anything about being stupid? I just said let me handle it on my own. You don't tell me what to do, now!" I said.

"Like I said, be stupid if you want to. That's you," he said.

"Shut up talking to me. I know what I'm doin! You don't even know what you're talking about!" I said.

"Yeah, you know you're stupid, but go on and be stupid if you want to," Scootie yelled back.

"You're stupid!" I retorted.

We found it easier to stay in our own space with our separate cliques. We always argued when we hung out too much together. I didn't want him trying to fight everyone for every little thing they said. Boys were always saying or doing things. It was silly to try to fight everyone all the time. I wanted to be independent anyway. Independence was my way of trying to find myself in the midst of what seemed like a struggle to be seen and heard beyond a boy just noticing my neat figure. I wanted to prove to them that I was much more than just a body so I became competitive and a tomboy. I didn't need Scootie coming to my rescue every second. If he walked up in the middle of me confronting a boy he'd just take over.

"Tweety, be quiet. Let me handle it. You just go over there and sit down," he said.

The boys admired him for being brave enough to stand up to bigger and older boys. Daddy taught him not to be scared of anybody. He also taught him not to ever run away. Daddy would make Scootie go back outside if he ever caught him running in the house to avoid a fight. He made sure Scootie was brave. He would even stand there and watch Scootie fight without jumping in.

"Go on Lil Joey! You can knock him out. You stronger than he is. I don't care how big he is," Daddy would say to Scootie.

Scootie wanted to make Daddy proud so he often proved Daddy right.

I played football mostly when Scootie wasn't around because I went to Mama and asked her to make Scootie stop keeping up trouble about the boys looking at me or saying things to me all the time. I assured Mama that Scootie was paranoid and exaggerated the situation. Scootie was frustrated with me.

Either Scootie would tell the boys he couldn't play or he'd quit when I came around to play. He acted angry with me as he walked away, I wasn't just standing on the field. I could catch better than a few of the boys, and could throw the football straight and far enough to astound all them. I had finally proven my skills to a point where the boys would beg me to play with them because I was a good asset to their team. They would choose me over some of the boys who couldn't catch or throw from too far away. I had a good, strong arm.

"Did you see that? Got dog! Man, did you see Tweety catch that long throw?" One of the boys yelled.

If I fell I just got up and dusted the dirt off, even if I skinned my knees.

"Hey, you alright Tweety?" The boys would ask.

"Yeah, let's play. Throw the ball," I would say.

"Damn man, she tough," the boys would respond.

They would even fight over me sometimes. The captains would always take turns picking one player at a time until everyone was either on a team or left out. I was never left out.

I felt good when they laughed and bragged over me faking out a boy and making a touchdown while Paulina, Anita and Lanette watched the game from the Community Porch acting prissy. Sometimes they would demand to play too because I was getting all of the boys attention. I was just happy to be catching their attention in the right way. The other girls always made a fool out of themselves on the field behaving too delicately.

A football was thrown way down field to Paulina who jumped back, too afraid to catch the ball because she might get hurt, or Anita would catch the ball and then complain about her arm and stop the whole game, acting like the catch damaged her arm for life. Lanette caught the ball and then froze in her tracks screaming with her eyes closed as the tacklers came towards her. She threw the ball down and said, "I give up!"

It got to a point where the boys would only let them play if they felt like clowning around or showing off, but not in a serious game. A lot of times in the more serious games the losing team had to pay up a little money.

Antonio was really nice. He never tried to feel on me. He always joking around. After I made a touch down and our team won the game, Antonio got excited about our team winning. He surprised me with a kiss on the cheek. I didn't cringe. As a matter of fact, I liked his cheek kiss. It was a safe kiss and it felt decent.

"That's my baby right there!" Antonio yelled with a gorgeous smile.

My crush suddenly appeared. Oh my God! I was never going to wash that spot on my face again. I had daydreams about his kiss for a long time after. I sat at the dinner table unable to eat for daydreaming. I continued to daydream after picking at my plate of rice and stew meat with sweet cornbread. I never imagined a kiss could make me feel so giddy. It was something about his kiss that seemed as if he was respectable. I think it was because he stayed in the boundaries of what I felt was safe. Other boys tried to kiss me sloppily in the mouth, and they always crossed the boundaries of what reminded me of Granddaddy. I always hated the thought of kissing until now. I even stopped kissing Daddy on the lips.

Scootie noticed I hadn't put one bite of food in my mouth. He was ready for seconds. Sonia, who was the slowest eater, was even almost done with her plate.

"What's wrong with you Tweety? How come you're not eating?" Scootie asked.

"Oh, well, I'm just not hungry," I replied.

"Uh oh! Call the ambulance, Sonia. Something's wrong with Tweety!" he said.

"Shut up! Ain't nothing wrong with me. I'm just not hungry," I said.

"Not hungry? Naw, naw, something's wrong with you. You ain't never not hungry!" Scootie said.

"I *said* nothing's wrong with me. Leave me alone!" I said.

Scootie was interrupting my daydream of being kissed by Antonio on the cheek. I never wanted to stop dreaming about him kissing me. I could just dream all night. Scootie reached for my plate and started eating. He was surprised I wasn't eating at all.

"I know what happened! Aliens done abducted her, Sonia! This isn't really Tweety sitting right here," he said while he ate from my untouched plate.

"Shut up! It *is* me. I'm not hungry, darn! Leave me alone!" I said.

"Sonia, I'm *telling* you, that's not Tweety. If I was you, *I* wouldn't turn my back on her tonight. She's gon try to eat you tonight. You seen "Body Snatchers?" he joked.

Sonia's eyes got big.

"Tweety, are you Tweety for real?" Sonia asked.

"Yeah it's me! Don't listen to him Sonia. He's just playin," I said.

"No I'm *not* either! They programmed her mind to talk like Tweety, but I'm telling you, you *better* believe me or aliens are gon come and get you too," Scootie continued joking.

"Scootie quit it! I'm not playing with you! You're trying to scare Sonia. You better quit it 'fore I punch you!" I yelled.

"Aaugh! Don't hurt me! See Sonia, she's gonna zap me with a lazer beam!" Scootie said.

I punched Scootie who exaggerated my punch by falling and screaming as Sonia's eyes got even bigger.

I yelled upstairs. "Mama! Tell Scootie to quit it! He's down here scaring Sonia!" I said.

"Okay. Alright Sonia. I was just kidding. You believe anything, don't you? Dog," Scootie finally said.

"Don't you talk to her! You're sitting up here scaring her like you crazy and you know it!" I snapped at Scootie.

I punched him again.

"Alright now, you're gon make me hurt you. Quit hitting me," he said.

"Make me!" I said.

"Hit me one more time and see," he warned.

I punched him again. He pretended to charge at me causing me to flinch.

"Aah ha! See there. That's why you jumped, 'cause you know I'll be done hurt you. You *better* be glad I don't hit girls," he said.

"I don't better be glad of nothing, now," I said.

Scootie laughed and started calling me an alien, again. I resigned to just ignoring him. Of course by bedtime, we were all laughing and joking again as if we were never arguing earlier. Sometimes I pushed Scootie too far with my punches and got shoved or punched hard on my shoulder.

I went back to daydreaming about Antonio's kiss as soon as our night talk ended. I lost my appetite for an entire week.

Because the boys still talked about how they sneaked in a touch on my butt or how juicy my booty was or how it jiggled when I was running, Scootie would overhear them talking behind my back and he would be infused with anger. He finally couldn't take it anymore and told Mama and Daddy unbeknownst to me. They finally suggested in a matter-of-fact way that I should stick to doing girl things and let the boys be boys. It was a nice way of telling me I couldn't play ball with the boys anymore.

CHAPTER SEVEN

"JAN"

I became more involved in the church every day. We hadn't been over to Grandmamma Lola Mae's house in a while so we dropped by. My cousin Jan was over there. I hadn't seen her in months. I was excited to see her after so long.

Jan immediately started telling me about her different boyfriends. She gave me details about kissing them. I admitted I had not kissed a boy before. I couldn't count the little cheek kiss Antonio innocently gave me.

"Well then I guess you don't know how to French kiss then?" Jan said.

"What's a French kiss?" I asked curiously.

Jan shook her head at me. "I see now, I'm gon have to teach you a thing or two!" she said.

Grandmamma Lola Mae asked Daddy to take her to the store. I stayed with Jan and my Great Aunt Goose. Aunt Goose was Grandmamma Lola Mae's sister. My Great Aunt Mae who named me Tweety, had passed away. Grandmamma Lola Mae and Aunt Goose lived together now. Aunt Goose was upstairs putting away laundry. My brother and sister rode to the store with Daddy to see what they wanted to buy. I almost left with them but Jan was begging me to stay with her.

"I guess you and Neecy *both* have a thing or two to teach me. Ya'll are so *fast*," I joked.

"Girl, and you know it! I'm gon *git* mines baby. Ain't *nobody* stopping me from havin some fun. I be makin 'em beg for mo'!" Jan responded proudly.

I started laughing. Jan grabbed her purse and came back in the kitchen where we couldn't be heard by Aunt Goose. Jan pulled out some lip gloss.

"Okay Tweety girl, let me tell you what me and my boyfriend be doin. Better yet, I'm gon just show you so you'll know what to do when it's *yo* turn to kiss a boy. Let's go under the pantry. Aunt Goose don't need to hear what I'm 'bout to tell you." she said.

I started giggling. I waited to hear what she was going to say.

"Okay, you ready?" she asked.

"Yeah!" I said eagerly.

"Okay, this how me and my boyfriend be kissing." She came over to me. "Okay, you gon be me and I'm gon be him," she said.

"Okay," I agreed.

Jan walked over towards me "pimping," the way cool guys walk. We both burst out laughing. Jan stood in front of me.

"Stand right there and just look at me cuz I'm gon show you *exactly* how me and my boyfriend be kissing," she said.

"Okay," I replied.

Jan got close to me and started leaning towards my lips demonstrating. "Ooh baby, come on over here and let me taste that sweet tongue of yours," she joked.

I burst out laughing. She backed up.

"Girl, you wanna know or not?" she asked.

"Okay, okay, I won't laugh," I said.

Jan started leaning towards me again, pretending to be her boyfriend. "Ooh baby, I just wanna taste those sweet sugar lips," she continued to act out.

I couldn't help but start laughing again. I couldn't believe boys talked like that. Jan stopped again looking exasperated. She was trying to act mature, but I kept laughing. I guess I was immature.

"You don't wanna know, 'cause you keep laughin. I'm trying to show you so you'll know how to kiss a boy when it's yo turn to kiss somebody so yo butt won't be actin all scared and stuff. You don't wanna be standin there actin all stupid girl, do you?" Jan said looking frustrated.

"Okay, for real this time, you can show me right quick. For real though," I said trying not to laugh anymore.

"Well quit actin like you scared then. If you act like this when a *real* boy try and kiss you, he gon just walk away and leave yo butt *standin* there," she said.

"Alright! I said I'm ready. Okay, wait a minute." I let out one more good laugh before straightening up. "Now, I'm ready. For *real* though. For real for real this time," I said.

I stood still and Jan inched closer. This time she actually kissed me. I closed my eyes trying to pretend she was a boy as she kissed me softly on the lips in slow motion. I wanted to laugh again but I held my laugh in. I opened my eyes to Jan smiling at me.

"That's it? I mean that's all I have to do?" I said.

"Well, naw, that ain't *all* my boyfriend did to me. He put his tongue in my mouth," she said.

I stepped back. "Ooh, that's nasty!" I gasped.

"No it ain't girl. That's a French kiss," Jan said.

"Oh, so *that's* what French kissing is? The boys around where I live call it tongues. Well, tongues is nasty," I said.

"No it ain't neither! Girl you crazy! Let me show you. You'll see. It's not nasty the way *we* do it. Hold your mouth open." I obeyed and opened my mouth wide. "Not like that stupid, do it like this," she said.

Jan demonstrated by barely holding her mouth open. I opened my mouth like her.

"Now, this is how my boyfriend be kissin me for *real*," she said.

Jan started sticking her tongue in my mouth grabbing me close. I didn't know whether to laugh or not. I let her show me.

"Girl, nall, you ain't doin it right. You gotta close yo eyes," she said.

"Well I don't like no boys putting their tongue in my mouth though. I *gotta* do it?" I asked relunctantly.

"If you wanna be with a boy then that's what you gotta do. You just gon have to grow up. You a big girl now honey child. You can't be actin like no baby talking 'bout you don't want no boyfriends. Come on, open yo mouth like this," she said anxiously.

I closed my eyes and she kissed me again. We backed up against the wall while she was moving up against me. I wondered when the demonstration was going to end. Jan stopped kissing me but kept moving up against me.

"Girl, when boys be kissing you and stuff, they be moving up against you just like this, and then they start grabbing yo titty like this and squeezing it," she said as she continued to demonstrate.

Jan was touching my breast and squeezing it. I just stood there and let her continue to demonstrate. I found the experience stimulating. I never thought about intimacy with a girl before but I felt if a boy was rubbing up against me, it would feel uncomfortable like it felt with Granddaddy. She felt soft. Nothing hard was poking me. Boys seemed so rough. She was starting to pull my dress up and talk at the same time.

"Girl, I had a dress on just like you and my boyfriend pulled my dress up and touched me like this," she said while she touched me intimately.

Jan started rubbing up against my panties.

"Then he squeezed my butt like this," she said as she gently squeezed my backside.

Although it was stimulating, I wanted to pull my dress down because I felt ashamed. Jan's eyes were closed and she was aggressively grabbing me. My inner voice was telling me I shouldn't. Jan started reaching for my panties. I reached to pull my dress down. Jan grabbed my hand.

"Don't stop me. Let me show you what he did," she said, almost sounding winded.

Jan was attempting to pull my panties down breathing heavy. She let out a hiss that let me know she was pulling down my panties for her enjoyment now. It may have started out a demonstration, but now I realized it was turning into something else. She wanted us to be two girls doing something together. I felt guilty so I resisted but she started pulling down her panties and telling me to come on and lay down so she could lay on top of me. I didn't move so she started sliding down my panties and rubbing up against me. She was rubbing my butt and grabbing my breasts and doing everything to entice me to lie down, then we heard the door open.

I quickly adjusted my panties along with my dress before coming from behind the pantry. Daddy was calling me. It was time to go. I kissed Grandmamma and yelled upstairs to say "I love you" to Aunt Goose. I went out the door quickly with Daddy.

I wondered all the way home if what I let Jan do to me meant that I was gay. It bothered me excessively. I didn't want to be gay. I started thinking about how much I talked about boys when I hung out with my crew at home. I couldn't be gay! I had a crush on Antonio.

I didn't understand that I was only experimenting. A lot of girls and boys my age went through experiments out of curiosity. I couldn't believe I let her do those things to me and it was stimulating. The stimulating part was what had me confused. If it felt good then I must be gay, I kept thinking.

I went to church and listened to Pastor Nichols' message the next day. He talked about God's wrath and how all sinners were going to hell. My eyes got real big. I was scared listening to his message. He described how it was going to be in hell. People were going to burn forever and ever because of their sins. Pastor Nichols talked about repentance. I prayed real hard asking for a lot of forgiveness.

The next day we ended up going back over to Grandmamma's house. Jan was still over there. I was hoping we could forget about what happened the other day. Jan ran to give me a hug. She was anxious to see me.

"Oooh Tweety, yea! Hey honey child! I'm so glad I git to see my cousin again!" she said.

"Hey girl," I said, sounding a little nervous.

Jan grabbed my hand leading me up the steps real fast while every one else was downstairs.

"Ooh girl I got something to tell you!" she said.

I didn't want to go upstairs alone with her. I frowned behind her back not wanting to hear more trash talk about boys and kissing.

"Ooh, girl, I been thinking 'bout you all night long. I can't wait to git them panties off you. I'm gone climb on *top* of you with *both* us naked! Take off all yo clothes right quick," she said with anticipation.

Jan had lost her mind! She was saying how she had been dreaming about me all night long. She was using explicit language. She was shocking me with all her crazy behavior.

"I'm fixin to tear that pussy up!" Jan grabbed my hand. "Come on girl, let's go over to the bed," she said.

She locked the door. Jan was acting crazy! She started reaching for her panties. "Girl, come on! We probably ain't got much time!" she said.

All I could think about was Pastor Nichols' message. He said God was watching everything we did and He knew our hearts even when we weren't honest. I already asked God to forgive me for all my sins and I didn't want to sin ever again. I prayed and asked God not to let me be gay. I looked up at Jan.

"Jan, wait a minute. We can't," I said.

"Why not?" she asked.

"Girl, don't you know we can go to hell if we do that?" I said.

Jan looked shocked. "What you mean?" she said.

I told her how the Bible said all sinners were going to burn in hell. I asked her if she wanted to burn in hell. She said no. I told her to pray and ask God for forgiveness like I did so she could go to heaven. Jan was disappointed.

"Well I guess we better not do it then," she finally said.

I hugged Jan. "Good. Now we can both go to heaven," I said.

We went downstairs with everybody else. Jan still tried to talk me into doing it one last time. I kept moving away from her and avoiding her. I prayed to myself for her a lot. She was acting so desperate and I felt uncomfortable.

After we left, I didn't see her for a long time. She must have been possessed with a demon because she acted so sex crazy. Pastor Nichols talked about people who were possessed with sex demons. She acted like she was going to die if she didn't get me in bed and climb on top of me. She kept begging and saying she needed to feel me naked underneath her. Every chance she got, she whispered desperate things in my ear. I wanted to keep her away from me from then on. She was acting as crazy as J Bug.

I didn't see her again until we were in high school and she was pregnant. She had quite a reputation by then.

"Healing Roads Journal"

For me, there was an inability to know how to heal and allow God to fill my empty voids left from the stigma and the pain, due to my molestation. Instead of God being the one who completed me, I became dependent on others who weren't capable of filling my voids or completing me. Now, I realize no human being is perfect enough to fill my voids or complete me. Healing comes from within me. I need to know who I am as I stand alone in the mirror and feel good about the person I see in my reflection. I was blessed to have God intervening in my life during my period of experimentation, even though I still didn't know how to allow the same God to fill all of my voids and make me complete. I still had much more to learn about my Creator and his purpose for me.

CHAPTER EIGHT

"Love Birds"

At church I became best friends with a new girl named Tameka, who lived around the corner from the church. She attended the same school as Mikey and Nae Nae. Mikey's current girlfriend, Julia, was considered the prettiest girl in church. She had a perfect smile, long hair and cute dimples and she was Mikey's age. I felt like a little girl compared to her, being that I was still only in the sixth grade. Tameka was in the eighth grade and Mikey and Julia were in the ninth grade.

Tameka liked Mikey as well, but he was in love with Julia. They always held hands and talked outside after church. Mikey seemed to only be attuned to what he would consider the stereotypical pretty girl with long hair. He criticized me constantly because I was dark skinned and my hair was not very long, especially since Sonia cut my hair while I was asleep during the summer going into the fifth grade. She thought she was fixing my hair up pretty, but she cut my hair all around the edges. Mama had to work magic with braids to cover up my bald spots.

Mikey picked at all dark skinned girls even though his sister was the darkest girl in church. He acted like the perfect world was filled with bourgeoisie girls like Julia. I couldn't stand him because he always looked at me with a smirk on his face whispering and laughing.

"That girl must thank she something wit her lil black baldheaded self. Look at her walking round here like she somebody," Mikey muttered to J Bug as I walked by.

"I don't *have* to think; I *know* I'm somebody and at least I'm not as black as you. You the one think somebody *wants* your behind, now," I retorted.

"I don't have to thank somebody want me! Look at my girlfriend and then look at you," he said.

"So, *look* at your girlfriend. That doesn't mean anything," I said.

"It mean she pretty and you *ugly*, and she wit me, so what that tells you?" he said.

"Awe shut up talking to me," I said.

"You *better* say shut up 'cause you can't say nothing else," he said.

"Oooh you make me sick!" I said.

"That's what the hospital..." he started

"Just shut up talking to me! Stupid!" I interrupted.

I was glad he was obsessed with Julia instead of my new best friend. Tameka kept staring at him all the time.

"Tweety if I tell you something you promise you not gon tell nobody?" Tameka asked.

"Yeah, what?" I said.

"Promise me you not gon say nothing first. I'm for real," she said.

"I promise. Now what is it?" I said.

"Don't look over there but I like that boy with the white shirt and dark brown pants sitting back there next to yo cousin," she said.

I looked back to see who she was talking about.

"No! Don't look. I told you not to look," she said.

"Who are you talking 'bout? Mikey?" I asked.

"Shhh. Yeah, be quiet," she said.

"Eeew, Tameka why you have to like him?" I said.

"Because he cute," she said.

"Not to me. J Bug look *way* better than him to me," I said.

"Not to me," she responded.

"Anyway, you see that girl sitting over there with the long hair smiling?" I said.

"Who you talking 'bout? The girl with the pink on?" she asked.

"Yeah, her. Her name is Julia. She and Mikey go together," I said.

"You for real?" she asked.

"Yeah, where have you been? They have *been* going together," I said.

"Well don't tell nobody I said that I like him," she said.

"I wouldn't do that to my friend. You don't have to worry," I said. I was trying to figure out why all these pretty girls at church were talking about wanting to have a chance with Mikey, because I didn't like him. I was curious and caught myself staring at Mikey a lot. I wanted to find out exactly what the other girls saw in him. He always seemed to be the best dressed boy in church. He had a slender build and was somewhat shorter than the other guys. He had tiny brown freckles on his nose that were only noticeable when you got really close up to him. His dimple showed on the left side of his face when he smiled. Either the girls liked his smile or the way he dressed. Then again, it could be his "too good" attitude that made the girls want to get his attention. If he noticed you, it was only because you were really pretty; otherwise, he totally ignored you or picked at you if you ever got on his bad side.

He was a goody two shoes if you asked me. I had never done anything to him. It wasn't my fault other boys constantly talked about me around him. I had turned every last one of those boys down, so he thought I felt like I was too good.

He accused me of twisting my tail around trying to tease all the boys. It was just my natural walk. When he caught me staring, I looked him up and down from head to toe a couple of times in exaggeration and rolled my eyes with focused resentment.

"Oooh I can't stand that girl right there, man. She thank she cute," he would say to the other boys sometimes.

I stopped dead in my tracks and turned around and just stared at him with scrutiny. Every time he said something I just kept staring without blinking, the entire time until he shut up. I stared him down with such evilness till he couldn't take it anymore. I lowered my stare down to his feet and slowly stared all the way back up to his face in an uncomfortable silence. Even after he turned away he knew I was still staring. I waited till he looked up again before putting a smirk on my face and turned away with the satisfaction of making him feel uncomfortable with my concentrated focus on him. It felt better than any words I might ever think of saying because he always shifted his body uncomfortably. It shut him up for days.

I looked up to Mikey's sister Nae Nae. She was smart and carried herself in a respectable way. Her report cards were always straight A's. Nae Nae was in the eleventh grade.

Nae Nae discovered I knew how to braid hair and asked me to braid her hair one day. I spent the night with Mikey's family. They lived upstairs in the house above the church. Mikey's mama and daddy were both very nice. I enjoyed sitting around talking with them and Nae Nae.

Mikey was sitting on the porch by himself. His girlfriend Julia hadn't been to church in a couple of weeks. I knew she was sneaking around with my cousin PJ behind Mikey's back. I wanted to tell him. When Mikey glanced up at me, he looked so mean. I started to walk away, then I figured, he might be angry because Julia hadn't been coming around.

"Hey, I have something to tell you," I said.

"What you want?" He sounded mean.

I turned to walk away.

"That's okay," I said.

Mikey called me back.

"Hey Tweety, what you was fixin to say to me?" he asked.

I hesitated.

"What you got to tell me?" he asked again.

"I don't know if I should tell you because you might get mad," I said.

Mikey was talking calm. "I'm not gon get mad, so tell me."

"Okay, well I know why Julia hasn't been coming to church lately," I said.

Mikey's eyes lit up when I mentioned Julia's name. "Why?" he asked.

Before I went to spend the night over to Nae Nae's house, my cousin PJ came over to our house to visit. He was bragging about talking to Julia.

"PJ, you just telling a big story! You ain't talking to Julia and you know it," I said.

PJ picked up the phone and called Julia in front of me. His conversation with her indicated they were seeing each other. I couldn't believe Julia was cheating on Mikey, even if I didn't like him much.

After the whole PJ incident, of all people, here I was spending the night with Mikey's sister, feeling guilty about not letting Mikey know about his cheating girlfriend. I looked to observe Mikey's demeanor before telling him.

"Okay, well, Julia's been going with my cousin PJ behind your back," I said.

"Oh really?" he said, sounding surprised.

"My cousin came over our house and called her and let me hear them talking. I even heard them talking about how they kissed and everything," I replied.

"Wait a minute! She kissed him?" he asked.

I nodded yes before answering. "I heard them talking. PJ was telling her how much he enjoyed the kiss they had and he was asking her when she was going to come back over there."

"So she was at his *house*, huh?" he asked.

"Yep she sure was. I just thought you had a right to know," I said.

Mikey didn't talk for a minute. "Okay then. So, Julia is going wit yo cousin PJ now, huh?" he asked.

"Yep," I answered.

"What you do, go tell everybody?" he snapped.

"*Naw*, I didn't tell nobody. It's not everybody's business. So, what are you going to do now?" I asked.

"I'm gon *quit* her. What you think!" he said.

"Well good for you," I said.

He asked me a point blank question. "You can't stand me, can *you*?" he asked.

"Nope!" I answered.

"Why not?" he said.

I tooted my nose before answering him.

"Cause you're too smart mouthed. You're always getting smart with people," I said.

Mikey looked me dead in the eyes.

"You mean I'm always getting smart with you?" he said.

I didn't back down. "Yep!"

Mikey started laughing.

"Well, look at you and how you be acting. You the one who

uppity! Always tootin yo nose up and lookin me up and down," he said.

It was silent for a minute before Mikey spoke again.

"So, stop treating me like that and I'll stop gettin smart with you. I mean, what you think you is anyway? You think you better than everybody?" he asked.

"No, I don't think I'm better than *anybody*! I'm still not going to let anybody treat me like they're better than *me* though," I answered.

"Well, just stop lookin down on me like that. You probably a nice person, but I just wouldn't know it. I mean, I don't like you for a *girlfriend* or nothin like that because you not my type, and then again, you too young for me," he said honestly.

I interrupted. "I don't like you for a *boyfriend*!"

"Well I figured as much, but that don't mean we can't be friends. Right?" he said.

I agreed. We were actually civil to one another the rest of the day. He really wasn't so bad after all. We even laughed at a couple of each other's jokes sitting around the table with his family at dinner time.

His sister Nae Nae was extra dark skinned, but she had beautiful smooth skin and a pretty smile with perfect teeth. A lot of boys liked her. She was also good at karate. She took karate at school so she was pretty tough. She still carried herself in a lady like way. She was the first dark skinned, short haired girl who I felt was as popular as any of the other popular girls who had long hair or was light skinned. She made me comfortable with being dark skinned, especially with her being much darker than me.

For some reason, Nae Nae moved out of the house and went to live with her real father a short time later in the month. I couldn't believe she moved away and stopped coming to church. I didn't see her anymore.

I guess Mikey wasn't so mean after spending the night with their family. I couldn't wait to tell my friend Tameka he was quitting Julia. She still had a big crush on him.

CHAPTER NINE

"Pregnant"

My sixth grade school year was the first time we didn't celebrate Christmas. No one knew the actual day of Jesus' birth, therefore we were taught it would be a lie to celebrate Christmas. Daddy still bought us something the week of Christmas so we wouldn't feel left out among the rest of the neighborhood.

Mikey and I continued to be civil to one another at church from then on. We didn't really talk to one another much, but he was always hanging around my cousins, Bow Leggs, Weiner, and John John. I was always kidding around with my cousins as well. We wrestled and played around a lot since I liked to do tomboy things. Mikey would smile every now and then at something funny we did or I would occasionally laugh at something funny he said or did, but for the most part we stayed out of each other's way. We didn't act the least bit interested in one another. I didn't roll my eyes at him anymore and he didn't talk about me anymore.

Our Pastor challenged us to read the Bible from *Genesis to Revelation*. We all competed to see who could finish the entire bible. I read a book from the Old Testament as well as the New Testament everyday.

I got into heavy reading about The Virgin Mary. This story fascinated me because I was a virgin. I wondered if something like this could happen today.

While playing at home the next day, my stomach started hurting me most of the day. I ignored it as much as I could until I remembered the story about Jesus' Mother named Mary. I didn't realize I was cramping and swelling. Mama never talked to me about these kinds of changes. Out of curiosity, I ran upstairs to the bath room and pulled my shirt up to look at my stomach. It appeared to be poking out as if I was pregnant. I panicked looking at my bloated stomach.

"Oh no!" I yelled, thinking about the Virgin Mary.

I immediately believed God was using me just like he did The Virgin Mary.

"No! God, please no! I don't wanna be pregnant! I can't be pregnant. Please, God don't make me be pregnant! I'll do anything else but this God," I begged as I stared at my bloated and cramping stomach. That explained the uncomfortable feeling in my stomach; I was pregnant.

I started pushing my stomach in as hard as I could, then I punched my stomach over and over thinking I could stop the pregnancy.

Scootie and his friend Mark were downstairs and heard me panicking upstairs, even though they couldn't hear what I was saying.

"Man you need to go check on yo sister and make sure she alright," Mark said to Scootie.

"There's nothing wrong with her, man. She's always trying to fool somebody. She thinks she's slick," Scootie said.

"I don't know man. She sound serious. Tweety, what's wrong with you?" Mark yelled from the bottom of the stairs.

I forgot the bathroom door was cracked and they could hear me. I was embarrassed to tell anyone what was happening to me.

"I can't say. I think I'll be alright in a minute," I said, thinking I could beat my stomach and make everything go away.

"You sure?" Mark said.

I looked at my stomach again. It was still slightly bloated.

"Oh no!" I said.

I beat my stomach with my fists harder.

"Tweety?" Mark continued to call from the bottom of the stairs.

"Wait a minute! I can't talk right now," I yelled back.

I slammed my bathroom door all the way up. I looked at my stomach again and it looked as if it shrunk back down. I sighed in relief and went back outside answering Mark as I ran out the door.

"I'm fine now," I said.

I went back to my normal routine of playing and joking with my friends outside. Mama was downstairs in the kitchen cooking while Daddy was watching TV in his room. It got later in the evening. I was outside on the Community Porch when suddenly I felt funny in my stomach again. It felt like something was moving around so I ran in the house again and went upstairs to the bathroom. I pulled my underwear down and sat on the toilet to pass water thinking I might get some relief afterwards.

My jaw dropped when I saw bloody underwear. I had no idea what I did to myself. I immediately thought it had something to do with me beating the baby out of my stomach. I wondered if I had made God angry. I cracked the door and yelled downstairs to Mama.

"Oh my God! Mama! Mama come quick! It's an emergency! Oh no!"

Daddy ran out in the hallway and I closed the door real quick.

"I need Mama. Daddy you gotta go and get Mama real quick!" I yelled.

Daddy went downstairs to get Mama. I had no clue what was happening to me and I was scared to death I might be dying. Mama took a long time to come upstairs. I panicked more when I noticed more blood falling in the toilet.

"Mama! Please hurry up! Mama I think I'm in trouble!" I yelled.

I started crying, but Mama still took her own sweet time. Scootie walked in the house and heard me yelling and crying. I saw him running upstairs to ask me if I was okay. I slammed the door again.

"No, I'm not alright. I need Mama to come real quick and she won't come!" I yelled.

"Well, Tweety, what's the matter?" he said.

"I can't tell you. I need to see Mama. I need to see Mama now! I'm in pain. Please go get Mama for me. Tell her I'm bleeding," I yelled.

"Where about?" he asked.

"I can't tell you! Tell Mama to come here real quick please!" I said.

I heard Daddy calmly speaking to Mama at the stairs. "Mookie gon and see 'bout that child now. You hear her up there. Gon and see what's goin on wit her Mookie."

"Ain't nothing going on wit her Ranch. She gon be fine and you know it," Mama said.

"No I'm not Mama, I promise I'm not! You have to come here right quick Mama, I need you!" I started whining out my words. I felt frustrated about Mama acting like nothing was wrong. "I've been calling you for a long time now and you haven't even seen what I'm talking about!" I yelled.

Mama came upstairs taking her own sweet time while everyone else stayed downstairs. I just knew Mama was going to call the ambulance once she saw all the blood. She would feel sorry she took so long. She casually walked in the bathroom and closed the door behind her as I showed her the blood on my underwear. She barely looked and then she opened the cabinet in the bathroom and pulled out a tiny thing covered in plastic.

"Tweety, just like I thought. Ain't nothing wrong with you. You done started yo cycle," she said.

"Cycle? What does that mean?" I asked.

Mama sighed. "It means you can get pregnant if you have sex! Now," she snapped.

"But Mama, I haven't had sex! I promise I haven't had sex," I explained. I wondered if I needed to tell her about my episode earlier when I beat the baby out of me.

"Tweety, I didn't say you had sex. When a girl reaches the age where she can get pregnant she bleeds like this for five to seven days every month and if you ever have sex, you know you pregnant 'cause you don't bleed no mo," she explained.

"All girls do this?" I asked.

"Yeah! Now stop acting dumb," she snapped again.

"Well what do I do about all this blood? I can't go no where like this," I said.

"When you take those underwear off, you gon get a bucket of bleach and cold water and soak 'em in the bucket until tomorrow and then you gon wash 'em on yo hands and hang 'em up on the clothes line," she said.

Mama got me a new pair of underwear and she gave me instructions. "Now I want you to pay attention 'cause I'm gon show you one time, and one time only how to put this tampon on," she said.

I had no idea what a tampon was but I nodded. Mama showed me how to push it out of the plastic but I was confused. I didn't understand how far it could go inside me so I thought it was supposed to stop at the tip of my body. I never knew anything could even fit inside of me. I didn't even understand how sexual intercourse worked yet.

Mama already had left me alone to figure it out. She refused to come back upstairs when I called her to show me again. The tampon thing didn't stay in. It fell in the toilet. I sat there crying and begging Mama to come. She let me cry and call her for thirty minutes. Daddy made her come back upstairs again. I didn't know why Mama was so agitated with me.

"Look, I'm gon show you one more time and you better do it right this time, you hear me?"

"Yes ma'am," I said.

This time Mama stood with her back turned and waited for me to insert the tampon. I couldn't insert that thing inside me. I felt a lot of pain everytime I tried. I was crying and telling Mama it wouldn't go up inside me. Mama was angry with me.

"You better figure it out! It will go up in you! You ain't trying," she yelled.

"Yes I am Mama. I'm trying, see." I wanted her to look at me trying.

Mama wouldn't look. "You better hurry up 'fore I leave you in here," she threatened.

"But Mama look. It won't fit," I cried.

I tried again and it hurt, so I started crying more.

Mama gave me the whole box of tampons and as she left, she told me I'd better figure it out. She refused to look at me. I sat in the bathroom and cried and cried trying over and over again but failing. I felt sore from trying to insert that thing inside of me. At long last I finally got one inside of me. I wiped my eyes and smiled because Mama was right. It would go in if I tried hard enough. I got up and washed up slowly. I was afraid to touch the tampon so I carefully washed all around the tampon. I didn't want it to fall out again.

I was not about to go through all that pain again. After I finished washing and drying, I pulled up my new clean underwear and went downstairs. I walked slowly because I was afraid that thing inside of me might fall out. Mama told me I could go back outside. I was surprised. I thought I had to stay seated at all times.

I was afraid to stand up outside so I stayed seated for two hours before Mama called me in. When I stood up, I felt nauseated for some reason. I also felt light headed. I had no idea the tampon was causing my body to go into shock. I was more concerned with walking than I was with feeling sick. I was afraid to walk but I got up and walked carefully lying about sore legs to my friends as I walked slow and funny.

Mama told me I had to change into a new tampon now. I went upstairs into the bathroom and pulled on the string as Mama instructed me. I felt immense pain and I immediately halted. I called Mama, but she told me to figure it out again.

I pulled again and felt even sharper pain. I let out a huge sigh of pain.

"Mama! It won't come out." I yelled from the bedroom to her.

Mama ignored me. I sat in the bathroom trying to pull the tampon out and calling Mama for almost a whole hour and she never came. Daddy told her to come see about me and she still refused.

It took me an entire painful hour to pull the tampon out of me. I wrapped it in tissue and tossed it in the trash as Mama told me to do. I called Mama and told her I had done everything she said. I begged her not to tell me to use another one of those tampon things. Mama told me to wrap tissue around my hand and place it in my underwear until Scootie came back from the store.

Scootie begged Mama not to make him go to the store and get Maxi Pads, but she made him go anyway.

When Mama showed me how to use the pads, I had no problem for the rest of the week. My friends at home and at church made me feel like I had something to celebrate when I confided in them about my cycle starting. They told me I'd become a young lady. I felt more mature and therefore acted more mature.

In 1979, I noticed a lot of changes in my body. I was even more developed in my hips and backside. My muscular thighs had even filled out quite a bit.

As time went on during my sixth grade school year, I had my friends in my neighborhood, but I bonded even more with my church family.

At church, Tameka and I always stuck together. We helped each other with answers during bible study. She was Mikey's new girl-friend. At first she was considering talking to J Bug. She asked me which one she should pick, and I said Mikey. Mikey was more re-spectable of the two of them. She confided in me about J Bug feeling on her a couple of times.

"Girl, he makes me sick with his old nasty butt. He's always try-ing to feel on somebody," I said.

"He tried to feel on you too?" she asked.

"Girl, ask me that question again," I said sarcastically.

"Uh uh honey child. Now I know I won't be going with his lil fresh behind!" she said.

"I know that's right," I replied.

I regretted Tameka and Mikey being together because she hung with me less, giving most of her attention to Mikey. I backed off when service ended so they could go off to talk alone. Mikey hinted whenever all three of us were together as if I was a sore thumb.

Some of the other boys at church who were around my age asked me to be their girlfriend. I wasn't interested in the boys who asked me so I turned them down. A couple of the boys got on my nerves trying to flirt. All those boys were interested in one thing. They all thought they'd have the ability to take advantage of me sexually, but I was nobody's fool. I didn't want a boy to touch me inappropriately. I certainly didn't want to have sex with anybody. Just the thought made me want to run as far away as I could from boys. If only I could find a boy who wasn't out to take advantage of me. Someone who really liked me for who I was; just a nice girl to spend time with.

Tameka's aunt started coming to church. She had six boys. I really liked one of the boys. His name was Bean. He looked mixed. He had curly hair and a nice smile. He never once behaved inappropriately around me.

Tameka had another cousin named "Q" who was also handsome. I liked him at first, but once I got to know him, he acted too goofy, even though he seemed respectable.

Bean was the only boy who I would not have turned down had he asked me to be his girlfriend. He liked me too, but he was too scared to ask me to go with him. Maybe his goofy cousin Q told him he was going to ask me for a chance so he backed off. Q did ask me but I turned him down politely. I just told him I didn't want any boyfriends right now. He asked me if there might be a possibility in the future and I lied to avoid hurting his feelings because he was such a nice boy.

"Yeah, maybe," I said.

This might be the reason why Bean wouldn't ask me for a chance, because I knew he liked me. Tameka already told me he was in love with me. He probably thought I was going to turn him down like I did his cousin and everybody else. Whatever the reason, he never asked me. Of course, I never asked him. He was the one respectable boy who I liked enough to have as a boyfriend. Other than Q, he was the only boy who didn't seem mannish. He just wouldn't ask me.

He stopped coming to church because he had to live with his daddy for a while along with his other two older brothers. His baby brothers stayed with their mother.

I already knew Q was going to ask me for another chance since his cousin Bean was no longer around. Q knew I liked his cousin because Bean and I hung around each other all the time whenever he came to church. He would sit next to me and everything. His other brothers were cute as well. A lot of girls talked about how cute the three oldest boys were which included Bean.

I really missed Bean. We always played around after church. He would grab something out of my hand and I would run and chase him. He'd find some kind of way to hold my hand by trying to take something from me. He never touched me inappropriately. We came so close to kissing. There was this time when I tried to get my quarter out of Bean's hand. We were alone on the side of the church. We looked eye to eye and Bean started leaning towards me. I was going to be kissed for the first time by a boy, until an adult walked up on the side of the church. Our lips never touched. He's the first boy I was going to let kiss me and I felt like I was finally ready. I wish he had asked for my phone number before he left.

Mikey's family moved to a new place on a different side of town after Nae Nae left home. They moved to a nice area in some apartments where Bean's mother lived also. Tameka and Mikey spent even more time together because she spent the weekend over at her aunt's house.

The adult who caught me and Bean about to kiss, told my mama and daddy about it, so they said no when Tameka asked if I could go over to her aunt's house with her to spend the night. Tameka said Bean was never over there any way. Bean was angry with his mother for making him and his two other brothers go and live with their father. Bean's parents had recently divorced.

CHAPTER TEN

"Pastor"

There were a lot of new members who were continuing to join the church during the spring of my sixth grade year, in 1979. We had a new Pastor who also presided over the youth ministry. His name was Pastor Jacobs. He was engaging and he made Bible study a fun place. Pastor Jacobs came up with games and contests to get us to study the teachings of the church and to learn the scriptures. He had a beautiful wife, Sister Jacobs, and they had three children. Sister Jacobs was pregnant with another child. Sometimes Sister Jacobs helped with bible study. She was really compassionate.

Pastor Jacob's niece named Quanetta had her mother to ask me if I could spend the night with them one day during the summer so I could wash and braid Quanetta's hair. I had become quite the expert at braids in those days. I braided a lot of hair when I was at home. I didn't mind, so we asked my mama if it was okay. Mama said okay. Quanetta was younger than me, but she was a part of our church family. I liked her family. Quanetta's mother and father were ministers in the church. She also had three little brothers.

A lot of the adults who didn't work, including Mama, attended what we called day time "Watch Services." They spent an hour or more praying, then they talked, read and asked questions about the Bible. They also asked Mother Jordon for all types of advice. Watch Services were from nine in the morning to one o'clock in the afternoon except on Fridays. Most of the men were working except for the pastors, so the majority of the Watch Services were filled with a lot of the women in our church. The majority of the women in our church did not work. Quanetta's mother also attended "The Watch."

I washed and braided Quanetta's hair while we both baby- sat her brothers. Her mother was at The Watch and her daddy was at work. Pastor Jacobs pulled up. They were excited to see their uncle. They referred to him as Uncle J. They all ran to his car yelling.

"Uncle J, Uncle J!"

They were asking him for candy and money. I smiled because Pastor Jacobs reminded me of Daddy. I realized how much Pastor Jacobs was like my father. He was always making you laugh. He was exciting to be around.

Pastor Jacobs came inside the house. I wondered why he wasn't at The Watch. He sat down in the kitchen and told Quanetta her mama sent him by to check up on us. Quanetta's mother obviously told him I was over there too because he wasn't surprised to see me.

Pastor Jacobs started joking around wrestling with the boys who were jumping all over him. Quanetta and I laughed at the boys and Pastor Jacobs wrestling. They were having a lot of fun. Pastor Jacobs had a lot of energy to be able to keep up with them. Daddy would have been out of wind by now.

Pastor Jacobs finally told the boys he was tired. He calmed them down by pulling out some candy. He gave us all butterscotch, caramel and peppermint candy, then he started joking with me about having boyfriends.

"How many boyfriends you got Tweety? Probably five or six, huh?" he said.

"No way! No, I don't either!" I yelled.

Pastor Jacobs laughed at my reaction then he started counting down. "What then, four? Three? Two? One?"

I was laughing so hard by the time he got to one because I shout-ed out "No!" several times by then. Pastor Jacobs made an obscure face.

"Tweety, come on now. I know you got about two or three boy-friends at home or at school somewhere, don't you?" he said.

We were all laughing.

"Pastor Jacobs, I don't have any boyfriends and I don't want any boyfriends!" I retorted.

Pastor Jacobs sang in aggravation. "Tweety got a boyfriend,

Tweety got a boyfriend!"

I covered my ears. "I'm not listening Pastor Jacobs!"

"Tweety, you not telling a story, is you?" he said.

He probably wanted to give me a lecture about boys. At bible study, he talked to the girls about not getting caught up in compromising situations with a boy just because he said he loved you. He role-played with us to test us.

"No Pastor Jacobs. I don't have any boyfriends. Boys are stupid anyway!" I responded.

Pastor Jacobs asked me to let him whisper something in my ear that he had heard. I leaned over expecting him to tell me some possible gossip at church about me and some boy.

"Um gon make you my lil' girlfriend," he whispered.

He was either testing me or joking and being silly. I laughed again. I waited on the test, but he didn't say anything else about boyfriends afterward.

Somehow Pastor Jacobs talked us into playing a game in which we could win his money. He offered to take us to the store and buy some treats. Quanetta and the boys would compete against me and him to see who was the strongest. Quanetta immediately protested.

"Naw Uncle J! Y'all gon have the advantage!" she said.

Pastor Jacobs disagreed. "Quanetta, you gotta be kidding me! Me and Tweety against all four of y'all? Yo brothers are strong 'cause they just finished wrestling with me and I couldn't beat 'em! Ain't no way me and Tweety can beat y'all cause you ain't weak yo self!" he argued.

"Naw Uncle J, I'm telling you it still ain't fair 'cause you bigger than us!" she said.

"Okay. I tell you what. Let's see who right then. Um gon go to the swingin door round here and all y'all stand on this side and let's see who gon push the door open. I bet y'all beat me!" he said.

"I bet we don't neither," Quanetta said.

"Okay, we gon see!" Pastor said.

Pastor Jacobs had all of us stand at the swinging door holding it while he walked all the way around through the hallway and living room to make it back to the other side of the swinging door. It was a lot of trouble to walk all the way around when he could have just gone through the door, but we waited patiently until he got to the other side. He stopped at the kitchen and lined up the kitchen chairs across the first hallway as a way of keeping us from walking around to where he was. He said we might try and cheat. He walked around to the other side and insisted we couldn't peek at him or try to cheat in any way. We all laughed at his antics.

"Okay y'all, I'm at the door so when I say go, I want y'all to push as hard as you can and I'm gon try and push the door open on my end. If y'all beat me then all y'all get a dollar," he said.

We got excited about getting a dollar. We told the boys to push with all their might when it was time. Pastor Jacobs had muscles. He looked really strong. He told us to start so we pushed against the door. It was a struggle but we beat him after some time. It took all our might and all our breath as well. Pastor Jacobs was out of wind on the other side of the
door, too. Quanetta asked for our dollars. Pastor Jacobs gave each of us a dollar. He was sitting on the floor as if we had really worn him out. We laughed and pointed at him breathing hard on the floor. Pastor Jacobs finally stood up.

"Okay now I got my breath back. Let's go again, but this time I'm gon need some help on my side, so Tweety's gon help me this time," he said.

"Uncle J, you know we can't beat both of y'all together!" Quanetta said.

"All y'all against me and Tweety and I'm weak too? Shoot! I think that's only fair. Y'all gon have to give me a fair chance to make my money back. I tell you what. If y'all beat us, then I'll give the boys fifty cents each and you get another dollar. Tweety automatically git another dollar if you get one 'cause she y'all guest. Now keep in mind, I'm real tired now so y'all have a real good chance of beating me 'cause Tweety's gon have to do all the work just about by herself," he explained.

Quanetta agreed to play along. Pastor told me to follow him back through the other side of the swinging door while Quanetta and the boys got positioned at the door on the other side. He had to move all the chairs just to get through to the other side. I wondered why he just didn't go through the swinging door. He placed all the chairs back as a way to block anyone from coming around to our side.

"I don't know, y'all might cheat. Me and Tweety gotta watch y'all 'cause y'all be trying to cheat," he joked.

Pastor told me to hold on a minute before I stood at the door. He said he wanted to strategize. He stood thinking for a minute.

"I know what Tweety. Um gon make you as tall as me so we can push the door at equal levels, and that way we might beat 'em. If we beat 'em, I'll tell you what, I'm gon give you two dollars instead of one, okay? Be quiet though, don't say nothing to Quanetta them," he said.

Pastor put a long wide foot stool at the door and told me to stand up on it.

"I'm scared, I might fall if they push the door open on us," I protested.

Pastor Jacobs told Quanetta and the boys to hold on a minute while we strategized more. Quanetta accused Pastor Jacobs of trying to be sneaky about beating them and he told her he was just trying to give me a fair chance against all of them. He convinced them to give us a chance to get a good position then he winked his eyes at me while he placed the stool closer to the door.

"Come on Tweety. Stand right here." He noticed my hesitation. "I ain't gon let you fall. I got you. I promise I ain't gon let you fall."

I hesitantly stood on the stool expecting for Pastor to stand next to me but instead, he told me to step down for a minute and adjusted the stool towards the middle of the door. He told me to stand back on the stool.

His tactics were crazy so I laughed but I stood on the long foot stool anyway. I would just have to trust him since he was the adult. Pastor Jacobs came up directly behind me and placed his hands on both sides of me on the door. The smile dropped off my face. I immediately felt a zillion butterflies in my stomach. I was nervous. I didn't want him to stand behind me with his arms trapping me. I felt him moving closer. He made a lot of body contact with me and it made me very nervous. I would have preferred it if he stood next to me. I didn't know how to address him, so I stayed quiet. He told Quanetta we were almost ready.

I was hoping he realized I was uncomfortable and changed positions. I was laughing and having fun until Pastor Jacobs stood behind me. I usually elbowed boys for coming up behind me trying to get all up on me but I couldn't elbow Pastor Jacobs. He was someone in authority over me. I felt powerless to defend myself or speak out and say anything. All I could do was pray he didn't touch my backside.

I felt his eyes on me. All of a sudden I could feel him breathing on me. *What was he doing?* Pastor Jacobs inched closer until he made full body contact. Oh my God! His body was up against my backside. He was not supposed to be touching my body.

On the foot stool, I was tall enough where his private parts almost met my backside but not quite. Pastor Jacobs got closer then squatted slightly to position himself perfectly behind me. I felt nauseated. My heart was racing because I was scared. My legs felt like jelly while Pastor Jacobs breathed down my neck.

I immediately dropped my hands from the door hoping he got the message. I wasn't participating in his game anymore. I was still too scared to say anything.

Pastor Jacobs was pressed up against me breathing heavy. I began to tremble. *What should I do? This was a grown man hunched over me!* This was Pastor Jacobs!

I closed my eyes tight and inhaled when his lips lightly brushed up against the back of my neck. I almost choked when he wrapped his arms around my tiny waist tightly as he continued to kiss my neck. I was afraid to breath. He reached for my breasts with one hand and grabbed my stomach with his other hand to hold me steady up against him. I froze completely. I was afraid I might suffocate because I was trying not to breath heavy.

Quanetta called out to Pastor Jacobs because he was taking too long. Pastor Jacobs told them to count to forty and to start pushing as soon as he said go. He continued to run his hands up and down the front of my body between my breasts and as far as he could reach almost to my private parts. When they were close to forty, he pinned himself tightly between me and the door and he placed his hands on both sides of me again. He planted a few more soft kisses along the back and sides of my neck and dropped one hand to hold me steady up against him. I didn't think they would ever get to forty. Once they got to forty, he put both hands back on the door and gave Quanetta the go ahead. He was holding the door effortlessly. He told Quanetta and the boys to push. He wasn't even straining to hold the door. He started holding the door calmly with one hand while having his way with me with his other hand.

I opened my eyes after he stopped kissing my neck. I tried to hold my breath the whole time to keep from letting out a heavy breath. If I breathed heavy, he might have thought that I wanted him to touch me because he was breathing heavy as well. I didn't want to sound like him because he seemed to be enjoying himself.

Pastor Jacobs was leaning into me like it was some kind of game to see how many moves he could make up against me. In between trying to touch me everywhere, he gripped my stomach tightly. He almost moaned out loud rubbing his body desperately aganst mine. I realized he planned this whole thing after he dropped one of his hands and grabbed me around my waist to squeeze me tighter. Quanetta and the boys were determined to keep trying to push the door so they could win more money. They continued to make lots of noise on the other side, straining without success to get the door open. I couldn't believe they tried for so long.

Pastor Jacobs' was still holding them back with one hand. I wanted to scream out. Quanetta and the boys were grunting and straining but Pastor Jacobs was far too strong for them to beat him even one-handed.

I knew he let us beat him on purpose just so he could get me by myself. What was I thinking, believing we had beaten him earlier? He was a strong bulky man with a very muscular build. He was in his early twenties, around twenty-three, so he wasn't that old, either.

Quanetta and the boys finally gave up after what seemed like forever. His hands were rubbing against my private parts. His touches were becoming bolder until Quanetta announced they gave up. I stood frozen in silence the entire time while Pastor Jacobs had his way. He was hunched up against me and started to sweat. His hand continued to roam up and down my body as if he was attacking me.

"Y'all give up?" he said, sounding out of breath.

"No we don't give up!" They yelled back. They really wanted to win the money.

After a little while longer they finally gave up and Pastor Jacobs was still all over me.

"Naw, Naw, y'all need to give it at least one more try. I know y'all ain't no quitters," Pastor Jacobs yelled out.

Oh God! I felt like I was about to pass out. I was trying as hard as I could to hold myself together. It felt as if he was about to swallow my whole body. I felt so helpless and so tiny up against his strong body. I was perspiring just as much, if not more than he was. Why was he doing this to me? Why did he want me? I was just a tiny girl compared to him.

I was so thankful when Quanetta and the boys finally gave up. As Quanetta and the boys raced around to the other side of the house, Pastor Jacobs had a hard time letting me go. I listened while they struggled to move all the chairs out of the way. I wished they'd hurry up. Pastor Jacobs didn't seem the least bit in a hurry to stop. He almost got caught. He took his time letting go. Quanetta had to run all the way down the hall, and through the living room. They had to open the door leading from the living room to the dining room after moving five chairs back in the kitchen. I still felt like Pastor Jacobs should have turned me loose the minute he heard all of them running around to where we were.

Pastor was still standing near me fully dressed in his suit. He took a step back calmly, smiling softly towards me. I was too embarrassed so I turned away from his stare quickly. Quanetta didn't think anything about him standing near me of course. My head drooped. My eyes were full of water. I felt traumatized. The feeling was worse than when Granddaddy touched me. I didn't remember feeling so shaken up before.

I had to sit down before my legs gave out. It took all my strength and muscles to stay frozen up against Pastor Jacobs. I was too afraid to move even an inch so every muscle in my legs locked in an awkward position. By the time I stepped down, I felt like I had been lifting weights with my legs until they were just about to give out on me. I was perspiring and I could barely breathe from trying not to breathe much. I made it to the living room and plopped down on the sofa. I didn't know if it was okay for us to sit on the plastic covered living room furniture or not but I had to catch my breath.

Quanetta and the boys were preoccupied convincing Pastor to give them the money he would have given them if they had won the bet. They didn't notice how shaken up I was. They were in the dining room.

When Pastor Jacobs finally wrestled the boys off him they came into the living room where I was sitting.

I had gained enough strength to get up. I headed to the kitchen and sat down away from Pastor Jacobs.

"What you doin Tweety?" Pastor asked.

I didn't want Pastor talking to me anymore. I wanted to be alone.

"Uhm, nothing," I answered dryly after taking a few gulps of water to attempt to clear my shaken voice. My hands were clasped together tightly. I struggled to stay calm.

"Well, come on let's all go to the store. I'm gon take y'all so you can buy some sweets with the money I just gave you. Since you the guest of honor Tweety, you get five dollars," he said.

"Naw Uncle J, that ain't fair!" Quanetta protested.

I didn't want five dollars, though. I didn't want to go to the store. I wanted to be left alone. I quickly accepted the money because Pastor Jacobs made skin contact with me when he put the money in my hand. He was trying to hold my hand but I moved away after accepting the money.

I nodded when Quanetta whispered in my ear asking me if we could put our money together and share everything.

"We can take some stuff to church tonight and watch everybody beg," Quanetta said with anticipation.

Quanetta was excited over the idea of having all the children be nice to her just so she could share candy with them. I had to re-member she hung with the younger crowd of children who could be bribed and controlled over something as small as a bag full of candy.

I could get Daddy to buy me some stuff. I didn't need Pastor Jacobs to be nice to me. He might have wanted something in return. I handed the money over to Quanetta.

"Just pick out whatever y'all want. I don't really care," I mumbled.

I was quiet when we got in the car. Pastor told all the boys to sit in the back. The girls got to ride in the front with him. I made sure I sat by the door and let Quanetta sit in the middle.

Pastor backed out the driveway and stopped the car.

"Tweety, you wanna learn how to drive?" He still had that scintillating tender smile on his face. I was too ashamed to face him anymore.

"No sir," I said.

I turned my head facing the open window. I didn't want to talk to him.

Quanetta begged for a chance to learn how to drive. Pastor walked all the way around to my side of the car. He opened the door on my side telling Quanetta to slide down and get behind the wheel. Quanetta slid behind the steering wheel then Pastor Jacobs forced me to the middle as he slid next to me. The car was still running. Pastor told Quanetta how to position her feet on the gas and the brakes and he showed her how to put the car in reverse. He was reaching all over me purposely touching my breasts and body while he was instructing her.

I twisted around to keep his hands away from my breasts. Don't touch me! I was screaming silently.

When Pastor reached down where Quanetta's feet were to see if her feet were on the gas and brakes properly, he laid across my lap leaning down. I felt his hand running under my dress up my thigh. I jumped when his hand inched up to my thigh, then Pastor Jacobs straightened up to cover up my reaction.

"Tweety scared you gon have a wreck Quanetta. Ain't you Tweety?" he joked cunningly.

He started tickling me and laughing except his hands kept squeezing my breasts.

"No! Don't! Pastor Jacobs, I don't feel like being tickled!" I protested.

I was extremely ticklish so I was squirming all over the seat bending down. This only made it easier for him to touch me inappropriately. He was grabbing me, hugging me and laughing while his hands roamed all over me as if he didn't know he was squeezing my breast.

"I don't wanna play anymore!" I yelled.

I was angry because I knew he had no right to put his hands on me. He was doing this on purpose. I still found myself afraid to speak out.

He finally stopped when Quanetta made it to the end of the long street and back down again for the second time. He told her to go back up to the end of the street one more time. It was a long dirt road and no other cars were around.

As he sat close to me touching my thigh, I felt my muscles tightening again. I stayed in a still position. If I moved just a little, I'd be making more body contact against Pastor Jacobs. I didn't want to encourage him or make him think I wanted him to touch me any more. He bent to whisper in my ear.

"I want you so bad, I wish it was just me and you baby."

He had one arm around me still trying to rub my breasts. Quanetta accidently hit the brakes real hard and Pastor Jacobs intentionally fell all over me covering up the fact that he was squeezing my breast firmly now. I reached down in an effort to try and push his body off me. His legs swung across my lap in exaggeration of Quanetta hitting the brakes hard and I accidentally touched his bulge between his legs. Before I could snatch away, his hand was covering mine as he pressed down. I wrestled my hands away. What I was feeling was scaring the daylights out of me. I shouldn't be touching grown men let alone knowing what they felt like. I refused to let my thoughts wander. I wanted to jump out the car and run. This was wrong! I had to pretend I never touched him. This never happened.

When Pastor finally took the steering wheel I made sure Quanetta got back in the middle. I stared out the window thinking about his beautiful wife and children and how much I liked her.

I was confused. Why me? There were a lot of other girls who

were a little older than me. Why not them? I could never tell anybody. Daddy might stop us from coming to church, or even worse, he might do harm to Pastor Jacobs. His wife would be angry with me. All the children would be angry with me at church if I caused Pastor Jacobs and his wife to break up or have problems.

A lot of problems and confusion might start in the church if I said anything. It would be my fault if a bad consequence happened as the result of me telling on Pastor Jacobs. Since I didn't see any good coming out of me telling on him, I decided I would rather just keep my mouth shut. I couldn't even say anything to my friends or it might get back to other people. I had to figure out another way to deal with this.

After we came from the store, Pastor Jacobs finally left. I was not the same smiling face anymore. I became withdrawn as my thoughts kept going back to what happened. Quanetta asked me what was wrong and I said nothing was wrong.

Quanetta's mama and daddy came home and they even asked me if I was okay.

"Yes sir. Yes ma'am," I answered.

"Well you sho is quiet," Quanetta's daddy said.

When we got to church, they told Mama I was really quiet, but I was a sweet girl. They insisted on paying me a few dollars for braiding Quanetta's hair.

CHAPTER ELEVEN

"The Escape"

During church, Pastor Nichols and Mother Jordon asked all the children going to the third grade and up to sit in the very front rows of the church. They said they were going to be specifically talking to us tonight. Daddy worked a lot during the week and came home late. Sometimes he even had to travel for a couple of days. I was glad he wasn't at church on this night. I sat towards the front as instructed along with Tameka. She sat next to me and Mikey sat next to my cousin Bow Leggs who he was close friends with. I was glad to be around my best friend. I felt normal again. Seeing Mama, Scootie, and Sonia finally walking in the church also made me feel normal. I rushed over and hugged them almost not wanting to leave Mama's side. Before I could start a conversation with Mama, Tameka called me back over to sit next to her.

We opened with prayer like we usually did. After prayer, we did what we called "Saluting One Another," which was when we shook hands and showed love to one another. We were taught to kiss the cheeks of the women and say, "God Bless You." We only shook the men's hands and said, "God Bless You." Women weren't to kiss men. Mother Jordon wanted to make sure there was never any confusion in the church.

I didn't go anywhere near the pulpit because I didn't want to face Pastor Jacobs. I made sure to move towards the back of the church and salute away from the pulpit.

Mother Jordon announced there had been some confusion among us children about who was talking to whom. She wanted to clear up all of the boyfriend/girlfriend misunderstandings. I must have missed something because I wasn't aware so many children were dating. I only knew about Tameka and Mikey.

I heard that Q had asked another girl for a chance so they might be talking. Other than that, I didn't know of any other couples.

Mother Jordon told all of us to get a bible. I didn't have one and neither did Tameka. Some of us were walking around to different adults trying to get bibles. I asked Mama, who had already given my brother her Bible. She told me to run to the car to get Daddy's Bible out of the car. I ran quickly to the car.

Mother Jordon and Pastor Nichols were teaching about fornication and appropriate behavior between boys and girls. They wanted us to behave like respectable young men and women. If we were going to talk exclusively to a boy or girl, then our parents needed to be aware of it as well as other girls and boys in order to keep down confusion.

Mother intended to have every single boy, heading to sixth grade and older to stand up and announce who they were talking to or who they liked. She told us girls if we thought a boy liked us and he didn't get up and call our name, to drop him like a hot potato.

I wasn't talking to anybody, so no one should be calling my name. I had already turned every one of those boys down. I was just interested in finding out about everybody else.

I ran to get the Bible out the car fast so I wouldn't miss anything. As soon as I closed my car door to head back around to the front of the church, I ran smack into Pastor Jacobs. We were in the back parking lot where it was dark. I was startled when I bumped into Pastor Jacobs. I didn't know who he was at first. I looked up and then I froze. *What was he doing out here?* Pastor Jacobs had a big smile on his face.

"Tweety," he said.

I dropped my head. I didn't want to look up at him. Pastor Jacobs leaned his head sideways and knelt to my level.

"Tweety, you didn't salute me," he said, speaking delicately.

Pastor Jacobs had kissed my cheek on occasion when we were in bible study if he was commending me about doing a good job on something. This time he was staring straight at me, even though I was trying not to look up. I could feel his eyes on me.

CHAPTER ONE

Pastor Jacobs held out his hand.

"God Bless You Tweety," he said.

I hesitantly reached my hand out to shake his hand. He was standing so close I could barely hold my hand out. Pastor Jacobs took my hand and shook it. *Why was he looking at me so serious? Why wouldn't he let my hand go?*

"Look at me Tweety," he was still speaking softly. "I been thinkin 'bout you all day. You know that don't you?"

He was sitting next to his gorgeous wife in church when I left. He started moving towards my lips. I dropped my head but he reached gently for my chin and lifted my head up. He placed his lips on my lips. I didn't make a sound. I didn't move my lips at all.

He was kissing me very softly and rolling his lips all around. His eyes were staring dead at me, so I closed my eyes out of fear. I didn't want to make eye contact with him. I didn't know how to stop him because I was afraid to speak out. He gave me a long passionate kiss like we were in love or something. I couldn't cover up my breathing. I had to breathe out of fear. I never kissed a boy before and here he was kissing me for an eternity. I finally felt his tongue on my lips forcing my mouth open. I was too afraid to resist as his tongue pried my lips apart. I was so shaky I lost my balance and stepped back. Pastor Jacobs reached out and caught me around my waist pulling me closer towards him. He was still looking me dead in the face. I dropped my head once more. I could still see him smiling out of the corners of my eyes.

"Tweety," he called out to me.

I refused to look at him. He chuckled softly and touched my chin again. *Why couldn't he see I didn't want to look at him? Couldn't he get the message? I didn't want him touching me! Couldn't he see I was afraid?* I was thinking.

Pastor Jacobs ran his hand across my cheek in a stroking motion and smiled as he glared down at me.

"Tweety, I like you 'cause you special. You my special girl. You not fast like some of them other girls. I been watching you for a long time and I said, I wonder if she like them other girls out here, but no, you different from them other girls. That's why I don't like all them other fast girls. You so sweet. You know that don't you? If I wanted to I could have any of these girls out here, but I don't want none of them. I chose you. Look at me Tweety. Look me in the eye. I don't know what it is about you, but do you know what you do to me? You know you driving me crazy don't you? I wanna tell you something."

He tilted my chin forcing me to look at him while I forced back tears.

"Tweety, I love you. See there. You done made me fall in love with you. You gon be my sweet lil Tweety bird, okay?" he said.

I wanted to scream out NO! He was serious about us being boyfriend and girlfriend. He couldn't be serious because I was just a child! I had to get away. Oh no! I felt I was in trouble. He loved me for real. That was not good at all. *Please God! This can't be happening to me!...* I thought silently. I was just a little girl compared to this full grown man. *Why me Lord?* I thought. I dropped my head in shame. I was too embarrassed to cry even though I wanted to cry. This was real bad! His wife would hate me forever. She would blame me for everything if she caught us.

"Look at you actin all shy my lil Tweety bird. Done made me fall in love." He was still stroking my face then he started running his thumb softly over my lips. "Wit yo lil sweet lips," he whispered.

I couldn't let him keep touching me. He looked like he wanted to kiss me again. I hesitantly started taking steps around him with my head still down. He chuckled and let me pass. I nervously walked back towards the front of the church. I wondered where he was. I didn't know if he was going to stop me again. I glanced back slightly. He was still standing in the same spot just looking at me smiling.

I walked faster until I rounded the corner. I breathed a huge sigh of relief once I made it back into the church. My legs were so shaky. I went straight to my seat. I collapsed in my chair like a frail cat. I put the Bible in Tameka's lap not even looking at her. I stared blankly. Tameka kept eyeing me, but I didn't notice until she shoved me back to reality. She was laughing at how weird I was acting. She asked me if I was alright.

I couldn't let her find out. She might get angry at what Pastor Jacobs was doing to me and tell because he was doing an unthinkable thing to me. She was my best friend and we took up for each other all the time.

"Yeah, uh, I just gave out of breath from running so fast back from the car," I mumbled.

Tameka was still laughing.

"You sure you're alright Tweety?" she asked.

I nodded yes again then I saw Pastor Jacobs walking in from the back entrance of the church which was usually locked. Now I knew how he snuck up on me when I was at the car. He sat back down in the pulpit next to his wife. I couldn't believe the first time I stood still and let somebody kiss me, it was a grown man. I wished it were Q or any boy for that matter. It would have felt natural being kissed by a boy, but the kiss with Pastor Jacobs wasn't normal at all. It didn't seem fair to me. I felt like he robbed me of something. What had I done to make him do these things to me? Maybe it was all my fault. I must've made him think I liked him in that way.

Mother Jordon was calling the boys to the front of the church one at a time asking them if they liked anyone or had a girlfriend. A lot of giggling was going on and some of the children were making jokes and carrying on. I didn't understand how, but I had earned a reputation for being considered "fast" by some of the gossiping women at church. A lot of boys approached me and I turned them down but some adults assumed I was giving them an incentive to flock around me. I didn't realize the boys were flocking around me. In my neighborhood, boys were around all the time just being boys. I didn't think anything different was going on at church. Sometimes we all hung out together in a crowd.

I knew what all the boys were after so I was not interested in any of them. It turned out that I was talked about the most among the boys. They said I was fine and had a "big butt." They knew better than to discuss any of my body parts directly to my face. I would have told them off. I heard them in passing and ignored them. Other children always told you what they heard someone else saying as well. I thought it was stupid to like a girl just because of her nice figure. There was much more to me than my body. If boys wanted me just because they thought I was fine, their only incentive was to use me for my body and then walk away. The ladies at church definitely had the wrong impression of me. Why did I have to be picked on just because I had a nice shape? I wasn't the only girl in the church with a neat body. I'd rather be skinny for all this grief. I was in trouble enough as it was with Pastor Jacobs. I wish I had never gotten my appetite. I was growing too fast. Everyone told me I looked much older than I really was. They all said I should be in high school, according to my mature body.

I didn't tell on boys a lot of times when they were being disrespectful because I was not a "tattle tell." I could handle the boys on my own. They knew not to touch me inappropriately after testing me. I always let them have it. My cousins Bow Leggs and them always had my back and all the boys knew it. They always protected me and asked me if I needed them to take care of anyone. My brother also had my back and he'd fight any boy who bothered his sister. He still kept his distance and wasn't around me nearly as much as my cousins were. We both preferred our space from one another to avoid arguing. I didn't run to him too much because I was scared Mama and Daddy might find out something and make a big deal out of nothing.

Rumors continued to spread among the adults. I didn't find out until later just how bad the rumors had gotten about me. I wasn't the way they thought at all. A popular female adult minister in particular had been heinously sabotaging my reputation with all sorts of wild stories of me and some of the boys. It would be some time before I personally discovered this. Because she was considered a trusted woman of God in the congregation, her lies were thought to be true accounts of my promiscuity. I continued to be confused by the attitudes of the adults around me as I remained unaware of the continual cauterization of my reputation. Obviously Pastor Jacobs had observed me more closely and saw a different, more respectful young lady. As our youth pastor he spent a lot of time with us.

Two boys stood up to express an interest in talking to me. Mother Jordon made me stand up and asked me if I liked them. I nodded no to both boys and sat back down. I felt out of place having my name called. I didn't want to deal with another boy or man for all I cared. Pastor Jacobs seemed to have seen me straightening out all the boys. He told me he liked me because I was special and not fast like some of the other girls. No adult in church would blame him. They'd all blame me because they thought I was fast, but I wasn't.

I felt Pastor Jacobs' eyes on me the whole time. Maybe I should have said yes to one of the boys. I wanted to feel normal again after looking at Pastor Jacobs. I'd rather have common experiences with typical boys and not men. Maybe if I kissed a boy, I might feel like I'm back in the ordinary world, I thought. Then again, I didn't need anybody else taking advantage of me.

I was full of anger. I wanted to tell every boy who liked me I was not just a body! My name was sung out when certain boys stood up. I found out a lot of boys young and old liked me. "Tweety, go on up there!" the crowd of children would say.

It began to be embarrassing for me. I assumed they only liked me for my body since I didn't consider myself very pretty.

I started praying no one else called my name or even looked at me. I sat in the church angry. Mikey and Tameka had an easy time because everybody knew they were together and it was no surprise even though other boys liked her. No other boy would dare say anything because they knew she was already spoken for.

An announcement was made regarding Q going with this other girl who was younger than me. She was really pretty with long hair down her back. As he stood up, I wished I hadn't turned him down. Although he was goofy, he was the only boy who was a real gentleman. I was desperate to feel normal again. He would have been the perfect boy to say yes to. Pastor Jacobs would have left me alone if I had a boyfriend.

Q stood up front and was asked the same question as the other boys. He shocked everybody when he announced he liked two girls instead of one. He must be the boy the two girls were fighting over. I had to admit he was very good looking. He had a perfect smile and a nice and neat afro. He also dressed very neatly. He just acted square.

He was asked to call both girls up. Oh man, this was about to be good! Q called up the girl with the long hair first. She came and stood next to him with a surprised look on her face as if to say, you haven't been honest with me. I wondered who might be able to compete with her, as pretty as she was, and then he called the second girl's name.

"Tweety," he said.

Everybody burst out laughing including my cousins. They all assumed I was a willing participant in being the secret second girlfriend. I refused to get up at first. I looked over at Scootie who was calling me stupid and looking quite upset. He thought I was going to make a fool of myself. I felt embarrassed. I didn't want to be in the middle of church gossip. I couldn't believe Q called my name. This girl was much prettier than me. I didn't want the church people to think I was talking to him the whole time knowing he had a girlfriend. This proved the gossipers to be right. I had to be both fast and stupid to go along with being the second girlfriend knowing Q already had one girlfriend.

Pastor Nichols told me to come up front with Q and the other girl whose name was Linda. I nodded no. Pastor Jacobs walked towards me waving for me and telling me to get on up. I nodded no again. Mother Jordon forced me to get up on my feet. I dragged up to the front shaking my head as if I was explaining to everyone who was watching. Q noticed I was upset.

He spoke very, eloquently to my surprise.

"Excuse me, but, can I just say something?" he said.

Mother Jordon gave him the floor. He looked at me apologetically.

"I didn't want her to be mad or anything, but for the record, Tweety didn't know that I was going to call her name tonight, and as a matter of fact, I caught myself by surprise. I really been secretly liking Tweety for a real long time now but I just didn't know how to tell her. I mean, I didn't mean to make Linda mad or hurt her but even though I like Linda, I really like Tweety the most."

Q then turned to the Linda.

"Now Linda, don't get me wrong, I think you are very beautiful and everything, but I just like Tweety the most and I don't want to lead you on like this anymore. I mean, I don't know if Tweety likes me the way I like her, but I just want to be honest, that's all."

I was relieved he gave his explanation to the church and cleared me of any rumors. I was also impressed with how well he addressed the situation. Q turned to me and got down on his knees. The church went crazy laughing and clapping. I turned away blushing and totally embarrassed. I refused to turn back around until he stood back up again. He realized he was embarrassing me because I had my head turned away and my face covered. He apologized.

"Oh, I'm sorry Tweety. I wasn't trying to embarrass you or anything like that."

The congregation was on their feet cheering Q on. I covered my face even more to hide my embarrassment. I felt like I was being made a spectacle of. Q asked me in front of everybody if I would be his special friend. I was relieved he didn't use the word girlfriend but Mother Jordon stopped him and asked what he meant by "special friend."

"Well, okay, well...I mean, uh...okay, I'll say it. Girlfriend!" he said.

Pastor Jacobs blurted out, "Alright Tweety, give him his answer!"

After hearing Pastor Jacobs sounding so sure I was about to turn Q down flat, I realized this could be the answer to my prayers. Pastor Jacobs stepped down from the pulpit laughing and moved my hands away from my covered face.

"Don't be scared Tweety, just give him a straight answer," he said.

At Quanetta's house, I assured him I didn't like any boys and would never allow a boy to disrespect me. I told him how stupid boys were and how they got on my nerves. I needed to make him think differently about me so he wouldn't like me anymore.

I stood there for a minute while Linda spoke.

"I quit him anyway!" she snapped.

Q had never tried to touch me or kiss me, and he seemed like a nice boy. I could put up with him being goofy especially if it would get rid of Pastor Jacobs. I nodded yes after a while. Q let out a big huge sigh. I was glad it was him instead of anyone else there. He was not like the other aggressive boys. He would never even think about touching me inappropriately.

Pastor Jacobs dropped his head and didn't look at me again except out of the side of his eyes. I felt relief rush over me when I went back to my seat.

After church Q was following me everywhere. He never left my side.

"You know, you don't have to follow me everywhere," I said.

Q acted goofy as usual.

"Oh, oh, uh, my fault, uh, I mean, uh, I'm sorry," he said.

"That's okay. I'm going to tell my mama something real quick and then I'll be back okay?" I said.

I rolled my eyes up towards the sky as soon as I turned my head away from Q. He was already getting on my nerves! Mikey talked to his friends and hung outside waiting around for Tameka to step outside and talk. He was trying to be cool, so he never followed Tameka in and out of the church.

Whenever Tameka was mad at Mikey, she stayed in the church until it was time for her to leave because she knew Mikey was too cool to run after her.

I went inside to ask Mama how long we were going to be. I was ready to go home. Tameka left me outside alone with Q. She went around the side of the church with Mikey. Everyone who walked by called us two love birds.

As I headed back out of the church, Pastor Jacobs was still in the pulpit. I tried to walk past real fast. He called my name motioning with his finger for me to come here.

"Shoot!" I mumbled under my breath as I walked over to him.

I had a cynical smile on my face because I knew he was going to ask me about Q. Pastor Jacobs looked at me real stern.

"Tweety, what happened?" he asked.

He wasn't smiling. I didn't answer. He called my name again. I dropped my head.

"Tweety, look at me," he snapped.

It took me a minute but I finally looked up. Pastor Jacobs looked sad and angry at the same time. It looked as if he even had tears in his eyes. I didn't do anything to him! He was a grown man. He had a wife! I had a right to have a regular boyfriend.

Pastor Jacobs stared me down for a minute. He made me feel ashamed and I didn't even know what I was ashamed of. He was disgusted with me.

"Well, Tweety, you can't be my girlfriend no mo. You gon be giving yo kisses to somebody else now," he said.

His eyes were watering up, but I didn't understand why. He was acting like he was actually in love with me for real. He treated me like I betrayed him. He made me feel like I did something wrong. I stood there not knowing what to do.

"That really hurts me. I thought you were special. From now on I won't talk to you no mo and you don't talk to me no mo. Don't even salute me no mo. Look at me. This the last time I'll ever be saying anything to you. I don't even wanna look at you right now. Go on back out there wit yo lil boyfriend. You can leave," he said in anger.

As I was looking at him, he had the most disgusting look on his face. He acted like he couldn't stand the sight of me. I didn't deserve his anger. I walked off feeling inadequate, but at the same time relieved. I found myself blinking back tears. I didn't know why I let him make me feel so ashamed.

I was glad to see Q's smiling face outside. He asked me if he could hold my hand. I quickly said yes, hoping he could make me feel good again. We held hands as we talked.

"Ooh, look at the two love birds!" Tameka yelled.

I was even glad to hear Tameka's voice. She made me laugh. I needed to laugh because I was having a difficult time shaking the guilty feeling off me. I was having a hard time blocking out the disgusting look on Pastor Jacobs face.

Pastor Jacobs stopped talking to me from then on. He turned his back on me treating my like I didn't exist. He made it obvious I was no longer respected by him. He spoke to every girl around me and left me out intentionally. He made me feel ashamed. He stared me up and down like I was an immoral person. He only looked at me with pure disdain. Bible Study was difficult for me. I got ignored every week. I raised my hand to answer a question about the Bible and Pastor Jacobs ignored me and turned away. He laughed and praised everyone but me. He bragged to the parents about how smart their children were, but he had nothing to say about me anymore.

After feeling mistreated week after week, I wanted to go up to him and ask him what I could do to get back in his good graces. But I knew I could never speak to him again or he might try to do something else to me. I just wished he didn't make me feel so dirty. Months passed and he still looked at me in a loathing way. He could be smiling one minute and as soon as he saw me his smile faded and he turned away from me. Tameka sat right next to me and he would talk and laugh with her and then walk right past me and talk to the next child as if I were invisible. One side of me wanted to quit Q and ask for his forgiveness, but the other side of me remained resilient. My stubborn side told me to pretend as if I didn't care even when I wanted to give in. This was the side that continued to win every week. My tactic was to stay away from him and not look at him. When he came in my direction, I learned to quickly walk away. When he looked at me, I turned and looked the other way. A part of me felt like I was still a bad person.

About three months later, they announced Pastor Jacobs would be having his own church services in the suburbs or as we call it, "The Country," where he and his family were moving. I was relieved because he was going to be moving away. I stayed close with his younger son who still hung around me from time to time until they moved.

I had always treated his son like a little brother even though I knew he had a crush on me. Many of the little boys had crushes on me. I figured it was because I was kind to them. I thought little kids got ignored too much when their feelings should have been acknowledged. One of the little boys asked me to be his girlfriend.

"Oh, that's so sweet! Well, I can't be your girlfriend, but you can be my little brother though, how about that?"

I wanted everybody to be treated as important so even the younger children mattered to me. I felt the need to make younger children feel important as a result of being made to feel insignificant.

"Healing Roads Journal"

In Pastor Jacobs' mind, he really was betrayed and hurt. He confused normal feelings of affection with misguided feelings towards children, similar to Granddaddy when he felt betrayed enough to allow me to go without food. Pastor Jacobs' feelings for me were as real as his love for his wife and children. This is a confused characteristic of a pedophile. Knowing this removed any self blame I felt as a child growing up. It has taken me many years of struggling with issues in my adult life to recognize it isn't my fault I was molested. It wouldn't have been my fault if problems had arisen from exposing what Pastor Jacobs did to me. Pastor Jacobs was yet another man that I loved and trusted who hurt me. It seemed to become a pattern with significant men in my life. Trusting men would become a huge issue with me as I grew up.

CHAPTER TWELVE

"Crush"

Once Pastor Jacobs moved away, Q and I broke up. I couldn't take it anymore! I really didn't want any boyfriends. I just wanted friends.

Q stopped coming to church after we broke up. The only thing we ever did was hold hands. I let him kiss me once on the lips. He normally gave me a goodbye kiss on the cheek everytime we said goodbye.

"Uh, Tweety, uh, I don't mean to be disrespectful or anything, well I mean, uh, well...nothing," Q said.

"What is it Q?" I said.

"Oh, uh, nothing. I mean, I'm sorry. Well just forget it. I mean, uh, can we please just forget it, uh, if you don't mind?" he said.

"Boy, go on and just say whatever you're wanting to say!" I said.

"Oh okay, uh, I mean, I'm sorry. I mean...do you think it would be okay if I kissed you? I mean, I'm sorry. I shouldn't have asked you that. You're going to quit me now?" he asked after stumbling through all of those words.

"For what? Just 'cause you asked me for a kiss?" I said.

Q stuttered halfway through an explanation. "Uh, I don't know. I mean, uh..."

"Boy please! You're making me mad because you should've just kissed me without asking. I don't ever see any boys asking their girlfriend for a kiss," I snapped.

"Oh I'm sorry. I won't ask again, he said.

"Fine," I said.

"But, if it's alright, I'm going to just kiss you," he said.

"Fine," I said.

"Uh, I know you're going to think I'm crazy but, do you know how to kiss on the lips?" he asked.

"Well if I have to tell you, just forget it," I said.

"Well then, can I put my arms around you?" he said.

"Why are you asking me again?" I said.

"Oh, yeah, uh, that's right," he said.

Q put his arms around me and went for my lips. "Ouch! What are you doing? You bit my lips Q!" I screamed.

"Oh, uh, I'm sorry. I told you I didn't know how to kiss," he said.

"Shoot! Is it bleeding?" I asked.

"I don't think so. I'm so sorry. You're mad at me aren't you?" he said.

"Naw, just forget it," I said holding my lips.

"You're sure?" he said.

"Yeah. Let's just walk back up to the front of the church okay?" I said.

Of course, we never kissed again on the lips. It was a boring relationship. All he did was ramble on nervously, follow me everywhere, or sit around quietly waiting on me to boss him around. He wasn't playful, or funny and he certainly wasn't cool like most boys. Q was mostly nervous acting around me. I started avoiding him until he got the message. He was too nice for me to tell him to his face that I didn't like him. After being left sitting alone week after week while I went off with Tameka and who ever else I talked to, Q got tired of me.

"Tweety, uh, I uh, I, well, I hope you don't get mad at me, but, would it be alright if I went back with Linda?" he said.

"Oh yeah, that's fine with me," I said.

"Well, I mean, I won't go with her if you don't really want me to, uh, but if you want me to, I mean, if you don't mind..." he said.

"Oh no, I mean, it's fine with me. I think we should just be friends," I quickly said.

"You're not mad at me or anything are you?" he asked.

"Oh no, really. I would like for us to continue to be friends. I wish you and Linda the best," I said.

"Well, would it be okay if I gave you one last kiss?" he asked.

"Well, why don't we just shake hands and hug and leave it at that," I said, extending my hands.

Tameka was interested in some older guy she met coming home from school. She broke up with Mikey, moved away, and stopped coming to church. Q stopped coming to church as well. Over the years growing up, I ran into Q every now and then. He always told me he was still in love with me. I still turned him down nicely.

Mikey and I talked more as friends. He asked my opinion about girls and everything. I wondered who his next girlfriend would be. I finally appreciated his good looks but he was just too old. He was three grades above me. My cousins hinted at him to ask me for a chance.

"Man, she too young for me!" Mikey would say.

I responded in return. "And he's too old for me!"

We just left it at that.

I knew out of three girls in the church who really liked Mikey, he would end up going with one of them for sure. One of the girls was my friend named Debbie. Debbie hung out with me and Tameka when she was still coming to church. Mikey surprised me when he told Debbie flat out he didn't like her right in front of me.

"You not really my type. I just like you as a friend." He was too honest.

I was surprised when Debbie said that she and Tameka talked on the phone all the time because I could never seem to catch up with Tameka and she never called me back. We were supposed to be best friends. I refused to believe she would just turn her back on me even though it was appearing as if Debbie had stolen my friend right from under me. Why would Tameka turn her back on me? I had been nothing but faithful and loyal to our friendship.

Our church had moved towards the end of my sixth grade school year in 1979. We started having service temporarily at Pastor Nichols' house. He had two large rooms in the front and back which equaled to the two rooms at the previous church. It was just smaller. The pulpit sat in the front room with the congregation. There was no room to shout as freely as people would like. They stood at their seats and danced as much as possible. The adults sat in the front room and the teenagers moved as far to the back room as possible. We talked more during service because the adults' backs were turned away from us. Pastor Nichols had a large porch in the front of his house with columns around it. After service, we hung out on the porch sitting on the steps and cement walls.

One day when we were all hanging out on the porch, Mikey asked me and this other girl in front of all the other teenagers if we liked him. I immediately said no. He asked me again.

"Tell the truth! You like me don't you?" he said.

I was very adamant. "No!" I lied.

He asked the other girl named Anita. She was pretty and old enough to be his girlfriend.

"Well I ain't gon lie, yeah I like you. I sho do," she said.

Everybody got quiet.

"Well, guess what Anita? I know you like me. I been knowing you been liking me, and guess what?" he said.

"What," she answered.

"I DON"T LIKE YOU!" Mikey blurted out as loud as he could.

Everybody on the porch burst out laughing. I was so glad I said no to his question.

Our church celebrated every traditional feast mandated in the Bible according to biblical scriptures and in accordance to biblical months. Every New Moon represented a new month and was set aside as a Holy day. We didn't attend school or work on those days.

The first feast we observed was "The Feast of Tabernacle" where we ate for seven days. The first and last day was a Holy day so no one worked or attended school on those days.

Next was "The Feast of Blowing of The Trumpets" which was one day. It was also a Holy day.

Before the next feast we had "Fast Day for All God's People." Everyone was required to fast. A fast in our church was complete abstinence from food or water from sun down to sun down. If we started on Friday evening at sun set, then we didn't eat or drink anything until the sun went down on Saturday night.

Mother Jordon prophesied that God would not let any babies suffer during a fast for obeying his commandment. When Mother

Jordon spoke, we all received her words with absolute belief. We believed she spoke the words of God and could not falter. Even the little babies fasted on this day no matter how small. I couldn't see myself making a little baby fast. I was glad I didn't have any baby brothers or sisters.

During our next feast, which was "The Feast of Passover," we ate unleavened bread for seven days. We gave up regular breads, sweets, chips and other things during this week. We replaced bread with Matzos.

The last two feasts were "The Feast of Weeks" which led up to "The Feast of Pentecost."

We ate the feasts together as a church family as if we were at home. The rooms were filled with tables with white tablecloths spread over them during the feast times. The helpers, one of which was Mama, spent a lot of time preparing food for the whole church. Whenever our parents were at Pastor Nichols' house preparing for the feast we came with them as much as possible, especially during the summer feasts.

Debbie, who was now best friends with Tameka, only came to church occasionally. She would brag about her fun times spent with Tameka. It was obvious that she had something to do with why Tameka never called me or came to church to see me anymore. I was hurt because I felt that Tameka should have known me better. I would never have done or said anything to hurt her. Everytime I asked Debbie for Tameka's phone number, Debbie lied and said she didn't know it by heart, or that she had changed her number and she didn't have the new number yet. My number had not changed though, and Tameka never made an effort to call me, even after an entire year had passed.

Mikey was always over at Pastor Nichols house with his mother during feast preparation. He had a close friendship with my cousins. They played sports all summer, which was why Scootie went over every chance he got. J Bug was also over all the time. He knew better than to mess with me. My cousins had him in check by now. He was also maturing and had a girlfriend he seemed to treat with respect. We got along pretty well. He could walk up to me and carry a decent conversation. He and Curly were the comedians among us all.

My cousins had a basketball goal in their back yard where they shot ball everyday. Sometimes I played and often lost. They were all too advanced for me. If I won, it was because they felt sorry for me. They also played football in the street almost everyday. I liked going with Mama so I could help with Sister Nichols' babies. She had thirteen children by now. She had a new baby every year.

I was also close with my cousins Bow Leggs, John John and Weiner. I stood outside and watched everybody play. They treated me with a lot of respect and gave me lots of attention. I became their good luck charm when they competed against one another. They scored goals for me.

"Hey Tweety! You want me to win this one for you right quick?" John John would call out.

"Tweety look, this touchdown is all for you. Watch me fake everybody out," Weiner called out.

They had become my favorite cousins in the whole world. They were my best friends, my confidants, and my playmates. I couldn't ask for more loyal cousins. I loved them all.

At the end of my sixth grade year, Mikey and I talked almost every day at my cousin's house. It was during the week of feast. Sister Nichols had three babies in diapers at the same time. The church teachings were against birth control so a lot of ladies were having lots of babies.

When I wasn't hanging out with the boys, I was combing hair, changing diapers or just holding babies. I never got tired or bored. I liked combing hair. Sister Nichols liked for me to come over because I was a big help with the children while she helped prepare the feast.

They had tons of collards, green beans, potatoes, mustards and turnips to cut up along with other vegetables and a lot of meat and other things to cook for the entire church. A lot of feast helpers gathered at Pastor Nichols house to prepare the feast and go shopping.

The church was full and they had to cook everyday for all the people. Each family paid feast offerings according to family size.

The money was used to buy all the food.

I was enjoying my time talking to Mikey even if he was asking me about other girls he was finding an interest in. We were learning a lot about each other. He admitted I was different from what he originally thought.

My cousins Neecy and Yolanda stopped by to spend the day over Sister Nichols' house. I wasn't expecting them. Yolanda was sixteen and pregnant now. Although the school summer break was just beginning, Mikey was going into the tenth grade. Neecy was going into the ninth grade. It had been three years since Mikey had seen my cousins.

Neecy was very beautiful with long hair and dimples. She had a gorgeous smile. Mikey complimented her on her smile. I noticed Mikey staring at her unable to take his eyes off her most of the time. Oh no! Now they were going to start talking.

Mikey lost interest in me the rest of the day. By the time Neecy was ready to leave, they announced they were boyfriend and girlfriend. My heart stopped. Shoot! Why did she have to come around? I was winning his heart slowly. There were times when I was sure he was close to asking me for a chance. He talked all around it telling me I was a nice girl. Eventually, he would have asked. He seemed so respectful. He was the only boy who had never tried to feel on me at the time. Even the older boys had a problem with respecting their boundaries and keeping their hands to themselves. I was intrigued with Mikey.

Mikey and I stayed friends while he talked to my cousin. He showed me a lot of the things he bought before giving it to her. He bought her necklaces, earring sets and perfume. I thought he was very romantic.

He asked my opinion about the gifts before giving it to her. I remained the good and faithful friend although I was envious.

By the time the summer was almost over, Neecy called me at home telling me she was quitting Mikey. I was surprised. He was the perfect boyfriend. I asked her why.

"Because, he too scared to do anything!" she snapped.

"What you mean by that?" I asked.

"I mean he too scared to go all the way!" she said.

"You mean to tell me you're going to quit him just because he won't have sex with you?" I asked, surprised at her.

"Girl, yeah, Mikey don't like to do nothing! He act like he scared to touch me. He don't even try. I need me a real man; somebody who ain't scared. I like to have real fun. I ain't got time for nobody that gon sit around and act like a lil boy. Girl like I said, I gots to have me a real man. Somebody like his friend Freddy! Now Freddy ain't scared to go all the way!" she said.

"Now, I know you're not talking 'bout Freddy who lives across the street from him?" I asked.

"Yeah, girl that's him, wit his fine ass. You seen him before?" she said, shocking me with her use of profanity.

"Him and his brother came with Mikey to Sister Nichols' house a few times," I said, still not getting her point.

"Well, I saw Freddy for the first time about two weeks ago when I was over Mikey's house and it was on from then on," she said.

"You've been over to Mikey's house?" I asked.

"Girl, yeah, I tole you Mikey ain't nuthin but a lil scared boy! I done gave him plenty of chances to do something as many times as I been goin over to his house.

Girl, I don't even go over to his house no mo. I rather go see Freddy. Freddy know just how to handle me. I ain't got to tell him nothing. He got experience. He ain't nothing like ole boring Mikey. We done went all the way plenty of times," she said.

"But Neecy, that's one of his so-called best friends!" I yelled.

"Girl, I can't help it if he know how to love a woman and Mikey don't! He knew what to do the first day we was together. Like I said, I didn't have to tell him nothing. He got real skills girl, he be making me melt," she said.

I was overwhelmed listening to her. Neecy was a Pastor's kid. She was supposed to be a respectable girl. She sounded as *fast* as Jan.

"Well Neecy, it seems like to me, if Mikey's not asking you for sex, that's a good thing. I'd prefer a boy who didn't ask for sex rather than to have somebody who wants to have sex, 'cause most boys aren't going to do anything but get what they want and leave you. I know you're not saying you would rather be used by somebody?" I asked.

"Girl, they won't be using me, I'll be using them! Anyway, girl I'm dumping Mikey, as of today! I just called you so you can tell him for me 'cause I know you see him at church and y'all is friends and everything," she said.

"You tell him! You're the one who wants to quit him for one of his best friends! Don't be asking me to tell him!"

"Well then, I guess he gon just find out the hard way 'cause I done already moved on! You the one seem to like lil boys so you can have him for all I care 'cause I gots me a real man. Girl, you don't know what you missing. You need to git wit somebody like Freddy who can show you a thing or two. Anyway, my daddy callin me so I gots to go. See ya!" she said hanging up.

I was disappointed in her. I felt sorry for Mikey. He was so in love with her. I had never seen him buy so many gifts for any other girl. He talked about Neecy every time I saw him. Mikey confided in me about his feelings for her while I put on my fake grin.

It was torture for me, but I never let him know my true feelings. When he told me he loved her, it was heartbreaking for me because I knew she didn't care about him. I couldn't bring myself to tell him anything. I asked him if he and his neighbor Freddy were still best friends.

"Yeah, we cool," he said.

"Don't y'all go to school together everyday?" I asked.

"Yeah, when he's not playing hookie. Why?" he asked.

"Oh, I was just asking. No reason," I lied.

Mikey went on about Neecy and what he was going to buy her next. He was thinking about giving her a ring. I wanted to tell him not to waste his money, but I didn't know how to tell him. If I told him about her, then he might think I was just jealous and trying to break them up. He probably had some idea by then I liked him.

Mikey bought the ring for Neecy, but he was having a hard time catching up with her. She was never at home. She stopped coming to see him. Whenever he called, she was always busy or at least that's what she told him. It was hurting me to not say something. Neecy's distance was bothering Mikey. He was sad whenever he came to church. Some of the adult ministers including Mother Jordon noticed he wasn't himself. He wasn't smiling like he normally did.

Mikey confided in Mother Jordon about how Neecy was avoiding him. Mother Jordon and Mikey were very close. Mother Jordon was like a second mother to Mikey.

During church, I kept looking at Mikey's despondent face. His eyes seemed watery at times. We all stood in church and quoted the traditional Exodus 20th chapter followed by the book of James 2:10-12. Mikey stood up but his mouth wasn't moving along with everyone else. All the children and adults knew all these chapters by memory. We usually smiled at one another going from one verse to the next with our bibles closed. Mikey was not smiling. When all the children were called to the front to sing the books of the Bible and the biblical months which we also knew by memory, Mikey was the only one still sitting.

I finally had to tell somebody, so I told Mikey's mother about Neecy and how she was going with Mikey's friend behind his back. I asked her not to let Mikey know I was the one who told her.

Mikey's mother told him what she heard without putting my name in it. She told him the Lord let her know about Neecy and Freddy. Mikey accused his mother of lying. He went over to his friend Freddy's house finding Neecy over there. Neecy told him she was in love with Freddy and in fact, she was pregnant by him. Neecy was only fourteen.

I didn't see Mikey for a couple of weeks afterwards. His mama said he was heart broken over Neecy. She said he cried real hard. My own eyes were watery. I felt his hurt. I felt so glum.

When Mikey finally came back to church, he didn't know I already knew what happened.

"Did you hear 'bout yo low down, dirty cousin and one of my 'suppose to be' best friends?" he asked me.

"No." I lied and looked clueless.

He told me the whole story. I told him not to worry because there was a better person out there for him. He told me he was leaving girls alone for a while. I told him I was also leaving boys alone for a while.

When I wasn't at church during the summer, I spent a lot of time hanging with my friends at home. I had experienced a couple of things at home by then. Mark and I became friends even though he was Scootie's best friend. Not long after we became friends he was begging me to have sex with him. I was disappointed in him. I got the impression he got friendly with me just to try and get in my pants. I despised guys who did that to me.

All the neighborhood boys had asked me to have sex with them at some time or another. I hadn't found a single boy who was interested in getting to know me and like me and not my body. John, Ralph, Murphy, RJ, Gregory, and of course Mark had all asked me for sex. This was every single boy I hung around at home, with the exception of Vance, who was a loyal friend to my brother and Antonio, who was too old, even though they both slept with my friend JC a while back.

Antonio reminded me of Mikey. I still had a crush on Antonio because he treated me so differently. He treated me as if I was special. That was just great. The only two boys who I would never have as a boyfriend were the nicest guys out of all of them. I sometimes daydreamed about Mikey and sometimes I daydreamed about Antonio. I wished I was old enough to talk to one of them. I often tried to imagine which one I would go with if I were old enough and they both asked me. Sometimes Mikey won in my daydreams; sometimes Antonio won. Then I came back to reality. Anyway, Mikey continued to tell my cousins I was too young whenever they suggested we get together: I continued to respond after him.

"And he's too old for me."

Antonio continued to make me blush and call me his baby kissing my cheek from time to time.

During seventh grade, I stopped wearing pants. The church taught against girls wearing pants. We shouldn't wear anything pertaining to men. Mother Jordon stressed in her teachings how pants were supposed to be worn only by men. Daddy didn't want to force me to stop wearing pants. Mama did. Daddy told her it had to be my decision. I made the decision not to wear pants except during gym when I had to wear my gym uniform. I wore mostly skirts.

Most of my friends respected my decision. I had a few friends at school and at home who made a couple of comments but I had to tell myself I didn't care. If my friends at church could be strong willed about obeying God's commandments, so could I.

I had a crush on this boy at school named Bobby but so did just about every girl in the school. He sat next to me in one of our classes. He was light skinned with an afro and slightly bow legged. He was very muscular because he lifted weights everyday and took karate. He was nice. He never made a move or acted as if he had any interest in me other than as a friend so I settled for friends. I didn't have a preferred group of friends at school. I was friends with whoever wanted to be friends, which was almost everybody. Sometimes I sat at one table at lunch and other times I might sit at a different table if someone asked me to. I may have been asked more times to sit with a particular group, but no one made a big deal out of me changing tables. It never mattered if I wasn't sitting with the more popular crowd. I liked everyone who was nice and respectful towards me. I showed extra sympathy to the people who were picked on a lot by making conversation with them. It bothered me to see people being picked on.

There were some days after school that I would go to Ms. Janice's house and hang out with Paulina. Sometimes I just hung out with Ms. Janice since she was so cool. I knocked on Ms. Janice's door after school one day wanting to hang out with Paulina.

"Yo, come in," Antonio answered my knock.

I came in and asked him where Paulina was.

"She gone to the store wit Janice. She'll be back in a lil while," he said.

"Oh, okay. Well tell Paulina I stopped by," I said as I turned to leave.

"Hey, hold up a minute! What you rushing for? Sit down and talk to me for a minute," he said.

"Oh, okay," I said. He caught me totally by surprise.

Antonio started talking about the boys in the neighborhood. He heard some of the boys talking about running a game on me to see which one of them could get me in bed with them. He was warning me. I told him I was already hip to their game and they weren't fooling anybody but themselves. I already knew what they were trying to do. He asked me if I slept with any of the boys.

"No way!" I yelled.

"Well, that ain't what I heard!" he said back, with just as much conviction.

"I know how boys try to talk about girls, but none of these boys around here or anywhere else can ever say they had me without lying. Boy, I'm not stupid! I hear how these boys be talking about the girls they be done slept with and stuff. Neither one of them will ever talk about me that way and I promise you that!" I said.

Antonio stood up, walked over to me and hugged me.

"Yo! That's my girl!" he said proudly.

He kissed me on the lips. I couldn't believe he kissed me. We stood there staring at each other, then, he slowly bent and kissed me again. I was enjoying the kiss because he didn't try to use his tongue. I automatically closed my eyes when his lips touched my lips. Kisses were embarrassing for me because of Granddaddy and Pastor Jacobs. Antonio smiled at me, hugged me again and backed away.

"Well, you take care, okay?" he said.

I was impressed he didn't try to go any further. See, I knew he was different from other guys.

Two weeks later, Antonio saw me walking past his door and stopped me.

"Yo Tweety, come here for a minute. Let me talk to you," he said.

I trusted him so I went up on his porch and of course he asked me to come inside. I came in and sat down. He was standing the whole time. I wanted to scream because he was absolutely gorgeous in his Levi Jeans and red Polo shirt.

"Hey, you ain't being stupid about these boys around here are you?" he asked.

"No. Why did you ask me that?" I said.

"I was just checking. I just wanted to be sure," he said.

"Well no. No I'm not. I told you not to worry about me," I assured him.

"Okay. So anyway, what you want to be when you get out of school?" he asked, changing the subject.

"It's between a teacher and a psychiatrist. I don't know which one," I answered.

He was actually taking a personal interest in me. I felt special.

"Oh. Okay, well then, tell me this! What kind of grades you make?" he asked.

"Mostly straight A's and a few B's," I answered.

"Uh oh, you smart! You thank you something 'cause you smart, huh?" he joked.

He made me laugh while he teased me. He put this really charming smile on his face. We talked for at least twenty minutes and not once did he touch me. He was perfect. Why couldn't I be his age? I know he'd ask me for a chance if I was older. I would definitely say yes.

"Yo, so what's the deal? You gon be my baby or what?" he asked, catching me off guard.

I started blushing. I didn't know if I should answer him or not. I didn't answer.

"Well, I guess that means no, huh?" he said, sounding disappointed.

I started scratching my forehead still smiling then I nodded yes. Antonio acted excited and rushed over for a hug like we had just won a football game or something.

"Whew! I can't believe it! You gon be my baby!" he said.

I wanted to ask him what exactly did that mean, but I didn't. I just smiled.

"Well, yo, can I have a kiss?" he asked.

I blushed some more, then nodded yes. He gently tilted my shame faced chin up and kissed me again the same way he did before. He didn't grab me in any inappropriate way. The kiss was so innocent.

"Okay. Well, I'll see you later, okay?" He backed away as usual.

I said bye and left. I asked myself all day, what did he mean by baby? I looked forward to the next time he called me. I enjoyed talking to him. He probably would never attempt anything more than a kiss because I was so much younger than him. I trusted him. My time alone with him proved all guys weren't dogs.

It was a couple of weeks later when he called me over again. I couldn't go in because Mama was getting ready to leave. I told him I'd knock on his door after Mama and my sister left.

Scootie was always at the gym or at band practice or sometimes at the neighborhood basketball court.

When Mama left, I was too afraid to knock on Antonio's door. I didn't want to seem eager to see him. I was glad he came back to the door again and called me. I went in his back door this time. He went upstairs.

"Yo, come ere for a minute, let me show you something," he said.

I trusted him as usual and followed him upstairs. He had a photo album out with pictures. We were looking at the pictures up in his bedroom. He wanted me to trust him. We conversed innocently while he kept his hands to himself. He turned the pages and showed me a picture of me he had in his photo album. I was pleasantly surprised. It was a picture Paulina took of me one day when we were clowning around with the camera. I stared at the picture hating my hips. The boys bragged about my Coca-Cola shape, but I hated it. I was relieved the picture showed me facing forward and didn't really show my large backside.

"Yo, that's my baby right there," Antonio joked with me while seemingly admiring the picture.

I smiled. All of a sudden he was kissing me. After some time had passed, he started leaning back until I was lying down on his bed. Antonio was on top of me kissing me all at once. I didn't stop him. I had on a long fitting skirt so I didn't even stop him when he raised it up some to adjust himself on top of me. I still had no intentions of letting this go on for too much longer. He'd respect my decision.

Antonio was breathing a little heavier and then he reached under my skirt until he felt my panties. I was hoping he'd stop without me having to tell him to, but he didn't. I reached for his hand and moved it away from my panties.

"What's wrong?" he asked.

"Nothing," I answered.

"Well, why you stop me?" he said.

"'Cause," I said.

"'Cause what?" he asked.

"'Cause I'm not ready," I said.

"Awe, man! Yes you are! You just don't know you ready. Look at all this," he said as he placed his hands under me and squeezed my backside. My skirt was raised revealing my pink panties.

I moved his hands.

"So, I'm still not ready," I insisted.

"Okay, I'm sorry. Let me get my self together here," he said.

He lay still for a minute just staring at me. Then he finally sat up pretending as if he were putting a cold rag on his face. We both started laughing. His eyes were glued to my body. I adjusted my skirt below my thighs and sat up blushing. I was impressed he didn't try to force the issue more.

"So you wanna save yourself for the right time huh?" he asked.

I nodded yes, amazed he understood.

"Well, when you think it's gon be the right time?" he asked.

"Well, I don't know," I lied.

I wanted to say, not until I get married, but I kept my mouth closed. I'd rather lead him on to keep him interested. I didn't want our kissing sessions to end. I didn't want it to go any further though.

"Okay, well, yo, you gon come hang out with me again sometimes?" he asked.

"I don't know," I responded.

"Well, we can just fool around. We ain't gotta get serious or nothing," he explained.

"Okay, I guess," I answered.

I got up and headed downstairs. He followed me downstairs and gave me a kiss at the door and patted me lightly on my backside.

"I'll be ready whenever you ready," he said.

I blushed while laughing nervously before I went out the door.

I was afraid to go back in his house to be alone with him again. Something instinctively told me going back in his bedroom could prove to be risky for me. I didn't want him to get the impression I was okay with how far we went the last time. He went further than I was ready for him to go. I was afraid of the thought of giving in to guys. I promised myself, after escaping Granddaddy, I would never let a guy get the best of me.

I didn't know if I could get Antonio to back down so easily the next time. From then on, I lied and made up different excuses whenever he called me. I told him my mama was at home or, I had a red light. Red light meant I was on my menstrual cycle. Sometimes, I told him I had to do something real quick and ran off. A part of me wished I could let my guard completely down with Antonio and trust he wouldn't hurt me, but I loved Granddaddy who let me down. How could I trust any guy if I couldn't even trust my own Granddaddy?

Sometimes, Antonio caught me in my lies.

"You just said you had a red light last week. Come on now. I said we don't have to do anything serious. We can just fool around and have fun," he said.

I just smiled nervously, too afraid to let my guard down and believe him. He seemed too anxious to get me in his house. Something inside of me wouldn't let me trust guys no matter how nice they seemed. Granddaddy and Pastor Jacobs were both very nice and look what happened. No matter how much I longed to experiment with my feelings, I refused to trust him anymore because he went too far the last time.

A short while later Antonio had a new girlfriend. She was very pretty and even more importantly, she was his age. I wouldn't allow him to use me at his own leisure anymore even if I wanted his gentle affection. He just wanted to play around with me and I was not his play thing. He had a girl now and he was still trying to get me alone. I wanted to keep my self respect. He got the message and stopped asking after a while. He asked me if I was still his baby and I nodded no. He had more girlfriends than I could count after some time. I saw girls coming in and out of his house all the time. All of them were very pretty, maturely built, and his age. He was a junior in high school. *Why should he be different from the other boys?* He proved I was right about not trusting him.

"Healing Roads Journal"

On the one hand, there was something very wrong about me in the seventh grade kissing someone in the eleventh grade but I was obviously too confused to know. On the other hand, in my subconscious, I knew it was wrong because if I didn't really have a clue something was wrong about us, I wouldn't have needed to be secretive about it. I understand now when most teenagers behave secretively, it's because they know what they're doing will not meet approval. Secrets are often indicative of shame. Being secretive about Antonio was really an act of rebellion because I knew it was wrong, but I did it anyway. Most children are rebellious as a result of needing to vent or needing to lash out. Granddaddy represented someone I gave love and trust to. He betrayed me with deception. He left me hungry and treated me mean. This showed me how people who are closest to you can hurt you the most. I'm afraid to let my guard down ever again.

CHAPTER THIRTEEN

"Tongue"

I went over Ms. Pookie's house whose building was right in front of ours. She had a set of twin boys I helped her with from time to time. I didn't think I'd ever stop loving children. I stopped by to see if she needed help with the twins. Her teenaged son Tongue was sitting on the couch.

I walked in without knocking like I usually did and started calling Ms. Pookie thinking she was upstairs. I ignored Tongue.

"What you want lil girl!" he snapped.

"Where's Ms. Pookie at?" I asked.

Tongue jumped up playfully snatching my pocket book out of my hands.

"What you want with my mama?" he said with a huge teasing smile on his face.

I tried to take the pocketbook back. He put it behind his back so I reached for it. He grabbed both of my hands.

"Boy, give me my pocketbook and let me go! I'm not playing with you!" I yelled.

Tongue grabbed me around my waist as he backed up and laughed.

"I'll give you yo pocketbook alright!" he said.

I was looking intentionally aggravated. I asked him several times to turn me loose. I couldn't break free. He tried to kiss me on the neck. I was fighting him off thinking he must be half out of his mind to put his lips on me. I told him to stop.

He started backing back towards the sofa which made me panic. I struggled to break free, but I couldn't. His smile was replaced by a determined look. My heart was skipping beats. I knew he wasn't going to stop.

He dumped me on the sofa climbing on top of me pinning my hands up above my head. He didn't have on a shirt. He was muscular like most of the boys in my neighborhood. They all pumped iron and competed showing off their muscles.

Tongue was too strong for me. How in the world was this happening so fast? All I did was walk in the door and this creep was suddenly all over me.

I begged Tongue to let me go. I started to cry, but he ignored me. He pulled my skirt halfway up and I realized I couldn't fight him off me. I was hysterically fighting a losing battle. My strength was no match for his hold on me.

He unfastened his pants. I just knew I was in trouble. He bent down to kiss my neck while I struggled against him. He pulled my skirt up and struggled to pull my underwear down. I didn't know how this could be happening. I never considered him a dangerous person before. I couldn't fight him so I started to beg him to stop. He pulled his pants off revealing his blue boxer shorts. He was moving so swiftly, before I knew it he was back on top of me kissing my neck and grabbing for my underwear. He was ignoring my pleading and crying. I sank my teeth into his bare shoulder breaking the skin. Tongue yelled out in pain, jumped up and looked at my teeth marks on his shoulder. I lay there fixing my clothes slowly attempting to rise up while catching my breath.

Tongue slapped me so hard I saw stars. I grabbed my face and inhaled deeply. I cried real hard afterwards. Tongue yelled at me as I cried. "I was jus playing wit yo ass!"

I didn't respond. I jumped up and ran out the door. As I stepped off the porch Ms. Pookie was walking up. I stood there crying telling her what her son just did.

"Tongue just tried to rape me!" I cried out.

"What?" Ms. Pookie asked, completely astonished.

I repeated myself. She told me to come in and tell her in front of Tongue. I stood in her door telling her everything he did. Tongue called me a liar the entire time but Ms. Pookie grabbed a hard object and hit him with it. The object flew across the room so fast, I didn't know what it was she hit him with. Tongue hollered out in pain still saying I was lying.

Ms. Pookie slapped him real hard. She told me to come slap him too. I didn't want to touch him. She begged me not to tell, promising me she was going to get him real good for what he did.

"Tweety, just go on and slap the shit out of him since he wanna act like he so crazy! Gon and knock the hell outta him! He ain't gon touch you," she said

I didn't want to touch him. He had a whelp across his face from her hitting him with the object which turned out to be an extension chord. His hand was over his face. He was crying. She beat him in front of me with the extension chord. I was flabbergasted she was able to beat him so badly because of his age. He was as old as Antonio but he was in a much lower grade because he had been kept back a lot. He skipped school most of the time.

She continued apologizing to me for what her son did. She kept begging me not to tell. I told her I wouldn't tell. She asked me to swear I wouldn't tell.

"I won't swear, but I'll promise you I won't tell. It's against my religion to swear," I assured her.

I left and never told another soul about it. Less than a year later, Tongue was serving jail time for raping someone. I have no idea who this person was he raped a year later. Ms. Pookie said she didn't believe he was guilty because he knew better. I guess she figured the beating she gave him for trying to rape me would deter him from ever trying to do that to anyone else.

"Healing Roads Journal"

Yet again, my journey was still just beginning. I understand now I can't control my abusers, their parents, my parents, my friends, or their family and friends, but I can control my reactions to their personal choices. I now understand that I am not responsible for anyone else's actions except for my own. No one has the right or the permission from God who created me, to abuse me. I in turn have the right to do whatever is necessary to stop them from doing wrong to me. Low self esteem was a major factor in how insignificant I saw myself over others.

CHAPTER FOURTEEN

"The Whippings"

I was over Sister Nichols' house helping out with my little cousins. Weiner talked back to his mother to my surprise. I expected for him to be in big trouble.

Everything was quiet and the babies were all sleeping, so I went outside with Weiner. After talking and laughing for a minute, we started wrestling after I snatched a secret letter he wrote. His brothers, Bow Leggs and John John, were at their summer track practice. Weiner and I were struggling with the folded piece of paper. We both had a hold of it. He got serious when we were wrestling close and tried to kiss me.

"Weiner! What are you doing?" I yelled out in surprise.

"I just wanna kiss you one time, that's all," he said.

I stood still not knowing what to do or say at that moment. Weiner was staring dead in my eyes like he was in love or something.

"Come on. Please?" he begged.

He started inching up slowly towards my mouth as if he was going to die out of desperation if he didn't kiss me soon. I put my hand up to his chest to stop him.

"Weiner, what's wrong with you? We're cousins! I can't kiss you!" I said.

"I don't care," he said. He came towards my lips again.

I still had my hands up to his chest but he was trying to kiss me anyway. I had to push him off me.

"Well I do!" I snapped.

Weiner had a pleading look on his face. He grabbed my hands and actually started struggling with me. He continued attempting to persuade me to give him just one kiss.

"Please? Please Tweety?" he begged again.

I kept telling him no. He was hurt by my refusals.

"Why you gon do me like this Tweety? I can't help that I'm in love with you. I can't help it, Tweety! I just need to kiss you and hold you one time. Don't you love me too?" he asked.

"I love you like a cousin Weiner. Not like a boyfriend. I can't let you do what you want 'cause it's not right Weiner!" I explained.

"But Tweety, I really love you and you just said you love me too so what's wrong if we love each other?" he asked.

"Weiner, no, it's not right." I answered.

He actually started crying heavy tears.

"You just don't know how I feel right now. I feel like you breaking my heart Tweety. Please don't do this to me. Just one kiss is all I'm asking for. Just one kiss and hold me one time. That's all I need. Please? Please Tweety?" he pleaded.

"Weiner, I told you, I can't! We can't do stuff like that. It's wrong," I continued to explain.

I couldn't make close body contact with my cousin. He wanted to hold me in the wrong way. He seemed meloncholy. I knew how it felt to want someone to hold you when you were going through a lonely period, but I also knew he was having misplaced feelings. He was hurt about a recent break-up with a girl. He was going through some things at home with his parents. He was hurting and confused. I sensed his desperation but I didn't know what to do to help him.

Weiner snatched away from me turning his back on me. I didn't want him to be angry with me. I walked over to him and touched his arm.

"Weiner, you mad at me?" I asked.

He didn't answer but he shrugged my hand off him.

"Please don't be mad at me. Please?" I begged.

I felt bad about hurting him. He and his brothers were my closest cousins ever. I felt befuddled. I felt pity for him but I couldn't love him the way he wanted me to. I would do almost anything for him. I just couldn't love him the way a girl loves a boyfriend no matter how much it hurt him. He didn't seem to be accepting my apologies for it.

My feelings were hurt as well. I walked off and went in the house. I picked up one of his baby brothers who woke up. I was glad the baby was awake. Babies always cheered me up.

After a little while Weiner came in the house. It never occurred to me that someone could have seen and heard us through a window. The next thing you know, Weiner's mama called him into her room. He walked out of her room talking loud.

"Git out my face! I'm tired of all this shit. You better just back off me." Weiner yelled as he snatched away from Sister Nichols and walked off into his room.

Sister Nichols was so shocked it overwhelmed her and she started crying and turned to go back into her room. The entire house was quiet, listening to their mama crying. Some of the children were crying after seeing their mama so dismayed.

Pastor Nichols was extremely ruffled when he walked in the door from the store and saw his wife crying. I couldn't make out what they were saying in her room, but I could hear her still crying as she was talking.

I sat in the family room towards the back of the house still holding the baby. I knew Weiner was in big trouble for his disrespectful behavior. I saw Pastor Nichols come out of his room and go into Weiner's room. I heard him telling Weiner to take off his shirt.

"You been asking for this beating for a long time now son, so I tell you what...I'm gon git you for everything today. You been gittin away with this mess for too long now. I'm fixin to show you who the daddy is around here. You may as well git ready," Pastor Nichols said.

I was still sitting down holding the baby. Pastor Nichols walked back into his room and came out with several belts. He tested the strength by hitting his own hand. He sat the belts down and went back into his room unsatisfied still looking for something. My eyes got big when I saw him walk outside. He came back in with long, thick switches that had sticker briars in them. Sister Nichols called him into the room. She must have asked him not to use the switches on him. Thank God! He would have beaten him bloody with those switches. He finally walked back into Weiner's room and told him to reach under the bed and grab a piece of wood. He pulled out a short wooden slack from under the bed, which was normally used to support the bed frame. I heard Pastor Nichols testing it before closing the door.

At first I barely heard Weiner crying. He was trying to be tough because he knew I was in the house. Pastor Nichols was correcting him with words the whole time he was hitting him. Sometimes he was audible and sometimes he wasn't. Weiner started yelling "Yes Sir." He was still trying not to cry loud because I was in the next room.

After a while, Weiner got louder because he couldn't help it. He whipped him for a long time with the stick. I started feeling grievous for Weiner. I heard Weiner warning his daddy he was about to break his back. The whipping seemed endless lick after lick. You could hear the licks sounding off through the door. My God! It had been going on now for thirty minutes. Surely, it was about to end now.

The beating kept going. Weiner was shouting louder and louder.

"Oooh Daddy! My back! My back gon break! Daddy, my back gon break!"

My heart was beating fast. Weiner started screaming fiercely.

"Daddy! You gon kill me! Daddy Um 'bout to pass out! My arm! You gon' break my arm Daddy! Daddy! Aaaah, My back! You 'bout to break my elbow!" Weiner screamed out.

"Then move it out the way then!" Pastor Nichols yelled back.

The beating still didn't stop. The minutes were ticking away. I wondered how long Weiner could hold up. Tears were running down my eyes. I was sure he was about to kill Weiner. He kept stopping and talking but starting back up again. He was getting whipped for everything he'd done over the past month.

Pastor Nichols prayed instead of whipping his older boys for everything they did during the last couple of months. Weiner had become rebellious and more disobedient, unlike his other brothers. He had a cocky attitude because he knew he could get away with it, especially since his parents had stopped whipping them and prayed instead. He seemed to be testing his limits. He had always seemed to be the most rebellious out of the three boys and had gotten the worst of the beatings in the past as well.

Every time Pastor Nichols stopped to talk between the whipping, he reminded Weiner of an incident and then he would commence to beat him severely for all the whippings he did not get.

I felt infuriated and I wanted to get up, scream out, burst into the room, and beg for Weiner's life every time the beating started back up.

All the little children were in the other room crying with his mama. I was seething. I wondered why his mama didn't stop Pastor Nichols from trying to kill her son. She stepped out of the room and looked up at me briefly. She saw me wiping my eyes, then she quietly walked back into her room and closed the door. Weiner was begging for his life. I didn't want Weiner to be beat to death. I wished Pastor Nichols could go to jail at that moment.

Weiner got struck until the wooden slack broke, then his daddy finally stopped. In my whole life, I never heard someone getting battered severely. I was so glad to hear Weiner crying. That meant he was still breathing.

Weiner had been begging for some air for awhile during the thrashing. His daddy told him to go get some water and some air and to come back into the room. Weiner walked out of the room blowing really hard. He didn't look up at me when he walked past. I was relieved he could still stand on his feet.

I looked up into his daddy's face with crossness. Pastor Nichols walked off and fixed a glass of water.

To my astonishment, when Weiner came back in the room, Pastor Nichols came out and grabbed one of the belts and started back up again with the lashing. Weiner made the worst sounds I ever heard. I went in the room with his mama to put the baby down then I rushed into the bathroom and broke down crying hard. He was about to actually kill him!

Sister Nichols finally knocked on the door and stopped her husband. All the children were crying really hard and so was Sister Nichols.

I couldn't bring myself to step out of the bathroom. I had my hands covering my mouth to keep from crying too loud. The house was so quiet. Pastor Nichols finally knocked on the bathroom door.

"Tweety, you can come on out. It's over now," he said.

He must have heard me crying.

"Girl, Weiner gon be alright," he said assuringly. I didn't want to hear what he had to say.

I had to stay over there until church that night. I found it hard to look at Pastor Nichols for the rest of my time there. I tried not to be in the same room with him.

Weiner finally came out of his room and walked out side.

"Where you think you going boy?" Pastor Nichols snapped.

"Outside to get some air sir," Weiner said in a frazzled voice.

Weiner didn't have on a shirt. I saw some of the bloody bruises and huge welts on his back from a distance. When he came back in, his daddy asked him where his shirt was.

"I can't wear no shirt, sir." He almost burst out crying when he answered his daddy.

Just leave him alone! You already beat him half to death! I wanted to shout out. I just gritted my teeth. I would never come over to their house again except for church.

I was so glad when Bow Leggs and John John made it home from track practice. I never saw Pastor Nichols behave that way before. He was so furious with Weiner.

Uncle Lynn, or Pastor Nichols, as we now referred to him, had always been a loving father. The rest of the day, he was back to the way I remembered him being. He spent most of the day talking, laughing and wrestling with the younger children and joking with Bow Leggs and John John as if nothing happened. Weiner never came back out of his room. I didn't see him in church at all that night. I started to wonder if I should've at least let him hold me earlier. He seemed so desperate for love. Maybe he wouldn't have been so frustrated and yelled at his mama.

Some days later he apologized to me for his behavior and asked me not to tell anyone. I never said a word.

Everyone in the church whipped their children a lot except for our parents. I saw children get slapped just because they asked, "Why?" You weren't supposed to question your elders.

The church teachings were being emphasized more about "Spare The Rod And Spoil The Child!" This had Mama and Daddy on us a little harder about the chores around the house and moving faster when they told us to do something.

Pastor Nichols had whipped his children so many times, especially Weiner, who seemed to be the most rebellious, till Mother Jordan felt sorry for them. She witnessed one of Weiner's severe beatings and asked their daddy to have mercy on them and just pray and leave them in God's hands for a few months. She was hoping the children would fear God's wrath and fall in line and be obedient. I guess Pastor Nichols was tired of leaving Weiner in God's hands.

Mother Jordan spent two days teaching the parents why they shouldn't spare the rod. She taught from the scriptures in the Bible. Parents began to fear their children would go astray if they didn't discipline them strongly. As the teachings were taught to the parents, the punishments were beginning to seem endless.

The greatest fear was that God's wrath could fall on disobedient and rebellious children causing severe tragedy or death. It had been emphasized to the parents in our church to discipline us before God's wrath caught us. The wrath of God had been drilled deep into our minds and was a source of guilt, shame, and fear. Whenever something troublesome or painful happened, we were taught we caused God's wrath to fall on us through disobedience of some sort. Even the adults believed they were being punished by God when things were happening in their lives. Because we are imperfect beings living on this planet, one can always find fault in failure if you are being trained to do so.

Mother Jordan and Pastor Nichols didn't intentionally set us up for failure even though our fears were resulting in us becoming a stagnant church instead of a growing church over time. Someone ill went in search of self blame. Someone with family problems went in search of self blame and carried shame along with them. There was no true source of healing. Issues grew stronger and we grew into a large dysfunctional body of believers.

I spent the night over to a couple of the girls' houses at church. Curly's mama and daddy were by far the strictest parents I'd ever seen in my life. Curly's daddy slapped her right in front of me, for not bringing him a cup of water fast enough. She was moving pretty fast to me.

Curly's mama beat her with the broom so hard until the broom handle broke. I watched in horror as her mother told her there was still dust around the fireplace. She ran her fingers across the furniture looking to find anything dusty. I'll be doggone if she didn't run her hands across the old unused fireplace which gave her a reason to beat the crap out of Curly.

Curly had to dust all the furniture all over again. I felt guilty and rushed to help her. Curly got beat with switches because one of the glasses had a spot on it after she finished washing the dishes. Her mama dumped every single dish right back in the sink and made her wash everything all over again. I went home and told Mama and Daddy how horrible a time I had and what happened. I never wanted to go over Curly's house again.

Every time my brother, sister and I were at church and we did any little thing, the other adults were all over our parents. "Ooh, my child couldn't ask this or say that," an adult would say.

They were "nitpicking." They called us spoiled. Daddy and Mama started getting on us about little things around the house like taking our time if we were trying to finish a sentence doing our homework when Daddy asked for water at the same time. They got on us about doing more cleaning and asking too many questions.

"I wished I had yo daddy or I wish I lived with y'all." We heard these words constantly at church from the other children. Our parents were more lenient with us because we weren't forced to fast every Sabbath and we got to be involved in various school activities, plays and sports, unlike the other teenagers. Mother even taught against extra-curricular activities in the schools saying that we should be in the world, but not of the world as the scripture said.

Daddy didn't force every rule on us. Daddy never made us fast except the one day out of the year mandatory, which was "Fast Day for All God's Children."

In fact, this was the only time Daddy fasted himself. Daddy would have us to fix sandwiches and we practically had a picnic basket made up on Saturdays because church lasted all day until the sun went down. Mama fasted three days a week, along with most of the other ministers in the church. Most of the children were fasting and knew we were tipping outside to eat and drink everything from sandwiches, chips, and cookies, to water and Kool Aid. We always came back in the church smelling like food. All the children wished they had a Daddy like ours.

My cousins had to fast three days out of the week as well, even during school season. Sometimes when I went over to their house on their fast days, they would cheat and we'd all sneak and have "hot sauce sandwiches." At first I thought it was weird, until I tried it one time. We promised them we wouldn't tell on them for breaking their fast.

On "Fast Day for All God's Children," the small babies were so incapacitated by the end of the day they couldn't even cry. Daddy always took us to Zestos Burgers for whatever we wanted after our day of fasting. I always ordered a "Nut Brown Crown" ice cream cone for dessert. Other children would fight for the chance to spend the night with us so Daddy could spoil them as well. We enjoyed Daddy spoiling our church friends whenever they spent the night with us.

Mother Jordon taught that God alone was your doctor. She taught us to have faith in God and not man. She prophesied that people who didn't have faith in God would lose their lives to man by going to the hospitals and doctors. Most of the people at church feared her prophesies and refrained from going to the doctor's except to deliver babies.

Daddy never stopped going to the doctor and he never let Mama stop taking us for our routine exams. He disagreed with some of the things we were taught and wasn't afraid to speak up about some of the things. Mother was fond of Daddy and showed a lot of compassion towards him. She was patient when it came to understanding that Daddy wasn't ready for some of the things she had taught on.

Daddy did have some fear because he didn't smoke or drink alcohol anymore. He was too afraid unfavorable things would happen if he didn't heed God and stop.

We were very healthy and rarely got ill anyway. I don't remember any of the children in the church ever being severely ill, other than the flu.

My cousin, Bow Leggs did break his arm one time. The bone was sticking out from his arm. His daddy didn't take him to the doctor. He pushed the bone in himself and wrapped it. I felt sorry for Bow Leggs because he was in so much pain. Mother Jordon said it was God's wrath because Bow Leggs lied about breaking the broom the same day his arm broke. She said this was why he was suffering. We feared Mother Jordon's phophecy more every day.

Sitting at the kitchen table, Scootie announced his new girlfriend. Mama was at church and Daddy was working late.

"Tweety, guess who I go with?" he blurted out.

"Who do you go with?" I asked.

"It's somebody you know," he said.

"At church or at home?" I asked.

"Neither. I'm talking about somebody at school. You know Treasa?" he asked.

"Skinny Treasa?" I asked.

"She's not skinny, so what you talking about?" he said.

"She is too skinny. She might be pretty, but she's still skinny," I said.

"That's right. She's real pretty, isn't she?" he said.

"Yeah, she's cute. You go with her?" I asked.

"Yep," he answered.

"Good for you. What you want, a hero cookie?" I said facetiously.

"Why? 'cause she looks better than you?" he replied.

"Shut up! She don't look better than me," I snapped.

"Augh! You're just jealous 'cause she's pretty," he said.

"I'm not jealous of that ole dumb girl. She's not even smart, now!" I snapped.

"Awe, don't be mad at her. Sometimes ugly ducklings turn into swans, so don't be jealous of her," he continued to pick.

"Awe shut up!" I said.

"Make me," he said.

"Keep on talking, I'll get up and punch you!" I yelled.

"You'll be done got hurt is what you'll be done did," he warned.

"No I won't. I betcha I won't," I countered.

"Hit me then," he dared.

Sonia sat quietly watching in frustration as I jumped up and punched Scootie on the shoulder.

Scootie jumped, pretending to leap towards me as I flinched.

"Awe, see there? See what I mean? You better be glad I don't hit girls," he said.

"I don't better be glad of nothing," I said.

"Look, like I said, one day you might turn into a swan," he said.

I jumped up and punched Scootie harder. He looked at his arm and burst out laughing again. I got angrier because he continued to pick at me. I pushed his whole chair down causing him to bump his head. Scootie lost his temper and jumped up and punched me hard on my shoulder. I grabbed my shoulder in anger. Tears rushed down my eyes.

Sonia was sad seeing me cry. Her lips were pouting. She was ready to cry too.

"Scootie, I'm gonna tell Mama you made Tweety cry!" Sonia yelled.

"What about what she did to me?" Scootie said.

"So! You shouldn't hit girls," Sonia countered.

I left the table and stomped upstairs as Scootie yelled at me.

"I'm gon tell Mama you left the table before everybody was finished eating too!" he said.

"So, tell her, now! Don't you talk to me anymore!" I slammed the bedroom door and fell on the bed pouting about my arm. Scootie hurt my feelings when he picked on me and then hit me.

Sonia followed the rules and waited on Scootie to clear the table. It was his turn to wash the dishes. Because Sonia and I both were afraid to stay downstairs alone, Mama made us all wait on one another until all the dishes were done. We had to sit at the kitchen table and wait until the last dish was washed and then we could all come upstairs together.

Sonia opened the bedroom door and saw me wiping my eyes from crying. My arm was slightly bruised. I cried every time I looked at it.

"Look what he did to my arm. Ole Black dog!" I said as I showed Sonia my bruise.

I knew I wasn't allowed to call Scootie such a name, but I was angry and venting.

"You want me to tell Mama on him for you Tweety?" Sonia asked, feeling sorry for me.

Scootie walked into the room overhearing Sonia and seeing her rub my sore arm as tears fell. I had a stubborn look on my face. I rolled my eyes at Scootie. I was an expert at making facial expressions. There wasn't a day when I didn't make several faces to express my point of view.

Sonia saw my face and knew my feelings were hurt.

"Scootie, you bruised Tweety's arm and I'm telling my mama on you!" Sonia snapped.

"No I didn't. Well then, let me see," Scootie said.

Scootie came towards me, but I turned my body away in exaggeration.

"Don't you touch me!" I yelled.

"I was just trying to see your arm," he explained.

"I don't want you to see nothing. You shouldn't have hit me like that!" I snapped.

"Well, if Sonia tell, I'm telling Mama what you did to me too, and both of us will be in trouble. So, here. Hit me back," Scootie suggested.

I continued to ignore him.

"Here Tweety. Hit me back. You can hit me back hard, okay?" he said.

I took a look at the bruise on my arm before wiping my eyes. I jumped up and started punching Scootie over and over. He mostly blocked all my licks laughing at first. I accidentally bust his lip trying to swing around his blocked hands. His lip bled and he became angry again once he felt his bleeding lip. He lost his temper again and jabbed me hard in my stomach knocking the wind completely out of me. Unable to catch my breath, I doubled over and fell to the floor. I felt the worst pain ever, but I couldn't make a sound.

I couldn't breathe. I almost passed out. Sonia was crying hard and Scootie was scared. He tried to help me up. It took a while, but I suddenly caught my breath, as I inhaled and then released the loudest scream ever. I continued to double over sobbing hysterically and clutching my stomach. Sonia was afraid I was seriously injured and she cried harder. Scootie apologized over and over. The pain eventually went completely away. I felt normal again. I slowly got up and climbed on my bed and lay down with my back turned to both Scootie and Sonia while they continued to hover over me.

Scootie was begging me to hit him back and Sonia was begging me to talk to her. I just wanted to be left alone.

When Scootie wouldn't leave me alone I yelled out a bad name again.

"Leave me alone you ole black dog!"

Mama came home and caught me. Sonia explained to her how we had been fighting and why I was calling Scootie names. Mama made us go pick switches outside and gave us the worst whipping ever. She used three long switches twisted together on each one of us. I jumped all around the room screaming yes ma'am, I didn't know how many times. So did Scootie. Sonia cried for us as she watched.

When Mama was done, she believed she had done the right thing according to the Bible, as the church had taught. She told us to go take a bath and go to bed. As the bath water was running, Scootie and I sat in our room examining our welts. I was fuming.

"She make me sick. Don't she?" I asked Scootie.

Scootie agreed.

"Look Scootie! Look at what she did." I showed him how the switch wrapped around my thigh and made a real long ugly swelling.

"See, it's almost bleeding," I added.

Scootie inhaled making a snake sound at the same time reaching towards the bruise.

I jumped back. "Ooh, don't touch it!" I said, still looking at my marks, "I'm not gon never whip my children like this!" I snapped.

"Me neither," Scootie agreed.

Scootie started looking over his own body then he showed me a really bad 'wrap around welt' across his back.

"That's nothing, look at this one!" he said.

"Ooh! That is a real bad one! That's gonna sting when you get in the tub," I said.

"Tweety, you'll take a bath first?" he asked.

Daddy came in the room from work while I was still huffing and puffing over the whipping.

"Daddy, look!" I said.

I showed him my swollen bruises. Scootie started showing Daddy his welts as well.

Daddy patiently examined every mark we showed him.

"Good Lord! Mookie! Mookie you need to come in here and look at what you done did to these children!" he yelled.

"Those children gon be alright," Mama yelled back.

"No they not either! Mookie, you need to come in here and see what you did!" Daddy insisted.

Mama took her time but she finally got up and came in the room.

"Ranch, I promise you, these children ain't gon die," she said before she even looked at us.

"I don't care if they ain't gon die. This right here is child abuse right here. You can go to jail for this!" Daddy snapped.

Mama started looking us over real good. She got quiet.

"You ain't gon whip my children with no switches no mo, and I mean that! I don't care what the church says!" Daddy continued to snap.

"Ranch, we use to get whippins with extension cords and everything when we was growing up," Mama replied.

"I don't care what we got whipped with! Just 'cause they...they... they beat us half to death, don't mean we...we gon...gon beat them like that!" Daddy said as he stuttered, showing his anger.

Mama didn't say anything else. This was a lesson for the whole house. Mama agreed with Daddy about the switches. From then on, Mama and Daddy stopped listening to the church folk concerning whippings. On the rare occasions we did get hit, it was always with a belt, but we never got caught fighting again. Not because we didn't fight; we just never got caught again. I forgave Mama for whipping us, but I never forgot that day.

"Healing Roads Journal"

Mother was a great prophet and woman of God. Mother was a faithful servant of God. Mother was a strong follower and believer in God. Mother has laid hands on people who have been healed because of their faith. Mother has spoken many things which have come true. Mother, however wasn't God. Even though Mother Jordon never said she was my God, she became my total source. It's not my duty to bring any criticism upon any of God's people. My only intention is to grow through observation based on my experiences and learn from my choices.

CHAPTER FIFTEEN

"Strict"

During school seasons I spent more time at home than I did at church. I had homework and studies. Mama was helping out a lot at church. Daddy was at work a lot. When I came home, I changed out of my skirts and put on shorts because it was too hot to be outside in a skirt.

"I thought you weren't wearing pants no more!" Mama said.

"Mama, I can't help it. It's too hot outside," I said.

People started commenting on my figure once again. They told my parents how nicely built I was when I had on shorts outside. They joked and told Mama and Daddy to watch out for me with that neat figure.

Daddy started coming home from work earlier than he normally did. He had a new job with different hours. I was not accustomed to Daddy being home before Mama on some days. When he was home, he watched me like a hawk. He must not have liked what he saw or who I was hanging around. I still hung around my usual crowd of people.

Paulina, Anita, Lanette, and sometimes this other girl hung out with us named, Sweetie. Sweetie was deeply involved with this older guy who we called "Pretty boy," because of his good looks. I knew he was taking advantage of her but we promised Sweetie we wouldn't say anything and we didn't.

Some days Sweetie didn't go to school but instead, spent the entire day with "Pretty Boy." He was in his early twenties. "Pretty Boy" had a muscular build like a football player and was slightly bow legged. His weight lifting build reminded me of my Uncle Kirk. He was right out of a dream-date magazine with his perfect smile.

Whenever the boys weren't at the basketball courts, at the swimming pool, or working part-time jobs, everyone hung out together.

They were around us girls every week. We hung out with Paulina's two brothers, Gregory and Antonio. Gregory was extremely bow legged. Antonio was slightly bow legged. Antonio was the nicest and cutest of the two. Gregory was also cute but he was very slim and not nearly as nice.

We also hung out with Anita's two brothers, John and Ralph. John and Ralph were also handsome. John was light skinned with a solid build, medium afro, perfect teeth and very pink gums. Ralph had deep dimples, medium brown skin and a short hair cut. He was slimmer than John, but not skinny. All the boys hung out lifting weights together and had nice upper bodies.

We also hung out with Murphy, whose mom fixed my hair a lot. Murphy was the heaviest of all the boys but he was muscular in his legs. His upper body was slightly flabby. He had muscles in his arms but not so much in his stomach and chest.

Sometimes, Antonio's friend RJ and his cousin Blackie came around as well, even though they didn't live in our neighborhood. They still lived nearby and attended the same school.

When we all hung out together, we clowned around a lot. We listened to music, played Uno, Concentration, Spades, and four square as well as sports and other games. We hung out until our parents called us in. Scootie and I were the first to get called in every day.

Lately, when Daddy came home early, he made me stay on my porch a lot. Even when he wasn't home, Daddy had Mama call me in order to check up on me.

"Yo Daddy said to stay in front of the door," Mama would call out to me.

I objected and questioned why.

"Because I said so!" Mama snapped.

Even when my parents made me stay on the porch, everyone would just hang out around my little porch. If my parents let me off of the porch, then we hung out on the Community Porch.

I couldn't understand why Daddy was being so strict. Mama called me constantly just to check up on me. I got checked up on every single day, throughout the day. If I was standing around the corner at the next building, Mama called me.

"Tweety!" Mama called.

"Ma'am!" I answered.

"What you doing?" she asked.

"We're just all standing outside in front of Paulina's door Mama!" I answered.

"Well, yo daddy said you need to come back around here where you can be seen," she hollered back

A quick phone call from Daddy while he was at work ruined my whole day. My friends picked on me a lot.

"Damn! You can't even stand right around the corner!" John said.

"I know. My parents be trippin," I said.

They especially laughed because Sonia could go further than I could. She could go to China's and other friend's houses her age and I couldn't go anywhere.

Sometimes, my friends had to beg Mama to let me walk to the store with them or let me go over to Ms. Janice's house with everybody else. Sometimes, Ms. Janice would call my parents and ask them personally to let me come over, and they said okay to her faster than they said yes when we asked.

Ms. Janice was cool because she used our slang. She was really humorous. She was the only adult who could hang with us without getting on our nerves. She didn't scold the boys when a bad word slipped out their mouth. Sometimes a bad word even slipped out of her mouth. She fed us all the time. I hung out with her when everybody else was at the swimming pool. I enjoyed talking to her. Daddy didn't trust me to go to the public swimming pool to hang out with everyone else. I was the only one not allowed to go swimming.

It was practically a ghost town in the summer from about four o'clock to six o'clock because all the neighborhood children went swimming. We had a very large indoor public swimming pool at the middle school I attended. Everyone went there. I had never been allowed to go. I had only seen the swimming pool during school hours. Scootie even hung out at the pool. Sonia was too young to go to the pool, but she spent her days at her best friend China's house playing with tea sets and dolls. Only children ages twelve and older were allowed to come to the pool unsupervised. I remember spending a lot of days sitting alone on my porch playing Jack Stones, jump roping on the sidewalk, playing with my Bolo Bat, Hula Hoops, or playing a card game called Concentration. Sometimes I even sat out on the Community Porch for a spell, doing some of the same things I did on the porch. Occasionally I'd notice a shade lifted up where some of the boys' rooms were and I figured they had their reason for not going swimming. It was embarrassing realizing I was being stared at for God only knew how long, with all my defenses down. I always dusted my backside and legs off after sitting. I bent carelessly to pick up things when I thought no one was looking. I probably even dug cheese out of my shorts every now and then. Even the thought of my behind bouncing while jump roping or turning in every direction to keep up with the Bolo Bat or Hula Hoop made me feel ashamed of being watched. I'd often wonder how much of a show I unknowingly put on for the boy who had obviously been watching me for quite some time. The shade would suddenly drop after I stared long enough confirming my suspicion. Whenever the boys were around I made extra sure to turn my backside away from them whenever I did things like hula hoop or jump rope.

Daddy was becoming more paranoid as time went on. He was limiting me from so many things.

"If I really wanted to do bad things, I could easily get away with it during the times you're not around because y'all are not around me twenty four seven," I explained to Mama in frustration. "I'm not stupid Mama. I know better than to sleep with boys. I don't even have any desires to have sex with any boys so why are y'all treating me like I'm a fast lil girl or something?" I asked.

"Well Tweety, I know you're not stupid. I don't believe you would sleep with any boys but right now, yo Daddy doesn't trust any of these boys around here. It's not that he doesn't trust you," Mama explained.

"It's not the boys Mama. Daddy acts like I be doing wrong and he makes me feel like I can't be trusted," I argued.

Mama took in a deep sigh after some more debating. "Well Tweety, I'm trying to help you to understand where yo daddy is coming from. All I can do is tell you to just go along with it for now and try to be patient and just understand that yo daddy loves you. He'll probably get over it after a while," Mama concluded.

I didn't agree with Mama, but I couldn't change her mind. Daddy was always spying on me whenever he was around. He stood behind the front door to watch me and my friends. I sometimes spotted his head barely peeking around the door or out the slightly opened window curtains.

"Yo, Tweety...there go yo daddy spyin on you again," Murphy whispered.

My friends spotted Daddy quicker than me because I couldn't see as well without my eye glasses.

There were probably just as many times we didn't see Daddy hiding and looking depending on where he hid. It was beginning to be aggravating and I didn't feel like he trusted me at all. I hadn't done anything to earn his distrust of me. Unbeknownst to me, rumors were starting up again and getting back to Mama and Daddy at church about me being fast. Unbeknownst to me yet again, the gossiping lady at church was starting to make up lies about what she saw me doing with boys or what she heard me saying. Because she was a minister, other adults believed what they heard her saying and the rumors spread rapidly.

I went to Mama for understanding yet again.

"Mama, Daddy obviously doesn't know me as well as I thought he did or else he would trust me more," I said.

Mama continued to assure me that she trusted me and that she knew I was not stupid. I could just hear the song playing in my ears repetitively. "You're a Big Girl Now... No More Daddy's Little Girl," I wanted to sing the words out to both Mama and Daddy to make them understand that it was normal for me to grow up and hang around my friends without so much supervision and suspicion. None of my friend's parents were being so strict and untrusting.

"Please just try to be patient with yo daddy okay, Tweety?" Mama would continue to ask me.

"But Mama! Me, Paulina, and Anita were outside practicing cheers from school and Daddy made me come in just for that. I can't help it if boys are outside sitting around. That's what we all do. All the girls were doing cheers. It's not like I was outside all by myself trying to seduce any boys. I wasn't even paying attention to those boys. We were just practicing cheers. Daddy come talking about I was trying to get boys to look at me. The last thing I want is boys looking at my butt. I can't even be a normal teenager. Day before yesterday, we were having a singing contest, the boys against the girls. We were seeing who could sing and perform the best so the boys sang and did their little dance steps and then all us girls sang, "You got the Best of My Love," and did our dance steps we had made up. We were all outside in each other's face arguing about who won. Daddy called me in and yelled at me for being all up in boys' faces when it wasn't even like that. I wasn't just up in their face trying to be fast or anything, we were just all having a big huge debate about who had won the contest," I explained to Mama.

"Well, Tweety, all I can tell you is to try not to be up in no boy's face when yo Daddy's around. You know how he is. I mean, yo Daddy's a man and he know how boys can be. You need to try and look at it from where he comin from being a man," Mama said.

"It's stupid to me," I replied.

"Well, I don't know what to tell you Tweety. What you want me to say?" Mama asked, as if to say, her hands were tied.

Daddy watched me like a hawk, even at church. I mostly hung around my cousins Big Boy, Weiner, and John John. For no reason, Daddy would come outside and call me in and tell me to stay inside the church. I got spoken to in a snappy way if I questioned him, so I gritted my teeth and vented on the inside. Unbeknownst to me my parents had to deal with hearing the gossip that was viciously being spread about me yet again by that same female minister in the church. By now, according to rumors, I was sleeping with a lot of boys and sneaking behind my parents back. Also, according to rumors I was deceiving them terribly and sooner or later I was going to end up pregnant, and my parents would realize just how sluttish I was all along.

I wanted Mama to come to my rescue and tell Daddy to stop being so paranoid, but she never did. Sometimes she looked at me with sympathy and tried to cheer me up because at times I was so livid

I had to wipe a tear or two from my eyes. I felt more confused everyday. The harder I tried to be good, the more I seemed to get punished. Some of my friends followed me inside the church anyway once they realized I couldn't come back outside. They were used to Daddy making me come in. I didn't know what Daddy expected of me anymore. I couldn't please him nor could I prove to him I was a respectable girl, no matter how hard I tried.

I told all the boys in my crew at home to keep their hands off me period, whenever my daddy was around. Don't tap me on my shoulder or come anywhere near me when Daddy's around. I explained how paranoid he was behaving about me and boys.

If Daddy was home whenever my friends and I were on the Community Porch, all I had to do was issue fair warning. "My daddy's home."

I said it dryly, but they knew how to carry themselves. Don't hit me, don't whisper in my ear, don't dance in my face, just don't touch me period. Sometimes someone would show up after the fact and become playful. Daddy was always standing there and he called me in or made me sit on the porch every time. This meant he had to be spying for at least an hour sometimes to catch what he did catch. All he needed to see was a boy touching me period, anywhere. They could even be telling me something in my ear and Daddy would punish me for it.

Gregory joked around dancing in my face to Anita Ward's "Ring My Bell" while every one laughed at his silliness. Daddy didn't think it was funny when he came to the door. I got yelled at for Gregory's behavior because Daddy didn't like the words to the song.

On another occasion, Ralph was clowning around in my face acting wild and he grabbed me trying to dance crazy to Wild Cherry's "Play that Funky Music." This wasn't a big deal to me. Obviously no one could touch me period without Daddy flipping out.

On yet another occasion all the girls had pretend microphones as we sang Glady's Knight's "Leaving on The Midnight Train" and Paulina invented moves to go along with the song as we performed. The boys clapped and cheered us on. Daddy accused me of flaunting my body in front of all the boys.

Sometimes I got tired of my friends constantly pointing, asking me questions like 'Where yo sister and brother at?' They were no where to be found.

"Why yo daddy making you sit on the porch?" John was bold enough to ask.

"I don't know. No reason," I answered.

"Well, if you got to sit on the porch for no reason, why yo sister and brother don't have to sit on the porch too?" John asked.

"Exactly!" I replied.

I didn't have any boyfriends. I didn't want any boyfriends. I was trying so hard to prove to Daddy I was a good girl. I went out of my way to show him.

I was becoming depressed. I cried about it. I begged Mama to do something about Daddy. He gave Mama instructions for me even though he was never around most of the time. Mama kept asking me to just try to put up with him and to try to understand where he was coming from. I got tired of hearing her saying this to me all the time.

I finally gave up. I stopped coming outside period. Daddy wasn't around to see me in the house all day long; he wasn't around to really see how much of a hard time I was having as a result of his strict rules.

When my friends knocked on the door, I told them I was busy. I always gave them an excuse. I stayed in my room and read books. I sat in Mama's window and watched everybody playing outside while I watched TV.

I was vexed with everybody in the house except for Sonia. Scootie had too much freedom. He went everywhere. He picked on me sometimes telling me I was just jealous because he was the oldest.

"Shut up talking to me! Don't say nothing else to me!" I yelled at Scootie.

I wanted to sock Scootie because it wasn't fair. He liked to watch TV in Mom's room when he was at home so I went in my room and slammed the door behind me. I kept library books in the room with me to read all the time. I also read "Harlequin Romance" novels. Mama gave them to me to read. There was nothing explicit to read but they were very romantic.

No matter how angry I was with Scootie, anger between us never lasted very long. By the time we sat down at the kitchen table, we engaged in our usual chit chat, joking, and sharing stories. In addition to the time we spent at the kitchen table every single day, we all shared a bedroom. We argued, aired our differences, then we joked and laughed all in the same minute. Spending so much time together every day and every night, forced a continual family bond and strengthened our love for one another. Scootie made me sick plenty of times, but at the end of the day, I loved him with all my heart. That was my brother.

There was only one TV in our house, in Mama's room. I stopped going in Mama's room when Daddy was home because I was ticked off at him. I watched a lot of programs with Sonia like "Sesame Street" and "The Electric Company," when it was just the two of us.

Mama tried to talk to me a lot when she and I were home alone. I saw parts of her wanting to stand up for me. She wanted me to know she loved me. Daddy's over protectiveness seemed like a harsh punishment for no reason. Mama seemed to know how I felt.

I acted nonchalant when Daddy told me I couldn't go swimming. I was too stubborn to show hurt even though he made me feel cheap.

"You done lost yo mind! Ain't no way I'm fixin to let you go swimming wit all them boys down there!" Daddy said.

Scootie's best friend Mark was the only boy I spent time with because he came over with my brother. We passed licks a lot and acted silly whenever he came over. He was only interested in my body and I knew it. He had lots of girlfriends. He got on my nerves asking me when we were going to do it again. He referred to what we did when we were little kids wrestling as if we had real sex before. I finally got tired of playing his game.

"Never! Now don't ask me anymore!" I snapped.

He got offended and stopped coming over. I didn't care. I sat on the porch everyday when everybody had gone swimming. I also started spending time with one of the elderly ladies who lived across the street. Ms. Lizzy would come get me to walk to the store with her and help her clean up around her house. I didn't mind. It was something to do. Daddy didn't complain about this at least.

A couple of days out of the month every other week, Daddy had to travel out of town in his big truck. I finally got a little freedom on those days. Mama wasn't as strict on me when Daddy left because I spent too much time in the house as it was. I did homework for the week. I was always ahead on my school work. I made straight A's because I had so much study time.

Daddy still took us to get burgers and joked around on the weekends. He still had a way of making me laugh at his jokes even when I wanted to be angry with him. It was hard to hate Daddy because of his many good points. He was attentive to our needs. I could ask Daddy to get me a chocolate shake from Burger King and he'd go back out and get it even though he was tired from working. Most children in the neighborhood considered us spoiled because Daddy was always giving us things all the time. We couldn't afford designer clothes and we were not the best dressed in the least, but we were taken care of.

On Saturday mornings we always ran late for church because Daddy had to watch "Bugs Bunny" and "The Road Runner" before we left. Sometimes I sat on the porch dressed and ready to go to church with some of my friends outside. They laughed because they heard Daddy upstairs guffawing over his cartoons.

I started hanging outside maybe once every other week. I spent the remainder of my time inside. I dreaded the week days when Daddy was off work. I didn't want to be in the house with him because he watched me like a hawk all the time. The few times I came out when Daddy wasn't home and spent time with the crew, I was flooded with attention from the boys. They treated me like I was the new girl in the neighborhood because they didn't see me as often as the other girls who hung out everyday.

The girls seemed to be getting jealous of the attention I got whenever I showed my face and we became more distant. They often teamed up on me and made me the brunt of their jokes in front of everyone. I noticed them leaving me out of things. They would go hang out somewhere else when they knew I had to stay in front of the door.

I went to The Big Field with Paulina and Anita one evening to watch a talent show that was being performed on a stage that was set up on the field. I was wearing a new church outfit because Mama was coming to pick me up for church during the feast once she was done helping out with the feast preparations. I wouldn't have time to go home and change so I had to go to the show dressed up. I saw Mama's car going around the circle by the time the show was almost done so I started heading home. Paulina and Anita decided to leave with me. I was looking forward to going to church in my nice, purple outfit with my high heels and panty hose on. I thought I looked very sophisticated and mature in the neatly fitted dress. I could easily be looked upon as a sixteen year old because of my shapely body, if you didn't know me.

As we were heading home, Paulina hollered out loudly, "Look at Tweety with her Holy ass, walking in them damn high heels and shit!"

I tried to laugh with them seeing her and Anita laughing loudly. That seemed to anger Paulina more.

"What the hell you laughing for you damn Holy Roller!" Paulina said.

Paulina and Anita high fived one another and laughed even louder. Their loud laughing was drawing attention to others. Paulina kept repeating "Damn Holy Roller!" and getting others to join in laughing with them. I was the only one dressed up outside so I stuck out like a sore thumb. They were being intentionally cruel for no apparent reason. I walked ahead as they continued laughing. I couldn't understand how your friends could try to hurt you for no reason.

I even stopped hanging out over to Ms. Janice's house with them because Ms. Janice bragged too much about me, which made things worse. She told Paulina and the other girls they needed to carry themselves more like me instead of being all over these darn stupid boys all the time. They were outside everyday with the boys, hanging out at the pool with the boys, and bonding stronger. I felt as if the distance I had created by not spending so much time with them was destroying our close bond.

After Paulina and Anita treated me cruel, a few days later, we would be talking and laughing again as if nothing bad was ever said.

I was very forgiving because I wanted so much to bond with my friends at home. When Paulina wasn't around Anita, she was never mean. I could tell that Anita just didn't want me around them anymore period, and I often wondered what she was saying to Paulina to turn her against me. I figured Anita out one day when I was knocking on her screen door to see if she could come outside with me but she wouldn't come to the door. I knocked harder when I looked through the screen door and didn't see her coming, but she still didn't answer the door. Paulina walked up and called Anita's name through the screen door and she suddenly answered. When she stepped outside with Paulina I asked her why she acted like she didn't hear me knocking on her door.

"Why the hell were you knocking loud on my door anyway? Don't be bamming on my damn door like you crazy and shit!" Anita said.

Anita and Paulina high fived and laughed while walking away from me. I heard them laughing and having fun at Ms. Janice's house from my porch but I didn't go over there with them and they didn't ask me. The boys always asked me to come over, calling out to me from the screen door. I always told them I had to stay on the porch. Every now and then, Ms. Janice would call me over to hang with them. I sat quietly trying not to be the center of attention. Paulina was going with Anita's oldest brother John. Anita, who was my age, was being mischievous with Antonio. They were getting close as anyone could tell.

Daddy talked about the girls being outside with the boys and letting the boys hit them on their backsides. He talked about Paulina and John always outside in the public kissing and being all up on each other. I wanted to ask him, *What you be standing there in the door looking so hard for? If you didn't stand there so long, you wouldn't see nothing!* Of course I only said it under my breath.

Ms. Janice made it harder for me by bragging in front of everyone, even though she didn't know it. When the boys started playing with me, I acted disinterested trying not to aggravate the girls. That didn't make the girls like me any better though. They still whispered among each other, rolled their eyes and ignored me. I was hurt. I told

Mama about them one day as I cried.

"They're supposed to be my friends and they treat me like they can't stand me. They're always talking about me and whispering behind my back on the sly. They treat me like I'm Poison Ivey or something. I don't want none of their stupid boyfriends," I explained to Mama.

"Tweety, if I was you, I wouldn't even worry 'bout them. They just jealous, anyway. You just keep yo head up and keep on being respectful. Long as you know you haven't done nothing wrong, don't even worry 'bout them old silly girls out there," Mama said.

"I know... but they're my friends Mama!" I said.

"Apparently they ain't who you thought they was, are they? I remember when I was just a little older than you...."

Mama told me one of her childhood stories in an attempt to cheer me up. I didn't bother to come out for weeks on end because the girls treated me bad or they left all together. I blamed Daddy sometimes. He was the reason I started distancing myself from my friends to begin with.

I was miserable the second half of my seventh grade year. I became more introverted. I spent more time at Ms. Lizzie's house.

"Healing Roads Journal"

On the one hand, I was carrying scars from Granddaddy. I just didn't realize it. On the other hand, Daddy's controlling behavior was way beyond normal. This was extreme behavior to control me and keep me from boys. Daddy showed too much mistrust and was becoming too possessive, especially once it got to the point I couldn't let a boy touch me.

As children growing up, our perceptions can be distorted when it comes to how we assess our friendships. The girls that I hung out with in my neighborhood could have just as easily felt that I was a "goodie two shoes." They may have even felt that I was jealous of them the same way I felt they were envious and bitter towards me. I'm pretty sure that if you were to sit down with Paulina, Anita, Lanette, and Sweetie each in separate rooms and ask them to talk about how it was growing up around each other, everyone would have very selective memories and all of our stories would be quite different. We remember the details of our lives based primarily on things that are most significant to us. I would never argue with anyone about how they remember our childhoods no matter how different they remember it because memories are mostly based on feelings that we hold on to. I respect every one today because we all have a voice and we all matter. I was young and still learning about life and so were the girls I bonded with growing up. I isolated myself as a result of my daddy's controlling behavior. I never confided in them about why I was isolating myself, so they could very easily express a completely different viewpoint of our friendship.

CHAPTER SIXTEEN

"The Boys"

I learned to play the control game really well with boys. During the summer of 1980, I was going to the eighth grade, and I decided to make a sport out of the boys in my neighborhood who conspired to play their sex ploys with me.

I was unimpressed with the boys giving me so much attention every time they saw me. None of the boys ever asked me to be their girlfriend. They all asked me to have sex with them. I was annoyed with the boys thinking I wasn't good enough to be their girlfriend. They must've thought I was only good enough to let them take advantage of my body. I got this idea in my head to beat them at their game.

I walked past Murphy's door, coming from softball practice. He always begged me to come over to his house whenever he saw me walking past. I usually made a thwarting face and kept walking. One time I stopped and went up to his porch when he hissed at me.

"Okay Murphy, what you keep calling me all the time for?" I asked dryly.

"You know why. Don't play dumb. You know what the deal is," he said smiling.

"No I don't. What?" I said playing dense.

No one else was around. He asked me to come in for a minute. I said okay. I had a plan. I had to make him think I was falling for his game.

He literally pleaded with me for a kiss. I kept saying no at first, intentionally to make him beg. We were standing at his door which was slightly pulled up so no one could see us. He was all up on me begging and trying to kiss me. I didn't like him at all. It was part of my game to allow him to make body contact and tease him. I finally kissed him. I hated kissing him because he darted his tongue in and out of my mouth. I had to play the game so I put up with his kisses and groping when he pinned me against the wall. I wanted to titillate him so I could walk away. He asked me about having sex with him. Bingo! The plot was working just as planned.

"Yo, so, when me and you gon do that?" he asked.

Of course we all knew what "That" meant.

"I don't know. Soon, okay," I said.

"Hey yo, you for real though?" he asked.

"I just said soon didn't I?"

I smiled while talking in a soft voice. He was surprised with my answer but he was buying it.

"Well, let me get on home now but I'll see you later okay?" I said with a teasing smile.

The next day, I hung outside on the Community Porch around the crew with a purpose. I hadn't been around the crew in three weeks, so the girls were treating me okay on this day. All of the boys were outside being silly as usual. Murphy thought he was going to win the bet with the boys. He flirted with me a lot running up behind me with his tail wagging behind him. I was loving the game. I was calling him stupid and all sorts of names in my mind. I suddenly felt empowered. Murphy decided to go to the candy store. He was trying to prove a point to the boys thinking he was about to win the bet they made over me. He shined all his teeth at me deliberately wanting the other boys to notice how obsequious he was being with me. I played along for the fun of it.

"Yo baby, you want me to bring you something from the candy lady?" Murphy asked me.

I looked over at the other boys who were watching intently then I smiled back at Murphy.

"Yeah, if you gon pay," I said.

"I gotcha baby. What you want?" he said.

"Bring me some Boston Baked Beans and some Lemon Heads and a cherry freeze cup," I said.

"Alright, I gotcha," he said with the biggest smile on his face.

Anita and Paulina looked curious wondering why he was buying stuff for me. Before he got far I asked for something else.

"Oh! And bring me some Now & Laters."

Murphy stopped to complain but saw my "I dare you" look and changed his attitude.

"Yo, what kind?" he said.

"Red!" I said.

I purposely yelled for him again once he got a little further up the street.

"And some Hot Fries!" I added.

"Wait a minute! Damn girl!" he yelled back.

I threw him a sideways glare. He walked all the way back over to where I was sitting. I was wearing cut off shorts on purpose. I wanted to look mature and show my figure off just to make myself more desirable to Murphy. Before he could say anything I jumped down off the cement wall with my hands on my hips making sure he got a good look at all of me. I dusted off my backside. I wasn't trying to be obvious to anyone but Murphy but the others boys looked at me as well. As much as I hated it, it was worth the stares just to prove my point. Murphy was captured by my body. I had him wrapped around my fingers just as I thought I would. I was in control. It felt good. He whispered in my ear.

"Now, you know what the deal is for real now don't you?"

"Nigger please! You the one know what the deal is," I said provocatively, talking in my slang language that I often used when I hung with my crew.

I was leaning close enough to kiss his lips. I made sure he felt me breathing, silently daring him to say anything else. He got my point quickly and started blushing at my bold gesture. Again I thought I was in complete control. I knew that as long as I wasn't in John or Antonio's face, the girls would not be jealous. The guys snickered at us teasing one another. I would at least get my money's worth for letting him kiss and touch on me in his doorway the other day. He winked at the other boys before walking off. He was dimwitted to think he could buy my body for a couple dollars worth of junk food. I was not for sale. I wanted him to find out the hard way. I wanted all the boys to find out the hard way. I waited until he was halfway up the street before yelling again.

"Yo! Murphy!"

He stopped in the middle of the street with his hands in the air not believing I was calling him again.

"Bring me a dill pickle! A big one!" I yelled.

"I got a big pickle for you alright!" he yelled back.

"Ha ha, very funny! I'm for real though. Don't forget my pickle," I said turning away, unphased by his gesture.

Anita yelled for something, seeing how generous he was being towards me.

"Hey, yo! Bring me a dill pickle and freeze cup too!" she yelled.

"Psyche! You better git yo own shit. What the hell you think I am?" Murphy yelled at Anita.

"You buyin stuff for Tweety!" she said.

"That's different. You ain't Tweety!" he said.

"Alright then. You remember that! That's okay!" Anita said.

"I know it is!" he replied smartly.

I was still going to softball practice in the late afternoon but I would see Murphy in passing. He was avoiding going to the pool some days trying to catch me coming from practice. A lot of times I would cut through buildings to avoid him. The few days I was able to hang out with the crew, maybe once or twice a week, I wanted all the boys to think Murphy was winning their silly game. Some of the other boys would ask me if I wanted them to buy me junkfood from the candy lady but I turned them down. I just kept on telling Murphy, "soon" everytime he asked me when we were going to do it. I continued getting him to spend all his money until he realized I was just making a fool out of him. I wanted him to get the message I wasn't the one who was the fool, he was.

After a whole month of spending his money on me and being super nice, he stopped me, sounding exasperated.

"You keep on saying soon, but you ain't did nothing yet. What's up? I mean, you gon do it or not?" he snapped.

No one was around. He caught me before I could cut through the buildings as I was walking home from softball practice. By the time we made it to the front of his building he questioned me.

"So, what you gon do? I mean, you just playin games or what?

I hesitantly walked up on his porch. I let him pull me just inside his door. He anxiously pulled me close and kissed me. He thought this was it. He had a look of defeat on his face. He boldly groped at my breasts. I had to think fast.

"Oh shoot!" I said.

"What?" he said.

"I forgot! I gotta go do something real quick before my mama gets home or I'm gon be in big trouble! I gotta hurry up too. My mama's comin home early today," I said.

"You for real?" he asked.

"Yeah, man, darn! Well, I guess we gon have to try this another day okay?" I said sounding disappointed.

Murphy was breathing hard and reluctant to end our session but knew he had to let me go. He believed me with his stupid self.

I was going to have to end this game. This was too close for comfort. I gave him several more excuses as I noticed him desperately staying home waiting for an opportunity to catch me coming from softball practice. I kept giving him excuses until he finally let me have it.

"You have a damn excuse every day! I been patient wit yo ass every day. I believe yo ass is playin games. I mean, we gon do it or not?" he snapped.

I looked him dead in the eye before answering him.

"Not!" I snapped.

"What?" he asked.

"You heard what I said," I replied.

"So you been lying all along?" he said.

"Yep," I responded.

Murphy looked me up and down with disgust. I had a sly smile on my face.

"So then, you a liar then!" he said.

"So. I'd rather be a liar than to be a fool," I said.

With that said, I walked off smiling.

Murphy rolled his eyes and didn't speak to me for two entire months. I felt vindicated. I could just see him trying to explain things to the other boys. Just the mere thought kept me smiling. It was all worth it even though I knew he was extremely angry at being made a fool of. I knew he would warn the other boys. I wanted the boys to know I was more than just a body. If this was all they thought of me, I needed to teach them a lesson. It was just a cry for help on my part but it came back around to bite me before my eighth grade school year started.

I played on the girl's softball team during the entire summer. We had practice in the middle of the day on The Big Field where the football team practiced during football season. I had to wear the team uniforms to practice. Our school colors were green and orange.

I had three pairs of shorts; two green, and one orange and I had the orange cheerleader skirt we wore when we had games. I always put my shorts on under the skirt because the skirt was so short. The other boys in the neighborhood sometimes saw me coming from practice wearing those little shorts or the short skirt when we had games. They whistled at me all the time knowing it was discomforting to me.

One of Anita's brothers, Ralph, flipped my skirt up before I could say anything but they only saw shorts underneath.

"Awe man!" they all said.

I started snickering.

"Do y'all think I'm stupid enough to not know how you think by now?" I said.

I knew it was bound to happen one day with the team skirt being so short. I made a point to flip the finger up at Ralph before walking around the corner. He thought he was about to embarrass me. Ah hah!

I was too busy to hang out. I was glad, because I was finding out the true nature of the girls around me. I didn't want to hang around with a bunch of two timing girls all day long.

Everyone still went swimming everyday around four o'clock because they wanted to go during the hottest part of the day. I was still not allowed to go swimming. I came home from practice around five and everybody was gone since they were swimming at the school.

When everybody came home at about six thirty in the evening, occasionally I came outside with them for a little while if Daddy wasn't at home. Late into the summer months the girls were starting to ask me outside more often. They saw me doing my own thing and not allowing them to bother me. They couldn't hurt me anymore.

The boys didn't congregate around them all day the way they used to. They had started moving on to fresher bait just like Daddy said they would. When I was outside, because I was seldom around, the boys flocked around so the girls automatically followed behind them. Now it seemed as if the girls wanted to use me to draw the boys so they asked me to come outside all the time. Even John had stopped hanging out on the Community Porch so much with Paulina. He was sneaking around behind her back most of the time. I heard him bragging from my window about other girls. When I did come outside to hang out with the girls, we sat around the Community Porch for a couple of hours playing Uno, and four square, and being silly. Paulina and Anita could dance really well so they often danced while I sat back and smiled. Murphy, Ralph and Antonio could also dance well. It was never boring hanging out with them, especially when the girls were being nice to me.

As the boys were growing older, they were becoming bolder with their bad language and sexual ploys. Even though I was outside hanging with them, I didn't want any one on one attention from them. The only boy I felt like tolerating was Antonio. The other boys got on my nerves pulling on me and playing all the time. I didn't see why the girls made such a big deal over these aggravating boys. They played and cussed too much. They always bragged about their sexual conquests with other girls, trying to impress one another while trying to prove a point with us. They wanted us to know they could get any girl they wanted. I liked Antonio because I never heard him bragging or cussing. He was respectful. It was still fun to hang around this silly bunch sometimes rather than sit in the house.

I still stayed in the house if Daddy was at home or else I went over to Ms. Lizzy's house and helped her when she needed me.

I practiced every day until about five and sometimes until six and then of course, we had our games on certain days. If we played on

Saturdays, it would be mostly in the evenings. Daddy made exceptions for me to get to the games on the few Saturdays we played, even though it was our Sabbath day.

I brought my uniform to church with me when I had a game. Sometimes, the coach came to pick me up from church, and sometimes my Aunt Dean or somebody else would drop me off at the school where I rode with the team in the van.

I had to change in the church bathroom because I had to go straight to the field for our games. I always slipped my skirt back on over my shorts if we were not wearing our short skirts. I stepped out of the church skirt once I was outside of the church. Pastor Nichols and some of the ministers who saw me leaving from the church window were very disapproving of the way I was dressed. Girls in our church didn't wear shorts and all of our skirts had to be below the knees at our church. Of course, none of the boys were complaining about what I wore to the games. They peeked at me from the church windows when I ran quickly to the van trying not to bring attention to myself.

My parents were confronted about me not needing to play on the softball team because of the way I was dressed, but my parents didn't agree with them. They wanted me to stay active. Daddy had less to worry about with so much of my time being occupied. Daddy complained about the outfits being so short but I couldn't do anything about that.

The neighborhood bet was on again between the boys about who could get me to have sex with them. They played this scheme on several other girls as well. Every chance one of the boys had, they tried to play their little mind games. I was so on top of their strategy I found myself getting tired of the boys. They were starting to piss me off. Who did they think I was to believe I would be doltish enough to let them just sleep with me? They didn't even want me to be there girlfriend, they just wanted to have casual sex. I knew they didn't love me and even more, I was not marrying any of them. I knew they had no other interest. Once they got what they wanted, they would be moving on to the next cretinous girl.

Scootie's friend Vance started making his little secret moves towards me behind my brother's back. My brother would have been upset with Vance if he had known what he was trying to do. I was surprised about Vance myself though. I never thought he even looked at me twice.

Vance was this real cool acting smooth guy who swept girls off their feet. He never approached me before because he and Mark were best friends with my brother. Mark had already tried to make his moves on me, so I knew what Vance was after. If he was sincere, he wouldn't have been trying to be so secretive.

He knocked on my door one evening when I was at home alone. I was just coming from a game and everybody was already gone to church. Daddy was working late. Vance asked for my brother. I told him where everybody was and that I just came home from a game.

"Well come outside for a minute and talk to me." He surprised me by asking me to come outside with him.

I went along with his little game for a minute like I did with Murphy. I stepped outside, joked around and laughed for a little while. He made his move and kissed me while we were sitting on my front porch. He had his game down packed. When I didn't resist him kissing me the first time, he kissed me again longer. He talked real smooth unlike Murphy. He told me how sweet my lips were then he pulled me up to stand. I didn't resist.

He talked so sweet till I got caught up in his seductive talk.

"Come' ere girl. Let me see how soft you feel," he said while leaning against the wall next to my front porch. He pulled me closer to him moaning. He started kissing me whispering all this stuff in my ear about how good I felt and how I was making him go crazy. I felt like I had power over him since my touch made him moan and groan. He even told me how soft I was. I never experienced someone expressing themselves so graphically. He filled my ear with the most erotic words I'd ever heard.

"Oooh baby, you sooo soft you make me wanna melt inside you. Damn, I never dreamed you'd feel this sweet up against me. You makin me wanna scream. Kiss me baby," he hissed.

He moaned and urged every kiss deeper and deeper telling me how much my kisses were exciting him. For a second, he had my inexperienced head spinning, especially when he started kissing my neck. It was very stimulating hearing him moaning and reacting to every touch.

He caught me off guard when he said he had to have me now. I was not ready for "now." He wanted to go in my apartment. I had to put a stop to his game before it got any further because he was moving too fast. He was good at his craft. I could see why JC gave in to him. He worked us both up to excitement with all his moaning and verbal language. I put my hands up to his chest even though I was turned on.

"Hold on! I think you need to slow down. You're moving a little too fast for me," I said, wishing we could kiss and play around a little longer.

"Awe, you playin games," he whispered.

He was breathing heavy. He didn't want to stop.

"No, you're playing games," I said with a soft shove.

"I'm right here ready to go baby. What you mean, I'm playin? Hey, yo, I'm serious as a dog! I can take you to pure ecstasy like you ain't never felt before. What, you scared? Hey, hey, yo, let me show you something," he said.

He started kissing my neck talking sensually and inching his way towards my mouth. I turned my head away.

"That's exactly what I mean," I said.

"Yo, I'm for real though. Hey, I want you so bad right now, I'm 'bout to explode baby," he said.

He started licking my neck. No one had ever done this to me before. I let him tickle my neck with his tongue enjoying the moment. I still had no intentions of going all the way with him. He made me giggle as he continued to taunt me, daring me to go into the apartment with him. He was really good at awakening my senses. He moved like a pro. I could very easily have gotten caught up erotically with him if we were in a room by ourselves. He could prove to be dangerous if I wasn't careful. Shoot, no wonder JC fell for him. Now I see what JC meant, but I have to keep a level head. This is just a game, I had to remind myself.

"Come on let's go in your house for a minute. Let me hit it just one time. That's all I need is just one time and I won't bother you no mo baby. I just gotta have you just one good time. I'm on fire for you baby," he said.

Bingo! That was all I needed to hear. "Just one time and I won't bother you no mo." It woke me back up to the real world. He moved towards my lips again but I turned away.

"Come on now Vance! You should know me better than that. Give me some credit. You actually think I'm gon be stupid enough to let you just walk up to me and all of a sudden we sleeping together and you're not even my boyfriend?"

"Yo, what that got to do with anything? Huh?" he asked.

"It's got everything to do with it Vance. I know what happened with you and JC and I can tell you right now, I ain't nothing like JC. I'm never gon be like her or any of these other stupid girls for that matter. I mean, a kiss is one thing but I'm a respectable girl. I don't know what you were thinking when we started kissing, but I'm not the type of girl who has casual sex. I mean, just 'cause you kiss good and all... and you might talk a good game. I thought you and my brother were supposed to be best friends anyway, but I see now, you're just another dog," I said.

"Hey, yo, look. You right, I don't know what I was thinking 'bout. I just lost it for a minute. Hey yo, check this out though. I respect you for real though. Hey, I mean, don't nobody have to know 'bout this but me and you. I can just walk away and yo brother and nobody ain't got to ever know 'bout what happened tonight, okay?" he said.

I started shaking my head.

"Why y'all boys be trying to use girls like that anyway? Y'all think you can take girls' virginity and walk away and think nothing else about it. You know that's not right. Don't you?" I asked.

"Well, hey, those girls ought not to be so stupid. I mean, hey, yo, I'm just a guy. What I'm suppose to do if they wanna put themselves out there like that. I mean, it ain't like we be forcing them or nothing. But yo, who say they virgins anyway? I know you ain't no virgin, is you?" he asked.

"What you think? I don't play that mess!" I said.

"Well, you don't know nothing to be trying to school me. You just a teeny bopper," he said after discovering I was still a virgin.

"That's exactly why I plan to stay the way I am! I mean, you don't love these girls you be sleeping with so they're stupid to just let y'all use their bodies like that," I said.

"See! They the one's who stupid! Hey, yo, I didn't tell them to be so stupid. It ain't my fault. I mean, hey, if they gon just give it up like that, then I'm gon take it! Shoot! But you, well, yo, you gon be like my sister from now on for real though. Hey, look, for real though, I swear I won't ever try to mess with you like that again. Yo, all though I know I could if I wanted too," he teased.

"Ha ha! You know what the deal is. Nigger you ain't stupid," I said.

"Hey, yo, I ain't gon say nothing else. But for real though... Naw, I ain't gon say nothing else. I was gon say something for real though," he snickered.

"What?" I said.

"I ain't gon say it." He looked me up and down in a lustful way. He burst out laughing. "Hey! Yo, but for real though, hey, we straight?" he asked.

"Yeah, we straight," I said.

He shook my hand and walked off. I had to give it to him though, he was the smoothest guy I'd ever known.

****

Anita joined the softball team later on with me. She wanted to get attention from those simpleminded boys around there in her shorts.

We went over to her house one day after practice to hang out. I assumed we were okay friends for the time being, even though I always kept my guards up. I had gone home, showered, and changed into a fresh pair of the very revealing team shorts because we had a game later that evening. I wore an orange jersey with green numbers and dark green tiny shorts that once again made me look sixteen or seventeen with my mature body. Her two brothers worked during the summer at McDonald's. They brought boxes of McDonald's hamburger patties and cheese home. Anita invited me over to have a burger with her. She cooked the burgers and put cheese on them with bread instead of buns.

Mama only allowed me to go over to Anita's house when her brothers weren't home. If they came home I had to leave.

John, who was still going with Paulina, came home. He hadn't seen me around in a while. He was real cute but he was going with Paulina who I still considered to be a friend. I mean, she still had my back if it ever came down to it. She and Anita could pick and make fun of me but she always protected me from outsiders. There were also the confusing good days I spent with Paulina where she seemed very caring.

John was going into the eleventh grade. I had a new crush on his brother Ralph who was going to the tenth grade. Ralph hadn't approached me about sex all year. He seemed to have turned into a decent boy, aside from trying to flip my skirt up earlier that summer. He seemed more mature since he started working. He stayed more to himself.

When John walked in the door, I told Anita I had to leave because I couldn't be over there when her brothers were home.

Mama hadn't made it home from church yet because it was about to be another feast time again. Some of the feasts were weeks apart. She stayed late shopping with the church and helping out a lot. I didn't want to get caught over at Anita's house when Mama pulled up. John grabbed me and hugged me to my surprise. He hadn't seen me in several weeks. I came home from softball practice and games and went straight to church because of the feasts at church. John was being silly. I giggled and told him to let me go. Anita was ready to go outside. John wouldn't let me go. I was still laughing. Anita seemed irritated.

"Tweety, let's go!" she snapped.

I tried to pull away from her foolish brother who had his arms around me still kissing my neck. It tickled me so I laughed and told him to stop. I couldn't help but to notice John's nice physique and handsome features while he was teasing me. I asked Anita to come and get her brother off me. She and Paulina had become best friends so she had an attitude. She thought I was two timing since I was guffawing so much. I was only chuckling because I was ticklish but I wanted him to stop. She walked out the door and left me.

"Okay John, that's enough playing around. Let me go boy!" I said getting serious.

"Who playin?" he said still teasing me.

He tussled with me playfully as he held me, landing kisses all over my neck. I fidgeted trying to twist away while he continued chortling. He asked me for a kiss.

"No!" I said.

"Why not?" he asked.

"Because, you going with my friend. That wouldn't be right," I said.

"So what! Maybe I'm getting tired of Paulina," he said still teasing my neck with kisses.

"Well, tell her that. Don't tell me. Now let me go John! I gotta go before my mama comes home."

"Yo, one kiss," he insisted.

"No," I said.

"Just one kiss and I promise I'll let you go," he said.

I tried moving his hands, but he held on tight. His laughing made it hard for me to get angry or be serious.

"You just making me pull you closer, so keep on fighting me." His smiling and monkeying around still made it hard for me to show anger.

"Okay, come on John. My mama might pull up any minute now. Let me go, please," I said.

"Yo, you better hurry up and give me a kiss real quick, 'cause I ain't gon let you go till you kiss me." He was all the way up on me and breathing hard. He was getting aroused.

"Damn, you feel good! Come on now. Just one kiss," he said.

"John, what you trying to do? Get off me! I told you already, this ain't right. You go with my friend Paulina. Just think about it. It ain't right," I said.

I pulled at his hands which were squeezing around my tiny waist but he was starting to grind into me. He was getting more turned on with me struggling with him. He was muscular and I knew he was too strong for me to break away from.

"I couldn't turn you loose if I wanted to now. You done got me too excited, with yo fine ass. Look at how hard I done got," he said.

John was moving up against me so I could feel how hard he was. I still didn't know what he was talking about. I didn't know much about a boy's anatomy at that point. I didn't picture John feeling or looking the same as Granddaddy who hurt me. John's rubbing up against me didn't hurt at all. I changed baby pampers and this was the picture in my mind when it came to a guy his age, but slightly bigger. I figured men's anatomies grew as big as Granddaddy with old age and since John wasn't old like Granddaddy, I figured he had a long way to go. I didn't know anything about size or shape in older boys I just guessed there was no need to be frightened. I just knew guys had a penis. I was curious about what an older boy's penis looked like as with any girl my age, but I didn't want to find out that bad.

I continued begging John to stop, but he kissed my neck anyway. I turned my head from side to side fighting him off me. He had my hands pinned to my sides while he squeezed me tightly. He wasn't hurting me but it was irritating when he didn't let me go. John thought it was funny.

I started worrying about the time and Mama. I couldn't believe Anita left me. She went across the street to the Community Porch. Paulina was at the pool with everyone else. Anita wasn't able to go to the pool because of practice.

I finally gave up. "One kiss and you promise to let me go?" I asked.

"One kiss and that's it!" he said.

He started bending to kiss me and I changed my mind again.

"I don't really wanna do this. We can stop now and Paulina won't ever find out. I thought you two were in love," I said.

"Hey, yo, I'm 'bout to break up with her. She old news," he said.

"Well ask me for a kiss again after y'all break up," I said. We both burst out laughing. "I'm serious!" I said.

John stopped smiling and spoke in a husky voice. He continued making body contact with me the entire time.

"I can't let you go now. I want a kiss right now."

John was bending to kiss me and moaning at the same time and I didn't stop him. I had my mouth closed when he touched my lips.

"Kiss me," he said.

He was muttering under his mouth. I felt just the tip of his tongue and I didn't know what I was supposed to do with his tongue. I didn't want to open my mouth. I kept my mouth closed.

"Kiss me back," he said again.

"See how ya'll boys are? You get what you want from one girl and you try to dump her for one of her friends," I said backing away from his lips.

"Paulina the one stupid. I ain't make her give it up. Besides, I know damn well you ain't fixin to give it up like that...is you?" he asked.

"Nope," I said.

"That's what I thought. I ain't even tryin to go there wit you. I just wanna kiss, so kiss me," he said.

John bent to kiss me again. I kept my lips sealed even when I felt his tongue.

"Yo, come on now. Kiss me back," he whispered.

"What?" I said.

"Do like this. Open yo mouth a little," he instructed.

John put his tongue in my mouth while I tried to figure out what to do with his tongue. He stopped.

"I see now, I'm gon have to teach you how to kiss," he said.

"Or you can just let me go," I said.

We started laughing again but he continued to come towards me again with his mouth. He instructed me to open my mouth slightly. I did what he said this time.

"When I stick my tongue in yo mouth you supposed to suck it like this," he instructed.

He put his partially opened lips softly up to my lips.

"Stick yo tongue in my mouth and let me show you," he whispered.

I hestitantly slid my tongue inside his mouth and he sucked up my tongue like a vacuum and began sucking on the tip of my tongue for a few minutes. He was gyrating and grinding up against my body while I leaned against the kitchen counter.

"Now, I want you to suck my tongue just like I sucked yours," he said.

His tongue tasted like "Big Red" cinnamon gum. He was talking real husky because he was excited. As we kissed, he slid his hand in the front of my shorts. I immediately reached down to stop him. I couldn't get his hand out of my shorts.

"Come on John! Turn me a loose! Get yo hands out of my pants!" I said.

He was still sliding his hand down further in my shorts. He was trying to be gentle moving his fingers in slow motion.

"John, stop it! I ain't playing no more now." I still couldn't break loose from him.

This wasn't funny anymore. John was holding me firmly and trying to kiss me. He had his hand up my crotch at the same time. He moaned as he touched me which aggravated me even more.

"Just kiss me one more time, come on now." he begged.

"No! Let me go now!" I demanded.

He continued to swirl his fingers gently around inside of my pants. A part of me wanted to let him continue exploring because his fingers were moving so skillfully inside of me in a way I couldn't explain. I knew I had to resist so I continued to struggle trying to pull his hands out my pants.

I heard my mama calling me. I looked at John.

"See there! You getting me in trouble now. I told you to let me go! Now my Mama done pulled up!"

John looked calm. He still had his hands in my pants.

"I'll let you out the back door. Now kiss me one more time real quick," he said dreamy like.

He started back moving his fingers around.

"No! Let me go! Yo sister up there where my mama is and my mama probably done already asked her if she's seen me anywhere. Now let me go before you make it worse," I snapped.

"So! My sister ain't gon say nothing. She know better. Now give me one mo kiss real quick," he said.

I shook my head no. John took his hands out of my pants, put both his arms around me squeezing me real hard up against him and rubbing his penis against my clothing.

"Yo, If you don't kiss me real quick, I'm gon hurt you," he threatened while grinding hard into my body.

I didn't believe him. He was not as big and old as Granddaddy so I figured he probably couldn't hurt me even if he wanted to.

"Let me go! I ain't kissing you anymore. You're just gonna have to hurt me," I said.

I knew he was just anxious. I was angry because he forced his hand down my pants even after I told him not to.

I called his bluff. I was more concerned about Mama calling me. She stopped calling. I had to think up a lie to account for where I'd been. John was still holding me trying to move up against me while moaning. I was pinned up against his counter.

"I'm 'bout to cry if you don't let me go," I said.

I looked serious. Mama hadn't found me and I knew she was about to go crazy by now. John let me go except for my hand.

"Damn! Done got me all excited and shit! What I'm suppose to do now?" he said.

"You're suppose to let me go and then wait for your girlfriend, I guess." He continued to hold my hand.

"Yo, you mad at me?" he asked.

"John, come on now, I gotta go!" I said.

"Tell me you ain't mad at me first," he insisted.

"Fine! No, I'm not mad at you. Now let me go please," I said.

"You promise?" he asked again.

"Yeah, I promise." John smoothed down my hair in a caring gesture.

I smiled so he would let me go. He walked me to the back door and then we thought of something I could make up to say to my mama before I walked out. Just as I came down their last step, I looked up and saw Mama standing at the end of the building. She saw me coming down the last step. John already closed his back door and walked away without knowing Mama was standing around the back.

CHAPTER SEVENTEEN

"Why Me?"

Mama motioned for me to come here with her finger. I had no choice but to walk over to her. She didn't say one word all the way to the house. When we got in the house, she went upstairs and came back with a belt.

"Now, what the devil were you doing at Anita's house while she was outside?" Mama snapped.

"Mama, John was holding me up, and he wouldn't let..." I started.

"I don't wanna hear that lie! Now I'm gon ask you one more time, and I'm not gon play no games with you, and you not gon play no games with me, are you?" Mama said sternly.

"No ma'am." I took a deep breath. I tried to explain again real calmly. "Okay, this is what happened. I went over to Anita's house with her after practice, and we had burgers. Neither Ralph nor John was at home..."

"Why were you sneaking out the back door?" Mama said.

She was so angry she wasn't giving me time to explain everything.

"That's what I'm trying to tell you. John came home after we ate..." I started again.

"Shut up! I don't wanna hear no mo lies!" Mama yelled.

"Mama, I'm not lying! You can go and ask John!" I said.

"Go and ask John my ass! Mama said.

Mama hadn't cussed in years since being in the church. She never in her life used profanity towards any of her children. I knew she wasn't going to hear me out.

"Mama, I'm telling you the truth," I said.

Mama got up and started beating me with the belt. When she

was done, she told me to go upstairs and stay up there. She didn't allow me to go to my softball game that evening. She put me on punishment for two weeks. I cried more over the fact I got whipped for something I had no control over. She never heard me out and she never believed me. I tried to tell Mama John was holding me against my will. I wanted to tell her how he forced me to kiss him and everything.

I stayed angry with Mama for a long time. I was angry with John too. When I was in my room crying after she had calmed down, she asked me where I was while I was in their house. I told her I was in the kitchen with John the whole time. She asked if we were upstairs at any point and time.

"Mama, I promise you, we were in the kitchen the whole entire time. He go with Paulina! I wouldn't try to do anything on purpose with any of my friend's boyfriends, and I don't have sex with boys!" I understood her insinuation.

"Well you was doing something! Whatever it was, kissing or whatever, you still didn't have no business doing it!" Mama said.

She walked out and closed my door behind her. I was even angrier about having to prove to her I wasn't a whore. She never let me explain what happened. At least I convinced her that I didn't have sex with John, but that was about it. Neither she nor Daddy trusted me after this. I wanted to believe Mama trusted me all those times she said it was Daddy who didn't trust me. I thought about all the times she made me sit on the porch and said it was Daddy. I wondered how much it was her now.

I decided to keep myself locked away in the house again. I came straight home from practices and stayed in the house.
I saw John occassionally coming or going and ignored him when he tried to speak to me.

After ignoring John for some time, he ran outside in front of me. I tried to walk around him and he kept stepping in front of me. I asked him to move.

"Not until you tell me why you mad at me," he insisted.

I told him I got in trouble and my mama whipped me for being over at his house. He apologized sincerely and promised me he would never hurt me on purpose. He told me he respected me for not being fast like most of the girls around and asked if he could just be like my big brother from then on.

We agreed and became friends afterwards. Every now and then, I confided in him about my feelings or asked his opinion about someone. He turned out to be real cool. I still kept my distance to a large degree because he was still dating Paulina who seemed extremely jealous and possessive over John. He didn't try anything else with me while he was going with Paulina, even though I knew he had other girlfriends at school.

A month later, I ran into Anita's other brother, Ralph leaving practice. He had to get the door key from his sister. He hadn't seen me in a while, so he called my name out when I was on the field. I looked up and saw him smiling at me. I smiled back but quickly got back into practice mode before the coach could yell out to me.

"Yo, where you been hiding lately?" he asked after practice. He was staring at me constantly as if he was noticing how mature I was becoming.

"No where. I be at home," I answered.

"Well, I don't never see you," he said with a smile.

He walked me home while we talked and laughed. I couldn't help staring back at his cute LL Cool J smile. I found myself struck by his good looks. He also had on a muscle shirt to show off his muscles. I knew why he was able to date so many girls outside of our neighborhood. He stopped messing with all the girls in the neighborhood, but I had heard him talking outside my window sometimes with the other boys about his many girlfriends in the past.

The next day, to my surprise, Ralph was waiting on me after practice.

"Yo, for real though, I came to see you miss the ball," he said, joking around.

I started laughing because Coach was on me about missing a ball that was hit my way during practice. We were getting ready for another game. We started walking together quietly. I waited for Ralph to say something else.

"Yo, you wanna be my girlfriend?" he asked suddenly out of no where.

I wanted to say yes right away, but I told him I'd think about it. He looked surprised. He must have been accustomed to girls jumping at the chance to say yes to him. I had to admit, he was very good looking with his deep dimples.

"Okay, well let me know on Friday, when I'm off work again," he said.

"Okay," I said.

Friday came. I didn't see Ralph because he had to work. I didn't see him again until the next week while sitting on the Community Porch with Paulina, Lanette, and Anita. Paulina was hugged up with John. They were kissing and carrying on. Antonio, Murphy who was speaking to me again, and Antonio's brother Gregory joined us outside as well. We were all a crew again. I knew who to play around with and who to keep at a friendly distance.

Antonio was flirting with Anita. They acted like they had a secret thing going on. It was her turn now since I told him I wasn't ready. I hoped she wouldn't be stupid since he wasn't her boyfriend, but I didn't know how far they'd already gone with one another. I could just tell he was working his game on her.

Ralph walked up. No one had a clue he and I were considering going together. Antonio grabbed me playfully by my ankles pretending as if he was going to pull me down off the tall brick and cement wall I was sitting on. The brick walls were designed for us to sit on them with smooth cement paved across the top of each of the four brick walls all around the Community Porch. There was a high brick wall with cement paved across the seated area, attached to a lower brick wall, with cement paved on the top in each corner of the large square porch. Ralph walked over.

"Yo! What you doing man? Don't be playing with her like that! She might fall for real," Ralph yelled.

Ralph grabbed me, lifting me down off the cement wall. I smiled because I thought this was cute. Everybody made a big deal out of him coming to my defense. Ralph kept staring at me like he was in love. Everybody noticed. They commented about him acting like he was in love with me to get a response from him. Ralph grabbed my hand pulling me away from everybody else. He asked for my answer. I nodded yes with my head all in a cloud because of his good looks again.

"Okay," he said while smiling and showing his dimples.

We walked back over with everybody else. They didn't know we'd been spending time talking after softball practice. Ralph decided to let the cat out of the bag by kissing me. I let him. He was close up on me with his arms around my waist. I was glad he kept his tongue in his mouth even though his hand dropped lower towards my backside.

Everybody was shocked. Ralph had to leave for work after our kiss.

"Yo, see ya, okay?" he said, smiling again.

I blushed and said bye and he walked off. Everybody was clapping. They still didn't know why I let him kiss me.

Antonio snatched me by the hand after Ralph left pulling me away from everybody else. He looked upset. He started mocking me.

"I'm saving myself for the right person," he mocked.

"What's that suppose to mean?" I asked.

"You know exactly what I mean! Disrespecting yo self out here in public!" he snapped.

"Huh?" I said.

"So I guess you gon be kissing the whole neighborhood now. Anybody can just walk up to you and kiss and touch all on you and you just figure you'll just stand there and let him, right? Putting his damn hands on you like that and you just gon smile like it's cool," he said.

I finally understood his point. He didn't give me a chance to speak.

"I can't believe you, disrespecting yo-self letting him just grab all on you..." he started.

"We go together," I interrupted.

Antonio was surprised. "What?" he asked.

"Me and Ralph go together," I repeated.

Antonio stood still for a minute. "Oh," he finally said.

Just then, Ralph was walking back up, coming towards me. Antonio turned making a public announcement.

"Uh oh, y'all here go the two love birds. Y'all know they boyfriend and girlfriend!" he announced.

He gave Ralph a high five. Everybody started congratulating us. I looked at Antonio. Well, well, Antonio does care about me after all. He wanted to make sure I kept my self respect.

Ralph wanted to know if I'd like a box of hamburger patties from McDonald's.

"Yeah!" I said in a hurry.

I didn't tell Mama we were going together. He brought a box of burger patties and a whole lot of cheese as well. I took everything to Mama and told her Ralph gave it to us because they didn't have room in their refrigerator. She told me to thank him the next time I saw him. We all enjoyed the burgers at home.

I didn't see Ralph much. He worked all the time. When I did see him, I didn't like the way he treated me. He played too rough. He hit me too hard when he was joking around. After we kissed in front of everyone it was a week before I saw him or talked to him again. He came towards me smiling and then he did the weirdest thing. He punched me on my arm like he was crazy. I chased after him, but I couldn't catch him so I got mad and started walking away. He turned around apologizing and chasing after me. He grabbed hold of me rubbing my arm. I snatched away. That same day when he asked me for my phone number, I was still angry about the punch he gave me because my arm was bruised and I told him I wasn't giving him my number even though he kept hugging me and apologizing. I picked up on an abusive type of nature. We studied "relationship abuse" in one of my classes last year.

We had two weeks before school started back. They had a picnic at the park for the teenagers in our church. I attended with my brother. Mama bought me a new sun dress to wear to the park. The dress had thin straps so I didn't have a bra on with it. I couldn't help but notice how developed I was becoming. The dress was a perfect fit and made me look sixteen showing off all of my curves. Mother Jordon's grandson was coming to church a lot. He was my age. He asked me for a chance. I quickly told him I already had a boyfriend. I didn't need another playboy. He bragged and flirted with too many other girls. I was still friends with Mikey. I still had a crush on him even though I was with Ralph.

I wasn't impressed with Ralph the way I thought I would be. I was hoping Mikey would notice me in a more mature way instead as this girl who was too young for him. Everyone was saying how much older I looked and how nice the dress looked on me. Mikey barely glanced up at me.

I had another cousin who was a year older than me, named Monica who suddenly showed up at the park. She went to church with Neecy's family. She suddenly decided to hang out with us at the picnic. She was another pretty face hanging around Mikey at lot. I noticed her following him wherever he went. Mikey, Monica, and Bow Leggs separated themselves from the group and talked among themselves the entire time. Oh no! Now he's getting with another one of my cousins. I may as well forget it because all of my older cousins keep coming around every time. He'll never see me as a mature enough girl with all my older cousins liking him. He and Monica talked casually the entire time at the park while Mother Jordon's son Eddie tried to make me jealous by flirting with everyone around me. I could care less about Eddie. I was more concerned about Mikey and Monica. I walked over to where they were and started up a conversation with Monica a couple of times and you could tell she was irritated at me for interrupting them, so I finally decided to stay with the others and leave them alone. I guess he was over Neecy by now. Of course two years had passed and Neecy was pregnant again by the guy she dumped Mikey for. I found out that Mikey and Neecy had never even kissed the entire time they were together because for some reason he never tried to kiss her. That baffled me because I knew he really liked her.

About a week before school started, I decided to break up with Ralph. He showed up a week later outside with the rest of my crew after punching me. He was cute with his dimples and all, but he punched me on my arm two more times, which left more bruises. After the last punch, I slapped him real hard in front of everybody and he in turn punched me again even harder and made me cry. He just walked up to me and instead of saying "hello," he would punch me extremely hard on my arm. I didn't accept his apology that last time. His brother John punched him for hitting me hard. He punched me so hard, everyone stood still with mouths hanging open. After the boys asked him why he hit me like that, he got smart as if it wasn't a big deal. John and Murphy grabbed him in a headlock while I punched him for making me cry. I realized I had to end the relationship in a hurry. He apologized a zillion times. I kept telling him to get out of my face. I hadn't seen him all week after he hit me. My arm was still sore. He was only sweet and kind after being physically abusive. He seemed to get a high off making me hurt and then all of a sudden he was all lovey dovey and apologetic. He had to have a reason to feel sorry for me in order to be loving and gentle. Something was definitely wrong with him. I felt it. I was not going to be his punching bag anymore. His bruises lasted for a few days at a time now and I wasn't easy to bruise with my brown skin. He had to hit me pretty hard for the bruises to show. It became a pattern every time we were together. He would just walk up to me and punch the daylights out of me for no reason and laugh as if it were funny. The last time I slapped him, he slapped me back. No one was around to help me. I grabbed my face and walked away in spite of him grabbing me and apologizing. He kept telling me he loved me over and over while kissing on my neck and begging me to kiss him back. This time; after slapping me, I didn't forgive him. I planned to keep him away from me that day going forward.

That Sunday, I went over to Murphy's house so Ms. Rae Rae could straighten my hair. Murphy was heading out the door to go over to Ms. Janice's house. He was hanging out with Gregory. I had stopped by Ms. Janice's house earlier that day to drop off a package from my mama. Gregory was downstairs and Ms. Janice was upstairs getting ready for church. While I was waiting downstairs in the kitchen, Gregory walked up to me and grabbed me roughly. He told me to kiss him. I told him no. He grabbed my arms tighter and pushed me against the wall. He threatened to bust my lips if I didn't kiss him. I started wondering what was going on with these boys;

first Ralph and now him. I didn't feel like fighting him. I didn't feel like being roughed up. I let him kiss me even though I hated it. He wasn't tender at all. He kissed me hard on the lips as if to make a point. I was thankful that Ms. Janice started coming down the stairs before he could really get in a good kiss. He had started groping my behind and quickly yelled out, damn, because he had to quickly release me so Ms Janice wouldn't notice what was going on. I had kissed every boy in my crew now, mostly by force. Antonio's gentleness stuck in my head.

At Ms. Rae Rae's house, the phone rang. Ms. Rae Rae had just started straightening some of my hair. She looked surprised after answering the phone. She told me the telephone call was for me. I picked up the phone sounding very curious.

"Hello?" I said.

It was Murphy strangely enough.

"Yo, Ms. Janice said to come here for a minute, real quick," he said.

"Now?" I said.

"Yeah, pickle head! Right now! She said you can come right back," he said.

"Okay then. I'll be there in a minute," I said.

I hung up the phone. Ms. Rae Rae put a ponytail in my hair separating the straightened part until I got back. I ran across the street to knock on Ms. Janice's door. The TV was turned up loud so you could hear the football game on. The boys were carrying on about the game. Gregory yelled hastily when I knocked.

"Yo! Who is it! Damn!" he snapped.

"It's me," I answered.

"Who is 'me'?" he asked.

"It's Tweety, Gregory!" I yelled.

Gregory was into his football game.

"Girl, what you want? Um tryin to watch my game!" he yelled back.

"Your mama wants me boy!" I said.

"Come in! Shoot!" he yelled.

I walked in and he was still getting smart.

"What you lookin at?" he said.

Murphy was also sitting on the sofa watching football totally ignoring me.

"Where's Ms. Janice at?" I asked.

Gregory didn't answer me. He had his eyes fixed on the game.

"Gregory!" I said.

"What!" he snapped back.

"Where's your mama at?" I repeated.

"Damn! I'm trying to watch the game! Ain't nobody thinking 'bout you girl! Leave me alone and gon upstairs where she at!" he yelled.

I made a face at him and walked upstairs. I called Ms. Janice's name out when I turned the corner. I didn't hear her answer. I called her name again as I walked into her bedroom. She wasn't in her bedroom. This was weird. I headed towards Paulina's room.

"Ms Janice!" I called.

No one was in Paulina's room either. I started getting a funny feeling in my stomach that something wasn't right. The only other room was the boy's room. I had a feeling I wouldn't find Ms. Janice in there either. I walked hesitantly towards the room anyway, hoping. I called her name suspiciously one last time. I looked in the boys' room and Ms. Janice wasn't there either.

I looked towards the stairs again. Both Gregory and Murphy were barreling up the stairs. Before I could take three good steps back, they were all over me. Dizzying thoughts raced through my head. I was stuck in my spot. I needed to stop them.

"Uh uh y'all! No way! I'm not playing with neither one of y'all! You bet not put your hands on me!" I yelled.

"Shut up!" Gregory yelled back.

Gregory yelled at me while he and Murphy attacked my body touching me everywhere. Gregory was the main aggressor groping my backside roughly and taking over. I couldn't fight him off me. He told Murphy to go downstairs and wait his turn.

Murphy asked him how long he would be, reminding him they didn't have much time. I felt a rush of anger.

"I don't know what y'all think I am, but y'all gon be in trouble if you don't let me go right now!" I said.

Gregory put his fist up to my lips clenching his teeth.

"Shut up!" he said.

"No! I'm not..." I started.

Gregory pushed my mouth in with his fist forcefully talking between clenched teeth.

"I said shut the hell up!"

He had his fist shoved hard against my mouth still talking between clenched teeth.

"Say one more thing and see if I don't bust yo lips wide open. You think I'm damn playing with you, you try me!" he said.

I shut up as soon as I felt blood on my inner lip. Gregory firmly pressed his fist against my lips hard enough for my teeth to cut my bottom lip. He had this evil look on his face while biting his lower lip. When I looked into his eyes, I knew he was ready to be violent if necessary. Gregory wrapped his arms around my back and buttocks then he started backing me towards Paulina's room which was the closest room from the stairs. I instinctively protested and struggled.

"Gregory what you doing?" I asked.

"Shut up! Don't you say nothing. Don't even open yo mouth or I swear fo God I'm gon bust yo lip wide open!" he said between clinched teeth.

It only took the sting of blood on my lips to convince me he was not playing around. I kept my mouth shut when he forced me to sit down on Paulina's bed. He sat next to me knowing he had to calm me down from crying in order to accomplish anything.

"Now listen. Listen! I was just playin wit yo butt girl. Shut up! If you let me do what I ask you, it'll be over in a minute," he said, laughing nervously.

"I'm not gon do it, whatever you're getting ready to say. I'm not gon do it!" I said sobbing.

"Well you just gon be making it harder on yo-self then. Now, do you wanna make it hard or do you wanna make it easy?" he said.

I didn't answer. My eyes watered back up.

"Now hold on before you start crying again and shit, ain't nobody gon hurt you," he said.

"Well let me go then!" I said.

"That's what I'm trying to do! Now you just gotta do one thing for me first and that's it," he said.

"No, I'm not gon do nothing with you! I told you to let me go!" Tears were flowing freely down my face.

"I'm trying to let yo butt go. All you gotta do is just give me one kiss and then you can go," he said.

I knew it was a trick.

"No Gregory! Let me go!" I yelled.

He pushed me down roughly on the bed. He tried to force me to kiss him. During the struggle I found myself pinned underneath him across the bed.

"Yo, come on now! Stop fighting and just calm down and it'll be over," he said.

He was grabbing at my breast and backside continuing to rough me up. I continued to struggle and cry.

"I'm tryin to be nice. Just come on and give me one kiss," he said.

His penis was grinding hard into my body causing discomfort. He was trying to hurt me on purpose. He bit down hard on his lips and grunted every time he grinded hard into me. There was nothing gentle about him. John threatened to hurt me that time when he held me, but he was gentle the entire time. I knew what Gregory was threatening to do to me. He was causing me a lot of discomfort and I wanted him off me.

"Get off of me!" I yelled out.

We struggled for a long time.

"See, we could've been done by now. I just asked for one kiss," he said.

I wondered if they had done this to any other girls or if I was the only one. I was not about to give up without a fight so I continued to wrestle with him.

"Check this out." He started gyrating hard and slow on top of me. "This is the most I'm gon do to you right here and then I want you to kiss me and that's it. Now that ain't bad is it? It'll be over in a minute I promise. Just one kiss," he said.

He stopped grinding with all his might and eased off just a little.

I was getting tired of him grinding on top me. He was taking advantage of me. I hadn't given him permission to touch me. I felt his boner pressing hard against me. He started back grunting and grinding hard into me.

"Mmmm, damn! Shit! Come on girl, just let me git in it real good one time. Got damn you fine! Look at all this. Oooh!" he said, ignoring me struggling to get free.

I was too humiliated to tell him his thing was hurting me. I tried to twist my way off the bed, which created a greater struggle.

My skirt was raised up all the way to my panties. I was trying to hold on to my panties while Gregory continued to touch me everywhere.

Murphy came upstairs while we were struggling and burst out laughing at Gregory moaning and grunting loud on top of me. Gregory was mad at Murphy for spying. I looked over at Murphy staring at my legs and I was hoping he'd feel sorry for me because Gregory forced my skirt up and was going too far.

"Murphy, please tell Gregory to get up off of me," I begged.

"Damn man! Yo, she damn fine as hell! I told you man," Murphy replied, ignoring me.

"Yo, give me a few more minutes and I'll be done worked myself into some skin I betcha," Gregory sounded too sure of himself.

"Yo, man just hurry up!" Murphy snapped.

Murphy went back downstairs.

We started going back and forth. I tried to talk him into getting off me while he tried to get me to kiss him.

It was getting exhausting. We were both out of breath and perspiring. His grinding was causing a throbbing pain around my groin area. I wanted the pain to stop.

"If I give you one kiss, then you're gonna let me go?" I finally asked.

Gregory sounded excited. "Just one kiss and that's it," he agreed.

"Okay, hurry up," I said.

Gregory started kissing me sloppily. He covered my entire mouth with his mouth. I felt drool running down my chin. I wanted to get it over. I couldn't stand his sloppy kisses. He groped my breasts squeezing hard and rough while moving fast and hard up against me. During the struggle he lifted my shirt up exposing my bra. My skirt was already raised up. The only thing between us was his clothes and my under garments. When I saw him trying to sneak his pants loose, I couldn't take it anymore.

I turned my mouth away.

"Okay, I gave you a kiss, now let me go."

Of course by now, Gregory was too aroused. He started to get rougher with me instead of stopping. He was bruising my arms trying to keep me down. He started begging for one more kiss. During the process he slipped his jeans off revealing his bony bow legs in boxer shorts. I was completely turned off. I was afraid of what he'd try next.

"What you take your pants off for? I didn't tell you we were gon be doing anything!" I yelled.

He quickly climbed back on top of me.

"Look, I just wanted to get a lil mo comfortable girl, damn. I ain't hurt you yet have I? What you actin all upset for? You act like you ain't never kissed no damn body before. Shit! All I asked you for is one mo kiss!"

"No, 'cause you lied! You think you're slick! You told me one kiss and I did it and you still haven't let me go yet!" I cried out.

I was sobbing again and my body was aching. I was tired of trying to keep him from pulling down my panties while he begged me for one look at my vagina. He warned me he wasn't going to be nice for much longer.

"I'm gon just have to take it if you don't come on and let me hit it real quick so it can be over. I just wanna lay on top of you one good time. I promise I'm not gon try and put it in," he said.

I broke down crying harder. Gregory couldn't calm me down anymore, not even with his fists touching my lips. I just wanted to go home. I didn't ask for any of this. Why was this happening to me? What made him think he could just treat me like a piece of trash doing whatever he pleased? All he saw was a body and nothing else. He didn't see a person with feelings and a right to say no and be respected and heard. Murphy suddenly ran up the stairs.

"Yo man, yo mama them just pulled up!" he yelled.

Gregory jumped up off me.

"Quit lyin man!" he said.

"Man I'm not lying," Murphy said.

Murphy noticed me crying hard and got scared.

"Hey, yo, look man, I didn't touch her! That's all on you!" Murphy said.

Gregory was going to the eleventh grade. He began to panick.

"Awe Shit! Get up and fix yo-self real quick! Dry yo damn eyes girl. Ain't nobody hurt you! Shut the fuck up! You alright. Don't even try an act, 'cause I ain't hurt yo butt yet! I was just 'bout to tear that pussy up though. Damn! Got me all hard and shit. Git yo ass on up!" he yelled because I was moving too slow.

Ms. Janice was standing outside talking to a neighbor as Paulina and Antonio headed up the porch steps towards the front door.

"Run out the back door real quick! Girl hurry up, shit!" Gregory yelled at me while grabbing my arm in a rush.

I got downstairs and headed towards the front door instead. I planned to tell on them. Gregory ran and snatched me back.

"What the fuck you doing? You ain't going out the damn front door, and you bet not say nothing to no damn body either! If you say one mother fucking word, um gon beat yo ass. You better remember that," he warned.

Gregory jerked my body towards the back door and shoved me out. Just as soon as I got out the back door, I headed around to the front door. I was determined they weren't getting away with treating me this way.

Before I could get to the end of the building, Paulina was running out the back door looking around as if she were trying to catch someone. She called me and I walked back over to the door.

"Did you by any chance just see a girl come out this door?" she asked.

I put my hands on my hips and started tapping my feet as my anger began to show.

"Yeah! Me!" I practically yelled out.

Paulina put her hands up to her mouth in shock. She was trying to hold back laughter thinking I was boldly telling on myself.

"Yo brother and Murphy tried to run a game on me."

She knew exactly what I saying. She was shocked at the boys' deception. She called her mother to the door.

"Tweety, tell her what you just told me!" Paulina said.

I told Ms. Janice everything. As I began to talk about some of the details, I couldn't help but cover my mouth and cry. Ms Janice started crying when she realized how much her son hurt me emotionally. I wanted to tell Ms. Janice how sore my body felt from him pressing hard into my body, but I was too embarrassed. Instead, I showed her my cut inner lip from Gregory's fist and I complained about my arms and wrists hurting from him rough handling me.

Ms. Janice was furious. She called Gregory to the door. She asked him if he had lost his damn mind. She was shaken up and could barely address Gregory.

"Boy they can put your ass under the jail for stuff like...Let me shut up fore I be done hurt you myself!" she said.

"Ain't nobody did nothing to that girl!" Gregory said.

"Shut up! Don't you say another word or else I swear I'm gon slap the tar outta' you!" Ms. Janice warned.

Antonio was also listening. They had just come from a long day at church.

Antonio promised he would take care of his brother personally.

"Oooh! I'm gon kill 'em Mama!" Antonio blurted out in frustration before he hit the door with his fist.

I didn't know if he was upset because his Mama was crying or because I was crying. Ms. Janice warned Antonio to let her handle Gregory for now before one of them ended up in jail or hurt.

Ms. Janice was left with no choice but to take me home to Mama and Daddy. We told them together what happened. We both sugar coated the details so it didn't appear so brutal. We just told them they were touching me and Gregory was trying to climb on top of me. Ms. Janice promised Gregory wouldn't get away with what he did. She was crying and apologizing to Mama and Daddy over and over telling them she didn't want to lose their friendship over this. Mama gave her a hug and consoled her with Daddy nodding in agreement to trust Ms. Janice's handling of her son.

Mama, Daddy and Ms. Janice, all took me to Murphy's house and we told his Mama what happened as well. She immediately called Murphy in the room and slapped and hit him for calling me up to Ms Janice's house under false pretenses. I asked if I could leave. I didn't want to look at Murphy. I didn't know who or what they thought I was to treat me in this manner. I was just as angry with him as I was with Gregory for what I went through. I left while they stayed and talked. Both parents assured Daddy their sons were not going to get away with what they did to me. Daddy warned them if this ever happened again it was going to be between him and the boys. He let both parents know the boys wouldn't get a second chance. He vowed he would be going to jail next time.

"The only reason I ain't put it on 'em myself is...is...is 'cause of ya'll. I respect ya'll and I know you mean good so I won't hurt the boys this time but I...I...I promise ain't gon be no...no second time," Daddy warned.

Daddy was extremely upset over this matter. He asked me several times if I was alright. He was stuttering all over the place. I knew if I gave him one hint I was hurting over what happened he'd go after the boys. I forced myself to stay calm and block the tears from falling so Daddy could stop being so upset. From that point on I learned to be strong and hold back tears. I didn't allow myself to cry anymore. I went home and finished my own hair determined to be stronger than ever.

The boys were put on month long punishments and not allowed to come outside except to go to school. Once school started they were to go straight home. Murphy got whipped on top of his punishment. He was going into the tenth grade.

Both boys were extremely angry with me. Gregory threatened to beat me up from his window. I told Antonio, who later told me he took care of him for me and to let him know if he ever threatened me again. I heard Antonio had given him a good butt kicking. I felt vindicated somewhat after hearing about his black eye. I felt somewhat avenged for my cut and swollen lip.

"Healing Roads Journal"

Gregory's aggression stuck in my mind for a long time afterwards. I kept thinking about how his fists shoved my lips in and how rough he handled me. He was cruel. I didn't understand the characteristics of a typical sexual assailent. He expressed power and anger. It was a pure reaction to his violent impulse, not sexuality. If he had succeeded in raping me, I would have been even more damaged. I didn't understand any of this at the time.

CHAPTER EIGHTEEN

"Deja Vu"

The following week before school, I was at home getting ready to take a bath. The phone rang. It was my cousin Monica who hung out at the church picnic all up under Mikey last week.

"Girl, guess who over here?" she almost screamed.

"I don't know. Who?" I asked.

She sounded excited.

"Girl, you ain't gon never guess! Let me give you a hint. He's fine and good lookin and he downstairs in my living room as we speak," she said.

I already knew who it was. I said his name real dry.

"Mikey."

She screamed through the phone at me.

"Girl yeah!"

"What's he doing over to your house? I asked.

"Oh, well, he came over here with Bow Leggs them," she explained.

"Bow Leggs and them over there?" I asked.

"Yeah, 'cause Mama bought me a brand new car and they came by to see it," she said.

"A car? How did you get a car in the ninth grade?" I asked.

"Girl please! I been driving all last year! Where you been?" she said.

"I don't believe you! Let me speak to one of our cousins. I'm gonna ask them," I said.

Weiner picked up the phone after a few minutes.

"Weiner, does Monica have a new car for real?" I asked.

"Yeah, it's nice too. She getting ready to take us for a quick ride in it," Weiner said.

I thought about Mikey riding in the car with her.

I knew I could forget it. My cousin was pretty, and she had a car too. I sighed in disbelief.

I hung up the phone expecting for Monica to call me back with the announcement she and Mikey were going together just like it happened with our cousin Neecy.

He had never kissed Neecy, so I felt no guilt when I daydreamed about us kissing. Now I could really forget it because if he and Monica go together, I'm pretty sure they will end up kissing. I could never imagine kissing someone who kissed one of my other cousins, especially now that I was old enough to know better. I wished I didn't have a crush on him. Why did Monica have to show up at the park with us that day? I knew I was heading for a miserable eighth grade school year.

I got in the tub. Scootie knocked at the bathroom door.

"I'm in the tub!" I yelled.

"Telephone!" he yelled back.

"I'm in the tub!" I yelled again.

"Weiner said it was important," he said.

"Tell him I said I don't wanna hear about Mikey and Monica! Tell him I said, big deal!"

A minute later, Scootie was knocking again.

"What! Stop knocking at the door!" I said.

"Tweety, it's Weiner again. He told me to tell you it doesn't have anything to do with Monica at all. He said he just needs to ask you something real, real quick! He said, you can get back in the tub, but just come here real quick!" Scootie said.

I was in a tub full of soap bubbles relaxing. I grunted then I jumped out the tub. I was sore from a softball game workout and needed to soak. I wrapped a towel around me running to the phone in Mama's room.

"Weiner, I had to jump out of the tub real quick, so what do you want?" I snapped.

"Mikey standing right here next to me and he wanna ask you something real quick," Weiner said.

194

I held the phone waiting for a few minutes. No one came to the phone. I got tired of holding the phone. Scootie was standing there trying to be nosy. I handed him the phone.

"When Weiner comes back to the phone, tell him to quit playing games. I'm getting back in the tub. They play too much," I said.

I climbed back into the tub having to run more hot water to soak some more. Before I could finish bathing, Scootie was knocking at the door telling me telephone again.

"No! Tell him I'm not coming! Tell him to quit playing!" I yelled.

"Tweety, Weiner said he's not playing this time for real! He said Mikey wants to talk to you for a minute for real this time!"

"What he want? He just wanna throw up in my face that he go with Monica now! Tell him I said, good for him! Now leave me alone! Dawg!" I yelled again.

"That's not what he wants to tell you," Scootie said.

"Well, what does he wanna tell me then? Just say it! Darn!" I said.

"I don't know what it is. He won't tell me what it is. Tweety, come and get the phone so they can stop calling here!" Scootie said.

I finished bathing and wrapped the towel around me again scurrying to the telephone. I was irritated about having to rush through my hot bubble bath.

"Okay, what is it?" I asked as I grabbed the phone.

"Tweety, don't hang up okay?" Weiner's voice rang out.

"What is it?" I repeated.

"Tweety, Mikey said, give 'em a chance!" Weiner blurted out.

I hung up the phone and walked off. Scootie was standing there.

"What does he want with you?" he asked.

"Nothing. They're just playin games," I said.

I washed out the tub. The phone rang again. I couldn't hear what Scootie was saying with the water running. I was irritated with their games.

"Ooh, they're acting so stupid!" I said.

Scootie called me again sounding irritated himself this time.

"Tweety! Come get the phone! I'm not answering it anymore! Dang!"

I hadn't even got a chance to put on my night clothes yet. Mama and Sonia were at church and Daddy had to work late.

I picked up the phone. Weiner was on the phone again.

"Weiner why are ya'll trying to play games with me?" I asked, frustrated.

"Tweety, listen, listen! I wasn't playin. Mikey did say it! I promise he did. I ain't lyin. Just hang on for a minute. Don't hang up! Mikey get the phone! Mikey man you gon have to get the phone and ask her yo-self 'cause she don't believe me!" Weiner said.

I stood there with my hands on my hips. I might as well just see what the punch line is so they can stop playing on the phone, I figured. Weiner was just trying to get me to fall for his game so he could psyche me out. I suddenly heard Mikey in the background.

"Yeah, I said it! Tell her I said it man!" Mikey said to Weiner, loud enough for me to hear.

"You heard him Tweety? That came out of his own mouth Tweety. I didn't say nothing," Weiner explained.

Weiner was still holding the phone. I didn't know what they thought, but I was not falling for it.

"Well, like I said, tell him to stop playing games," I repeated.

"He not playing games!" Weiner insisted.

"Well how come he didn't just pick up the phone and ask me himself?" I said.

Weiner got quiet.

"Just like I thought. Tell Mikey I said I don't have time to be playing games on the phone. I'm hanging up," I said.

I hung up in the middle of Weiner talking. I was angry with Mikey. I couldn't figure out why he was playing cruel games with me since he was supposed to be my friend. I betcha he and Monica were getting themselves a good laugh.

The phone rang again and I didn't answer it. Scootie didn't answer the phone either. Weiner just kept hanging up and calling back about ten times. Finally, I got tired of him calling so I picked up the phone. I didn't say hello at first. Weiner repeated hello's through the phone. I finally gave in, speaking in a deep dragging voice.

"Hello," I finally said.

It was Mikey on the phone. He paused before talking.

"Hey," he said.

I got quiet and waited after being caught off guard hearing Mikey's voice. I didn't know what to say or expect.

"Tweety?" Mikey called out.

I cleared my throat and straightened out my voice.

"Yeah," I answered hesitantly.

"So, what's it gon be? Yes or no?" he asked.

"Ah, I thought you were hooking up with my cousin Monica," I said.

"No! I don't like her like that," he said.

"Why not?" I asked.

"She not all that attractive to me," he replied.

"Who? Monica? Monica is real pretty!" I said.

"Uh uh. Not to me. I like you better. You real pretty from head to toe. Yo cousin kind of thick if you ask me. She not built like you. She not built nothing like you. Besides, you different from most girls," he said.

He hooked me with his last statement, otherwise, I would have rejected his advances thinking he was only interested in sex like most boys. Could I for once in my life finally talk to a guy who was actually interested in me because he recognized my heart and not my body! I lost faith that a guy like that even existed anymore these days.

"How so?" I asked.

"I can't explain it. You just different. More like the type of girl that I like being with. You not fast like most of these girls out here," he said.

I was surprised to hear Mikey saying these things about me. I was even more surprised he actually wanted to go with me. He was going into the eleventh grade and I was going into the eighth grade. He was as old as Gregory but at that moment, the only thing that mattered was that he was the only boy who showed an interest in me 'the person' and not me 'the nice body.'

"I thought Monica was liking you?" I asked still wanting to be sure.

"I already told Monica at the park I don't like her like that. I told her we can be friends, but that's it," he replied.

"Are you for real? I asked still unsure.

"Yeah," he said sounding anxious.

"Okay, well, where's Monica?" I asked just to make sure he wasn't playing a joke on me.

"I don't know. She outside somewhere I guess. I don't wanna talk about Monica right now. I wanna know bout you and me," he said.

He asked again what my answer was. I was still guarded about whether or not he was for real.

"Well, I say yes if you say yes, and I say no if you say no," I said, thinking about the crush I still had.

"So it's whatever I say then, huh?" he giggled.

"Yeah, I guess so," I answered.

"Okay then, well I guess we go together then," he said.

"Okay then," I said.

"Will I see you at church tomorrow?" he asked.

"Yeah, I guess I'll be there," I replied.

"You promise?" he asked.

I started laughing before answering.

"Yeah," I said.

We hung up. I stood by the phone and screamed. I couldn't believe what just happened. Scootie came in the room. I looked up at him and screamed again.

"What?" Scootie asked.

I gathered my composure.

"Me and Mikey go together." I grinned from ear to ear.

"For real?" Scootie said.

"Yeah," I answered.

"For real, for real," Scootie said.

"Yep," I said.

"Wow! Your first boyfriend!" he said.

He didn't know about Ralph. I had to officially quit Ralph in a hurry! I hadn't talked to him in three weeks since the last episode of punching and slapping me but I knew he was sadistic enough to think I was still his girlfriend.

The next day, I was over Anita's house looking at some of her new clothes she got for school. I decided to wear pants again my eighth grade school year. I wanted to go all out and enjoy my last year in middle school. I had a hard time convincing Mama to let me wear pants again. Daddy felt sympathetic and took me shopping for pants.

I ran home to get my baggy pants I'd be wearing the first day of school. I tried on my entire outfit to get Anita's opinion about which shirt and shoes matched better. Ralph came upstairs where we were. He caught us off guard. He got off work early. Good, now I can break it off with him.

I had to admit he looked so cute when he smiled at me showing his gorgeous dimples. I told him I had something I needed to talk about real quick.

"Quick though because I'm not suppose to be in here when boys are at home. My mama be trippin'," I said to Ralph.

"Yo mama know 'bout me and you?" he asked.

"No! I would've been permanently banned from your house by now if that was the case!" I said. We both laughed.

Ralph was being unusually playful and gentle. He approached me with a compliment telling me I looked beautiful and then he kissed me on the cheek and smiled from dimple to dimple. I had never seen this soft side of him before. He kept hugging and tickling me surprisingly. I laughed but I wanted him to stop. He was making it hard for me to do what I needed to do. I put my old clothes in the bag that I wore over to their house since I was planning on changing back into them once I got home. I sat at the top of the steps to talk to Ralph away from Anita.

"Ralph, I need to talk to you real quick before I go," I started.

Anita walked past me going down the steps.

"How long you gon be?" she asked.

"Give us about five minutes," I said.

Ralph sat down trying to kiss my neck. He was still playing. He had to be sweet today of all days. Why couldn't he have been like this all along?

"Naw, give us about ten minutes," he told Anita.

He started tickling my stomach before I could tell Anita not to listen to him.

"Ralph quit tickling me! I need to tell you something real important!"

"Yo, I'm serious, you look real nice," he said.

"Oh, thank you. This is my school outfit. I gotta go change, so I gotta hurry up." I tried to be serious. "Ralph, remember when I said I needed to talk to you?"

Ralph started joking around again.

"Yo, we can talk all right! Let's go in my bedroom," he said as he unexpectedly nibbled playfully on my neck.

"Come on Ralph, I'm serious!" I said, turning away.

"I'm serious too! Let's go in my bedroom," he said.

"Ralph come on now, I'm for real," I said.

I wanted him to stop playing so I could be serious. He started tickling me again. I couldn't control my laughter. Anita was tired of waiting for me. She came to the steps and frowned up at me. I laughed again and again. I wanted to tell her I couldn't help but to laugh because I was very ticklish. I attempted to ask her for help throughout my laughing episodes. I was also yelling at Ralph to stop.

"I'm gone. Y'all playing too much!" Anita said.

"No! Here I come!" I yelled.

Ralph wouldn't stop tickling me. He tickled me everytime I stood up to try and tell him it was over between us. I fell back down everytime I stood up laughing hysterically. Anita thought I wasn't taking her serious, so she left me.

Ralph was holding me and wouldn't let me go. I thought about his brother John. Not again! I had to get serious. I forced myself to become numb to him tickling me.

"I gotta go!" I snapped.

I stood up fighting Ralph off me wanting to display my anger so he would take me serious. Ralph grabbed me from behind dragging me up a few stairs and then he started backing up towards his room.

"Quit playing boy! You play too much! Let me go!" I yelled.

I snatched away with all my might.

"I'm not playing no more!" I said.

Ralph grabbed a hold of me tighter. He was no longer smiling.

"I'm not playin no mo either," he said.

He was biting his bottom lip as we struggled against each other. I started talking really loud.

"Let me go boy! I'm not playing with you! I'm not playing!" What the devil was going on with all these doggone boys these days?

He was winning the tug of war against my body.

We were at his bedroom door. I held on to the doorknob. Ralph violently snatched me away from the door into his room. I started screaming. Ralph covered my mouth to prevent me from screaming.

I collapsed limp on the floor to prevent him from getting me to his bed. Ralph handled me roughly. My mouth was hurting from his hands as they covered my screams. My strength was about to give out from fighting him so hard. Every time I got his hand away from my mouth, I tried to scream, but he kept covering it up again before I could make a loud enough sound. I tried to bite his hand. He pressed harder on my lips. I was tasting blood.

He was practically dragging me by my mouth and waist. I dug my nails into him and he grabbed my arm twisting it painfully behind my back till tears were running down my face. I yelled out in pain.

"You gon stop fighting me? You gon stop?" he asked as if he was warning me.

I was bent over screaming underneath my covered mouth. He loosened his hold on my painfully contorted arm that was still twisted up behind my back. My arm was limp. It began to drop. It felt like he broke something. I had no strength in my arm. I let it lag down painfully. I was burnt plum out of energy. I didn't know if I had any fight left in me.

Oh my God! This was nothing like when his brother John wouldn't let me go! He was too violent! He was going to rape me! He was going to actually rape me! Thoughts were racing through my head. I just escaped Gregory last week and now this. I didn't know which one I'd rather be raped by. Ralph was hurting me a lot more than Gregory did.

He lifted my body up off the floor. My arm was still throbbing and had no strength in it. He lifted me up from behind. I felt too debilitated to fight. We dropped on his bed. I fell backwards on top of him. I was waiting for the throbbing to stop in my limp arm to see if I could move it. He rolled me over to the side. He had to catch his breath. I started getting strength back in my arm.

If I had any chance of getting away, now was as good a time as ever. I struggled with all my might to get away from him even though my arm felt weak. I couldn't believe I ever liked him. How could I have been so stupid? He was just a violent person. I suddenly fought as hard as I could to get away from him.

Ralph rolled on top of me jerking and slamming me repeatedly against the bed. He bit down hard on his bottom lip then lifted me by my shirt and slammed my body violently over and over with all his strength until I couldn't catch my breath. I lay there so out of breath that I couldn't make a sound. I wanted to speak. He knew he knocked the wind out of me.

He bent to kiss me while threatening me.

"If you bite me, I'm gon take my pillow and smother you."

He had a cocky look about him as if he was anxious for a chance to hurt me again. He was almost smiling when he bent to kiss me. I saw pure cruelty in his eyes.

I laid there keeping my lips sealed tight. He tried to force my mouth open with his tongue. He was pressing down so hard that my teeth were cutting my lips. They began to throb. He was punishing me for not opening my mouth by drawing blood. Tears started to run down my face. Every time I opened my eyes, he was staring dead in my eyes unemotional. I was determined to keep my lips sealed even though I knew he was more determined than me to have his way.

My tears didn't sway him one bit. At least Gregory acknowledged my tears when he had me alone. Ralph was so cold.

How did I get myself in this situation? Why did Anita leave me again? I couldn't even get to the window. I contemplated what to do next.

He groped my breasts and dared me to say something then bent to kiss me again. I turned my head away. He calmly picked up his pillow and covered my face and pressed down with his elbow and arms. I struggled to get the pillow off my face finding it hard to breathe. When he finally lifted the pillow, I was gasping for air realizing he could have killed me.

"You gon fight me again?" he said.

I was busy focusing on catching my breath. He slowly bent to kiss me again and he dared me to turn my head away. I didn't turn away, nor did I fight to keep his tongue from going inside my mouth when he commanded me to open my mouth. I knew he could have taken my life with the pillow.

Ralph started reaching for my new pants. I couldn't just give up without a fight. I covered my button with the hand on my good arm. I was still trying to breathe. Ralph placed his hand over mine and stared straight into my eyes. He yanked the entire button off my pants and he effortlessly ripped the zipper completely apart. It was no longer about sex, but control. I knew he meant business. He planned to win this battle and have his way with me. He slowly and calmly bent to kiss me on the lips again. I turned my face away when he started sliding his hand inside of my pants. Ralph grabbed his pillow and smothered my face again. I tried to scream under the pillow, but he pressed even harder silencing me. I surrendered and ceased fighting as I prayed he would stop pressing so I could breathe. He lifted the pillow up. I took in deep puffs of air still too afraid to move.

I realized he could kill me if I didn't cooperate. He stared at me with cold eyes before slowly bending to kiss me again. This time I didn't turn my head away. I let him kiss me as I lay motionless still concentrating on breathing. His tongue was forcefully gliding in and out of my mouth while he kept his unemotional eyes aimed at my eyes. He wanted me to know who had the power. I closed my eyes not wanting to see the look of victory in his eyes. I began to realize I didn't have any control over my body anymore. Either I gave in or got hurt or even killed. I opened my eyes and looked into his unblinking eyes. I was hoping to see some kind of emotion staring back at me even if it was lust but I saw nothing but a cold, angry stare, as if he was looking right through me.

He calmly rose up casually peeking out the window. I lay there crying still trying to get air. Ralph knew I was helpless. I struggled just to rise up. I wanted to do something, but everything I tried so far had failed. He climbed back on top of me and I turned my head away avoiding his eyes. He lay still waiting for me to look at him. I turned my face to look at him and wondered why nothing was happening. He smiled defiantly before slowly bending to kiss me again. He wanted me to remember who was in control. I rebelled out of anger over him smiling in defeat. I turned away. He punished me by jamming his hand inside my torn pants. I instinctively wrestled with him some more when he fought to get his hands in my pants. He pinned my hands together with one hand while digging roughly inside of my pants with the other hand. He wasn't even looking at what he was doing. He was staring me down eye to eye making a point to bite down on his bottom lip hard. I freed one of my hands and tried to pull his hand away. He shoved his hand in my crotch. I cried out feeling a sharp pain.

"Aaugh, Ralph, please stop. Just let me go home. All I wanna do is go home. Please let me go!" I begged.

I moved my hand away from his hand when he jammed harder, roughly sticking several fingers inside of my vagina. I figured out enough to stop resisting so he could stop being so rough. It worked. He relaxed his touch, but he didn't stop shoving his fingers inside of me. I was not lubricated and he was being too forceful with my body. I tensed up and yelled out when he continued to thrust his hand deeper inside of me.

No matter how much I begged and pleaded, his hand seemed to be digging further and further inside me. He shoved his finger painfully into my tender flesh as I moaned out of discomfort. Common sense told me he was preparing me for penetration. I saw he wasn't showing me mercy so I collapsed sobbing loudly. This finally agitated him.

"I ain't hurtin you! What you cryin like that for!" he snapped.

"Yes you are!" I yelled.

"No I'm not! This don't hurt and you know it!" he said.

"Yes it does too!" I insisted.

"What you sayin? So you a virgin?" He smiled as if he was turned on more.

"What are you gon do to me? I didn't give you permission to touch me at all!" I sobbed.

"Shut up!" he said coldly.

Ralph unbuttoned his pants then unzipped them. He rose slightly off me to pull his pants down. He had on light blue boxers. He had a nice physique, but I didn't care. He continued to stare me down while he pulled down his jeans. I read his expression clearly but he spoke anyway.

"Don't move," he warned.

He stood straight up off the bed. I started rising up. He shoved me back down with an exaggerated noise coming out of his mouth like he was jabbing a punching bag.

"I said, don't move." His voice was calm and confident.

He was crazy if he thought I was going to just lie there and let this play itself out. I rose up again. He shoved me harder in my chest with his fists making a noise to exaggerate his determination yet again. My chest was throbbing and the wind was partially knocked out of me. He was daring me to try to get away so he could inflict more pain on me, to prove he was in charge. I realized he was waiting on a chance to hurt me again. I had to think about another strategy. I couldn't give up. He was confident, calm and insensitive.

He stepped out of his pants. I couldn't give him a fight because I'd end up both beaten and raped, if not dead. Maybe I should just talk to him without fighting.

"Please let me go. Just let me go please. Why are you doing this to me?" I asked.

He ignored me and unbuttoned my shirt one slow button at a time. Instead of fighting his grip on my hands when I reached for my last button, I asked for some tissue because my nose was runny from crying. My body felt bruised from all the slamming and shaking. I didn't want to fight anymore. He was silent for a minute. He picked up a white pillow and held it above my face before he spoke.

"You gon fight me?" he asked.

I nodded no and prayed he didn't cover my face with the pillow again.

"Why are you doing this to me? I'm not gonna fight you anymore. You win. Please let me go," I begged.

He bent over me and slowly unbuttoned my last button then pulled each arm out of the sleeves of my shirt before responding. He ignored my grimace when he moved my twisted arm. I didn't have on a bra. He exposed my bare breasts.

"Shut up!" he said.

He didn't seem interested in looking at my breasts. He just continued his cold hard stare as if he were looking right through my eyes.

He slipped his shirt off revealing defined muscles in his arms. His torso was a six pack of rippling muscles as well. You could tell he lifted weights a lot. I felt powerless. He stood still looking at me, daring me to try to get away. He had this look of power on his face after realizing he had me tamed. He walked over to the window and looked out one last time before he got ready to climb back on top of me. I knew he would catch me and hurt me more if I tried to get away but when he walked over to the window, it was as if he was daring me to try to run from him. He was just staring out of his window about twelve feet away in no rush to get back to where I was lying. The door seemed almost as far from me as his window so I knew I would fail if I tried to out run him. I decided to try to find words to convince him that this was a big mistake before having the final fight over my virginity. I also tried to gather strength knowing that I couldn't just lie still and let him remove my pants.

"Ralph, you don't have to do this. I won't tell my Daddy or nothing if you just let me go now. I won't even be mad at you," I said.

Ralph kept his back turned looking out the window.

"Awe shit! There go yo mama! Shit! Fuck! Git up and fix yo-self up!" he yelled.

"Healing Roads Journal"

Why couldn't a guy look at my face and like me because of my smile or because I had a nice personality? Why couldn't guys just think of me as a nice girl to spend time with? What was it about me? I couldn't seem to attract a guy for the right reason. I was determined they'd never use me for my body. I was convinced the boys would dump me as soon as they got what they wanted. I wished I could teach all men a lesson about trying to use girls.

It occurred to me how Ralph's usual pattern was to be abusive and then be nice. He changed the pattern by being nice and then abusive. His motive to hurt me never changed. I just never realized it until now.

My power struggle led me further away from learning the right lessons. My journey gets tougher.

CHAPTER NINETEEN

"Boyfriend"

Ralph ran to the bathroom and came back with some tissue. He threw it at me and said in a panic, "Yo! Here! Clean yo damn face off! Shit!"

I put my shirt on and started to close my pants. There was no button and the zipper was completely ripped. I tried to find the button.

"Yo, Hurry up!" Ralph snapped.

I spotted my button on the floor and quickly picked it up. I wanted to get out more than he wanted me out.

Ralph was looking me over.

"Fix yo hair girl! Damn!" he yelled.

I fixed my hair a little bit. I didn't care about my hair. I just wanted to leave as fast as I could. I looked out the window and saw Mama walking towards our house with grocery bags in her hands. I wanted to scream for my mama, but I knew better.

I bent down to put my shoes on, which he pulled off once he threw me on the bed. I felt stiff and had to move slower than I wanted to. He snatched me up and pulled me towards the stairs.

"Hurry up! Git outta here before yo mama starts calling for you," he said.

I opened their back door. Ralph was throwing my bag of clothes downstairs. I picked it up and left. I ignored him telling me to come back and get my hair accessory which came out of my hair during our struggle.

I thought about the whipping I got when John held me against my will. I decided Mama wasn't going to believe me. I snuck in the back door and tip-toed upstairs. I was relieved I had accidentally left the back door unlocked.

Mama was putting away grocery and preparing to cook dinner. She didn't hear me coming in the back door. I closed my bedroom door upstairs and took my new pants off to look at them. They were ruined. I changed into shorts and lay across the bed and sobbed. I cried myself to sleep and felt relieved that no one could hear me.

My body was sore. I had a few bruises on my thigh. I remembered trying to keep my legs together while he gripped my thighs hard to cause enough pain to let him spread my legs apart. My inner thighs had dark marks from his hands which gripped them forcefully. I remembered trying to swing at him a few times, but he blocked every swing. I could barely lift my arms. My lips were burning and swollen. I wanted to tell on Ralph. He treated me like I was worthless. He could have smothered me to death and he wouldn't have cared.

I cried because Mama would blame me for being over there the same way she did with John. Anita was outside when Mama pulled up the same way she was when John kept me in their house.

Anita was heading to Paulina's house when I came from around her building. She looked up and called my name.

"Tweety. Tweety. Tweety! Well don't answer then!" she said.

I kept walking towards my house. I felt emotionally drained.

I lay in bed knowing I would never be the same again. This was really getting to me. I battled with my emotions. I felt beat up on the inside just as much as I felt on the outside. I cried myself to sleep. When I woke up, I was angry at myself for allowing Ralph to make me shed tears. I didn't want him to win but the tears made me feel like he had defeated me.

I couldn't seem to shake this experience off like I did the other ones. I don't even remember how I made it through the rest of the day or the next day. When I came home from softball practice, I was home alone. I felt sad again but I refused to allow Ralph to have any kind of emotional control over my life. I had to get out of my room to escape the sadness. I decided to go outside. There was no one outside because everyone was at the pool.

I sat alone on the Community Porch feeling sorry for myself but refusing to shed any more tears. I had my back against the high wall with my feet propped up. I could see Ralph's window which was across the street. I didn't realize he was sitting in his window watching me for some time. When I heard his voice, I tensed up as anger filled me.

"Hey baby," he said in a sweet voice.

I sat straight up. I just knew he was not talking to me! I swung my feet around so my back was completely to him. He called me again.

"Hey baby. Tweety, I'm talking to you!" he said.

I didn't look back. I just wanted to block him out.

"Hey baby, you mad at me?" he asked.

I was boiling.

"Come here for a minute Tweety, let me tell you something!" he said.

When I didn't move, he started laughing.

"Tweety, baby just come here for one minute. Just one minute and you can go back," he said.

I sat still trying to block his voice out.

"You ain't gon come?" he asked.

I finally stepped down, walked across the street and looked up at his window.

"How dare you even say my name you bastard! How dare you even call me baby! I'm not your damn baby you mother fucker! You can kiss my ass and you can go to hell!" I said through clenched teeth.

Ralph was giggling, like it was funny.

"You finished sweetheart?" he asked.

"No, I'm not done! Don't you ever put your hands on me again, as long as you live! As a matter of fact, don't you even look at me no more. If you see me walking down the street, do me a favor and look the other way! I don't want you even looking at me. You don't even deserve to be walking on the same side as me you fucking bastard! If you ever put yo hands on me again, I will go in my house and I will get a knife and I will stab you! If you think I'm playing, you try me you son of a bitch," I said.

"Listen baby. Just listen for a minute, okay? Just calm down for one minute, damn. I know you mad. That's what I'm trying to say to you! I..." he started.

"You're damn right I'm mad. You ain't nothing but a sick bastard and as a matter of fact, I don't even know why I'm even wasting my breath with you. Don't say nothing to me again and I won't ever say nothing to you again, you got that?" I said.

I walked away as Ralph yelled back.

"Hey, I was fixin to apologize!" he said.

"I don't need your apology," I said.

"Awe baby. Come on let's kiss and make up," he snickered.

He was talking in a sweet voice, taunting me. I ignored him and went back to the Community Porch with my back turned to him. He was not going to make me cower away. I felt empowered knowing he was watching my back. I sat calmly swinging my legs.

I didn't walk around using bad language, but I was so angry I lost control. This was my way of releasing all the stuff pent up inside me. Later on at the end of the week, Lanette told me she was in her window listening to the whole thing.

"What was that about Tweety?" she asked.

"Nothing. Don't pay it any attention. We're just gonna let it go, okay?" I insisted.

I didn't go to church the rest of the week even though I promised Mikey I would come. I wanted to be home alone. I didn't feel like dealing with Mikey or any other boys. I told Mama I wasn't feeling good. She believed me because I always liked going to church. I spent a lot of time alone in my room. I allowed myself to cry the first night and promised myself no more tears. I couldn't let Ralph win. I had to be strong from then on.

When I finally showed up for church on Friday night, Mikey was quiet. He seemed a little upset. He had his head down.

"So, what happened to you all week? I mean, I been coming to church every night. Every single night and you didn't come one single night. Yo mother was here. Yo sister was here. I even saw yo brother a couple nights. What, you didn't wanna see me?" he asked.

Mikey had been there every day since Tuesday expecting to see me. He figured by Friday I didn't really want to be his girlfriend.

When I saw him at church, neither one of us knew how to approach the other. We avoided each other, even though my cousins were trying everything to get us to talk to one another. We were still having church services in Pastor Nichols' house. He was now ordained a Bishop. We referred to him as Bishop Nichols even though we still slipped up a lot and called him Pastor.

Quanetta's father was now an ordained Pastor. They also moved to the country in a different county not far from Pastor Jacobs. So far, we had churches in three different places. All the churches were preparing to come together and celebrate the "Feast of Pentecost." This was our last feast of the year. Everyone gave and received presents as if it were Christmas.

Mother Jordon and Bishop Nichols announced we would be in our new church home by the time we got together for our last feast. Everyone clapped standing to their feet. Bishop Nichols' house was very crowded particularly on Friday nights and Saturdays because of the Sabbath.

While sitting in the back room away from the adults during service, Bow Leggs tried to persuade me and Mikey to talk, but with no success. Neither one of us knew what to expect from the other. Finally, Bow Leggs tapped me on my shoulder asking me to come with him for a minute so he could show me something. I got up and followed him into the kitchen. In the meantime, Weiner had Mikey to follow him into the kitchen. I looked up at him as Bow Leggs spoke.

"What's the deal between you and Mikey?" Bow Leggs asked.

"What do you mean?" I played dumb.

"I mean, you mad at him?" he asked.

"No," I answered.

"Well, Mikey you mad at Tweety?" he turned and asked Mikey.

"No, I guess not. She the one playin games man," Mikey said, looking frustrated.

Bow Leggs sighed. "Well, you not mad at her and she not mad at you so ya'll officially boyfriend and girlfriend. Now talk got darn it!" he said.

Bow Leggs and Weiner then walked out the kitchen. Mikey had been getting on his nerves all week since I hadn't been to church. Mikey was too afraid to call me and ask me why. I'm glad he didn't call because I would've changed my mind about having any boyfriends. I needed time to get over what happened with Ralph. I was somewhat reluctant about being in a relationship with any guys after the episode with Ralph. A part of me wanted to tell Mikey to go to hell. Another part of me felt a little bad about wanting to blame Mikey and be angry with him because of what Ralph did. The more I looked at him, the more I wanted to at least give him a fair chance. His eyes were nothing like Ralph's eyes. I looked at him and actually saw compassion in his eyes.

Bow Leggs became our lookout while we spent time alone in the kitchen. If an adult came towards the kitchen, Mikey would run in the bathroom behind the kitchen while I pretended to get a drink of water.

I sighed because it was hard to explain why I didn't feel like being bothered. I was too embarrassed to talk about Ralph. I didn't want him to know I had a boyfriend at the time I told him we could go together. I was also embarrassed about being caught inside of Ralph's house, period. I had already confided in Mikey about his brother John and the situation where I got in trouble for being over at his house a few months back. He would think I was stupid for going back over there again. I told him I had to stay late for softball practice and was getting home too late to come to church.

"I thought maybe you were trying to play me or something. I figured you were going with Ralph or Antonio or somebody," he said.

I was suspicious when he mentioned Ralph's name. I wondered if Scootie knew I liked Ralph and Antonio and spilled the beans. Somebody told him something.

"No! That's not it at all. I don't have any boyfriends!" I quickly said.

"You sure you not talking to somebody else? I mean, you can just tell me if you are and I'll understand," he said.

"Nope. I'm not talking to anybody else," I said.

"Well, you know yo girl been trying to get back together with me." he said.

"Who, Neecy?" I asked.

"No! I'm talking 'bout yo other girl," he said.

"Now I'm confused. Who?" I asked.

"Guess," he said.

I stood there for a minute to think. The only other girl was Tameka. I knew it couldn't be her. I hadn't seen her in years. I hadn't even talked to her in years. She stopped talking to me and got her number changed. I never knew how to get in contact with her anymore. Her Aunt always told me she didn't have a number for her. I blurted out her name to Mikey and he nodded yes. Well, I guess he is going to tell me he wants to be with her. I was prepared to be disappointed by yet another guy. One way or another, guys kept letting me down. My heart sank. When I looked at his face, he was still smiling tenderly at me and it confused me somewhat. I didn't know how he felt about Tameka. Did he have feelings for her?

"Okay. What did you say to her?" I asked.

"Of course I told her hell naw!" he said.

"Well why? And why you say it like that anyway?" I asked.

"'Cause, I don't like that girl!" he said.

"Why? Are you angry with her because she quit you?" I asked.

"Naw, I'm glad she quit me way back then. I was getting ready to quit her anyway. She was too silly and immature to me," he said.

"But didn't you have feelings for her?" I asked

"Feelings for her? What you mean I had feelings for her?" he asked.

"Well, I mean, you loved her back then didn't you?" I asked.

Mikey burst out laughing. "Shoot naw I didn't love her. Where you get that from? I ain't never loved Tameka! She told you that?" he asked.

I started laughing as well because he was laughing so hard.

"I just thought you were in love with her back then," I said.

"I was in love with Julia back then, but I ain't never been in love with Tameka!" he said honestly.

"Oh, so you're still in love with Julia? I asked.

"No! I been done moved on from that. I got over her a long time ago. So, is there anything else you wanna know?" he asked.

"Does Tameka know you and me are supposed to be talking now?" I asked.

"I don't care if she know or not! That was a long, long time ago. I ain't thinking 'bout Tameka right now. I'm thinking about you! So, are we together or what?" he asked.

I nodded yes with a shy smile.

"Okay then! Come on. Let's go in there and sit down before somebody starts talking. You know how these church people is," he said truthfully.

I sat next to Mikey until service was over. Bow Leggs and Weiner kept picking at us the rest of the night.

"Look at the two love birds!" They kept saying and laughing.

After service was over, Mikey asked me to go outside. A lot of children were already outside. Weiner was outside hugged up to his girlfriend. J Bug was going with one of my friends named Erica. She had an identical twin sister, but I was real good friends with Erica. I was surprised as I noticed how respectful J Bug was being towards Erica. He held doors open for her and they walked arm and arm. They'd been together almost all summer. J Bug was finally seeming to be a pretty decent guy and he was still as handsome as ever.

Erica and her twin T'Erica were moving to the country where Pastor Jacobs' church was located. They would start their new school season in the country, which meant they would be leaving on Sunday. J Bug was being extra attentive because they would be apart after Erica moved.

When Mikey and I stepped outside he held my hand. It looked like lover's lane with about three other couples outside acting romantically in love. As we walked towards the crowd, Mikey yelled to everyone.

"Hey everybody, check this out!"

I didn't know what he was about to do. We hadn't told anybody we were together yet, so I figured Mikey was about to make the announcement. Instead, Mikey looked at me.

"Can I have a kiss?" he asked.

I blushed because I knew he was asking me to kiss him in front of everybody. I didn't answer, so he asked again. I nodded yes.

"Everybody check this out. I got a message for y'all to give to

Tameka the next time one of y'all see her," Mikey announced.

He kissed me real quick. It was not the kiss I would have liked. He covered my entire lips with his mouth wetting my mouth. I hated it. I let him kiss me anyway. It was quick. I had to wipe my mouth. Everybody clapped because this became our official boyfriend and girlfriend announcement. Mikey was excited. He got carried away.

"Hey Bow Leggs! This one for Neecy!" He kissed me again.

"Hey! This one for Julia!" he said as he kissed me yet again.

I wished he could have kissed like Antonio with a closed mouth. I had to wipe my mouth because it was very wet. When he was done he put his arms around me. I was okay with him hugging me. Everybody was taken aback. No one ever expected us to end up together because Mikey always said I was too young and acted disinterested in me. I in turn had acted disinterested in him. We always told everyone we would always be nothing more than friends.

Curly spoke up. "Doggone y'all, when did all this happen?"

I hunched my shoulders not knowing how to explain.

We stood around talking with the rest of the crowd. Things finally seemed normal again. We joked and picked on one another like we usually did. Mikey took up for me when Curly made fun of the way my daddy called me in to sit down. She mimmicked my actions and how I looked.

"Hey, leave my girl alone now. You need to worry about those shoes you got on tonight!" Mikey said in my defense.

Everybody looked at her shoes and burst out laughing. One had a hole in which her big toe was bursting out.

"That's alright! That's alright! Don't worry 'bout it!" Curly said laughing along as a way of handling being the butt of the joke.

"I ain't worrying 'bout it baby! You the one gotta wear those 'holy' shoes. I hear 'em speaking in tongues way over here!" Mikey continued to joke.

Everybody fell out laughing. I was not good at talking about people at all. Mikey, Curly, and J Bug were the funniest ones out of everyone among us. It was all in good fun when they picked on you, so you just had to take it and laugh along. I always did.

Daddy was working a lot of overtime so he wasn't at church a lot lately except for Saturdays.

Before I started talking to Mikey, I was beginning to feel like a sore thumb at church because my friends all had boyfriends hugging and kissing them outside after service. I stayed inside the church not wanting to interfere with them kissing and cuddling. When I did go outside, I hung with Erica some and came back inside to leave her and J Bug alone. Sometimes I went outside and played 'catch football' with my cousins. I preferred holding Sister Nichols' babies inside.

I finally felt like I could fit in with everybody outside. Mikey gave me his phone number the first night we became an official couple. Throughout the time we were friends we confided in one another during the times we spent hanging out at church but we never spoke on the phone. I never called any boys, not even Ralph because I didn't want boys to think I was chasing after them. I had no intention of calling Mikey when he gave me his phone number because I didn't want to appear anxious or desperate. I decided I would wait for him to call me.

Mama and Daddy never said I couldn't have boyfriends and we never really talked about it. I was scared to say anything to them so I would just let them find out on their own.

CHAPTER TWENTY

"I Love You"

On Monday, after the first day of school, I picked up my sister from her friend China's house before going home. I fixed us lunch and went into Mama's room to watch TV. Mama was at the church helping to fix up things. She called to say she would be working late at the church all week. They were Feast shopping and getting the new church ready for services to begin. They also had to prepare the feast room in the back of the church. They had a busy week fixing up everything.

Daddy was working overtime as usual. Scootie had to stay late after school for band practice everyday. It was his first year in high school. My coach cancelled softball practice for the first week of school. I had homework the first day of school. I did all my homework and helped Sonia with her homework.

Sonia told me all about her first day of school with her teachers and friends. Scootie finally got home late in the evening. He told us all about his first day and how bad the school was. He said fights broke out and people had guns and knives. He was making me fear high school. He was excited about the large band. Scootie seemed to have the most interesting day of all.

The phone rang and I was surprised when Scootie told me Mikey was on the phone. Mikey didn't call Saturday or Sunday. I figured he would play it cool and try not to appear anxious. I didn't expect to hear from him at all the first week. I smiled from ear to ear when Scootie said he was on the phone. Scootie teased me.

"You actually have a boyfriend calling you! You never had one of them before have you?" He grabbed both his cheeks in exaggeration. "Oh my God, my first phone call! What am I going to do?" He was supposed to be imitating me.

I waved him off and got the phone. I held the phone and stood there for a minute. I was nervous. Scootie was still picking.

"Hey Tweety, here's what you do okay? First, you put the telephone up to your ear right? And then you say, hello," Scootie teased.

"Boy, shut up! Get out of here!" I yelled.

Scootie got phone calls all the time. Daddy even let him bring a girl home when he was in the eighth grade and no one was at home. I mean, Daddy didn't tell him to bring the girl over when no one was at home, but he didn't say anything when he found out she was over when no one was at home.

I finally got the nerve to say hello. I didn't know why my stomach was doing summersaults. Mikey responded and asked me how I was doing. He sounded so gentle. I told him I was doing fine. We talked about each others day. We talked about Scootie's first day in high school. I gave Scootie the phone and let him tell Mikey about some of the fight stories. I got the phone back and we ended up being on the phone for two hours. He was at my cousins' house waiting for his mama who was helping out over at the new church as well. I also talked to my cousins about their first day of school.

It was getting late and Mama told us what time to be in bed if she wasn't home. I told Mikey I had to get off the phone. He asked why and I told him I had to be in bed by a certain time. He was surprised I had a bed time curfew.

"Oh, well I guess I need to keep remembering that you just in the eighth grade. When I see you looking so fine and all, I forget sometimes," he teased.

"Yep, I'm in the eighth grade," I said.

I also needed to remember he was in the eleventh grade. Mikey told me he didn't want to hang up.

"Well, I guess I'll let you go though," Mikey said reluctantly.

I said okay, we said bye and I hung up. I went to run my bath water. It was late so I intended to take a really quick bath before Mama or Daddy got home. The phone rang again while I was in the tub and Scootie said it was Mikey again. I asked him to tell Mikey to call me back in ten minutes. I finished my bath and got in bed. Mama finally put a telephone in our bedroom. When Mikey didn't call back in ten minutes, I kicked myself for missing him. Mikey finally called back in about twenty minutes.

"I won't hold you up but I forgot to tell you something," he said.

"Okay, what is it?" I asked, baffled.

"I just wanted to let you know that I love you," he said.

I froze. I didn't know what to say. I had never in my life told a boy I loved him. I had no plans of telling him I love you back. I just held the phone in silence.

"Hello?" he said.

"Huh? I mean, uh, yeah, I'm here," I responded.

Mikey started laughing. "Did you hear what I just said?" he asked.

"Umm hmm," I said.

He laughed again. "Well, you gotta say it back," he insisted.

I was silent.

"Hello?" he said.

I didn't answer.

"Tweety?" he called again.

I didn't answer.

"Tweety!" Mikey called my name a third time.

"I...I'm here," I finally said.

"Well, I'm waiting," he said.

Oh my God! I'm not ready for all this! He's moving too fast! Maybe he's too mature for me or something. I can't do it! I thought to myself.

"Oh you don't love me? 'cause I love you," he said.

"I, uh, well, yeah," I answered.

"Okay, well say it then," he said.

Oh no! Why do I have to say it! I exclaimed to myself.

"Okay... me too," I almost whispered. I felt extremely awkward.

What am I saying! This is getting too serious for me, I thought.

"Me too what?" he said.

"Uh... huh?" I said.

Mikey was cracking up with laughter. "Me too what?" he said still laughing.

I sighed really heavy. *What will it mean if I say this to him? I don't know anything about love! I'm too young for this stuff. It's too deep for me,* I thought.

"I gotta get off the phone before my Mama or Daddy comes home, so, I guess I'll talk to you tomorrow okay?" I said.

"I'm not gon hang up till you tell me you love me first," he said, still giggling.

"Okay well I... well I," I started.

"I what?" he said.

"I ...love...you," I said.

It was the hardest thing I ever had to say and it sounded almost like a yodel. Mikey burst out laughing. I felt totally out of place, like I said something I had no business saying. Mikey finally calmed down from laughing. I felt like a little child.

"See there! Now that wasn't so bad, now was it? Now I can let you go to bed. Now I'm happy," he said.

What did I get myself into? God, he sounds so mature all of a sudden! I thought.

We said our goodbyes and hung up. I lay there feeling like a total idiot. *Why did I say that?* I sounded so horrible! I hope he still likes me. As a matter-of-fact "like" was more the word I was looking for. That word sounded so much safer. *Why did he have to say love? He doesn't love me! We just started going together. He can't possibly love me.* I guess this was something mature teenagers said to one another. That's it! He probably said it to all his girlfriends. Well, I hope he still likes me tomorrow. I hope I didn't act too immature tonight.

To my surprise, Mikey called me the next day as well, from my cousins' house again. He caught the bus to my cousins' house after school everyday to wait for his mama to come and pick him up.

Mama and Daddy were out late that night as well. Before we hung up Mikey said I love you again.

Oh no! He already said it yesterday. Here we go again.

"Why did you say that again?" I asked.

"Cause I do love you. You didn't know that?" he asked.

"Nope," I replied.

"Well, I do," he said.

He was sounding too mature again.

"I'm gon say it every night so you may as well get used to it. I don't ever want you to hang up the phone unless you tell me you love me, okay?" he said.

"Okay. I love you too." This time I rushed through the words. I figured I had better get used to it.

There was no church service for the first two days of the week because all the ministers were preparing for the feast and the grand opening of our new church on Sunday. Mama asked if we wanted to go to church on Wednesday. Scootie had too much packed into his schedule on top of homework, but Sonia and I went to church with Mama at Bishop Nichols' house. I was not going to miss an opportunity to see Mikey.

After service, Mama saw us holding hands. In the car, she asked what was going on between the two of us. I told her we were going together.

"How old is Mikey?" she asked.

"I don't know. He's in the eleventh grade," I answered.

"He too old for you! You can't talk to him!" Mama said.

"But Mama, I already told him yes! We're already talking!" I said.

"Well, he didn't ask me or your daddy if it was okay for him to talk to you anyway!" she said.

"Mama, he didn't know he had to ask," I explained.

"Well, that's just too bad for him! You not talking to nobody that's in the eleventh grade!" she said.

"Mama, he's only three years older than me! You and Daddy were talking at my age!" I said.

Mama got quiet even though she was still shaking her head. "We just gon see what yo daddy has to say about this," she finally said.

I was asleep when Daddy came home. The next day, Mama told me Daddy said no to Mikey and I going together and no to me having boyfriends period. Daddy said I couldn't have a boyfriend until I was sixteen. I was devastated. I cried and argued my point until Mama told me to shut up. Scootie could have as many girlfriends as he wanted to have, but I couldn't have a boyfriend.

I was supposed to go to church with Mama but I didn't know how to face Mikey so I stayed at home. Daddy came home early and went to church with Mama. While they were gone, I made up in my mind to explain to Mikey how much I still wanted us to be together. I'd just be with him in secret.

Unbeknownst to me, Mama and Daddy had a private meeting with Mother Jordon and Bishop Nichols regarding Mikey and I talking. They advised them it would be in their best interest as well as ours if they allowed us to at least talk until I could date.

"Bruh' James, what if they decided to sneak and talk anyway?" Mother pointed out the obvious to them. Mother referred to Daddy and Mama by their last name sometimes.

"Look Bruh' Ranch, I know you may not know this but Mikey's really a respectable young man. He come over here everyday so I know him. He almost like a son to me," Bishop said. Bishop referred to Daddy by his nickname, "Ranch." My daddy's real name was Thomas James.

Mother Jordon also said Mikey was like a son to her as well.

"Now Bruh' James and Sista James, wouldn't ya'll rather have Tweety talking to someone in the church out in the open than to be talking to someone who was not involved in the church? Don't ya'll think it's better?" Mother Jordon asked.

Daddy argued. "Well, I don't want her talking to nobody right now in or out the church. I don't want her datin' period."

"Look Bruh' Ranch, you got to be reasonable here now. Tweety's a very mature young woman. She got a nice body. She noticing boys and boys show noticing her. If you let her talk to Mikey at least they have limited opportunity to do anything if they at church. It's practically harmless. Even if he came over to yo house, it would be only when you were home. You'll be able to keep a watchful eye over the situation so nothing got out of hand. Now don't that make sense?" Mother Jordon said.

Mother Jordon spent a lot of time with Mikey talking to him and helping him deal with his problems. He spent the night with her and Bishop Nichols a lot since she stayed at Bishop Nichols' house many weeks at a time. She promised Mama and Daddy that Mikey wasn't the type of guy to try anything inappropriate. Bishop Nichols added I might become rebellious and end up striking back by sneaking around with other boys outside the church or at school.

"Bruh' Ranch, I hate to put it like this but, Mikey probably gon have to slow yo daughter down some anyway. Look Bruh' Ranch, I'm telling you, I know how these young girls is these days. You'd probably be surprised if you knew everything there was to know about Tweety 'cause you can't let these young girls fool you. You shouldn't think of Tweety any differently than any of these other girls out here," Bishop Nichols said.

"I know how I raised my daughter and I teach her better than some of these other men teach they children," Daddy argued.

"Well, Bruh' Ranch, I'm not saying Tweety done slept with boys but then again, all I'm saying is you don't know so you really can't say," Bishop argued.

Bishop Nichols talked about how some of these girls are and shared his knowledge about fast, sneaky girls as if to imply I could be one of those girls.

"All I'm getting to Bruh' Ranch, is I feel like you'd be making a big mistake if you were to try and keep yo daughter away from Mikey. Mikey a good young man and at least he coming to church and serving God. He know the word of God, he fasts and prays, he's in school...I'm telling you Bruh' Ranch, you couldn't ask for a better young man for Tweety than Mikey."

Weiner eavesdropped on their entire conversation and told me everything word for word two days later. I was offended by Bishop Nichols' last comments because it was confirmation of how loose he thought I was. He didn't know anything about me!

Mama and Daddy came home from church and broke the news. Mikey and I could talk but we couldn't date. I smiled at them and thought, okay, whatever y'all want to call it.

I went to church the following night. All eyes seemed to be on me. I pulled Curly aside and asked her why everybody was staring at me and Mikey.

"Well, Tweety, I didn't really wanna say nothing but since you my friend I'll tell you. See, you know Mikey's mama been talking 'bout you to my mama don't you?"

"Sista Lynn's been talking 'bout me?" I asked.

She was always smiling at me and acting as if she liked me so I was surprised.

"Uh Huh! Bad too girl! She told my mama you just want Mikey to git up under yo dress and she tole Mikey not to fool wit you," Curly added.

"What? Girl please, I wish I would let any boy get up under my dress. I'm not about to sleep with Mikey or any other boys for that matter," I argued.

"Well I'm just warning you girl. All eyes is show on you so you betta watch yo back. Just don't tell nobody what I just tole you. I only tole you 'cause you is my friend and I don't wanna see you being made a fool out of," she said.

"Oh, I'm not going to say nothing to anybody, but thanks for the warning just the same," I said.

I wasn't aware that Mikey's mama was the female minister in the church who was starting all the rumors about me. She kept telling Mikey behind my back she wouldn't advise him to talk to me because I was fast. I had no clue that Sister Lynn had been inventing extreme stories about my promiscuity to many of the adult ministers in the church. She began to be a core source of information causing people to label me as this sneaky girl sleeping around with everyone. She told people she saw me sneaking around with boys and letting them do all kinds of disrespectful things to me. She invented these lies in her head for whatever reason. It would be years into my adult life before I would ever realize why I was being labeled a fast girl by many adults in church. She hugged me all the time. Everyone trusted her and believed her words to be true, including me. She continued to be extremely nice to me whenever I saw her.

Conversations started among some of the adults in church as they sat around and talked behind Mama's back. They talked about how I was probably going to end up pregnant now that I was with Mikey. Many eyes were on me with rumors all over the place about me. I was clueless about all these rumors. I hadn't done anything with a single boy at church to deserve this reputation. Other than Q biting my lip, I had never kissed a boy at church before I kissed Mikey.

Daddy instructed Mama to make me stay inside and talk to Mikey.

Here we go again. Mikey and I hugged as I left, which I liked better than kissing anyway. We spent most of our private time together on the telephone.

Most likely, Daddy had been hearing all these bad rumors and lies about me which explained why he was watching me so closely and being so strict again. I continued to be clueless. I became more confused about why Daddy didn't trust me when I hadn't given him a reason to distrust me.

Mikey asked me a lot of questions to test all the rumors going around about me. Even though I didn't know he was testing me, he realized I was respectable after our conversations. He tested me on the sex question, and I told him I didn't plan on having sex with a boy until I got married so we could have something to look forward to. I was remembering many of Mama's stories and used her answers to many questions. He asked me if I ever had sex with a boy before and I told him never. I told him sex was yucky to me.

"It seems as if that's all boys want these days. I'm not going to let anybody take advantage of me like that," I assured Mikey.

"You don't think you might change yo mind in the future?" Mikey asked.

"I'm not going to be anybody's fool! I mean, not if I can help it," I said.

"What you mean, not if you can help it?" Mikey asked.

"I mean, the only way a guy would take advantage of me would be if he raped me or something. Boys are too stupid. I mean, not that you're stupid or anything, but we have a long way to go between now and adulthood. I have college and everything," I said.

Mikey asked me one more time if there was any chance he and I might give it a try and have sex and I told him not unless we get married one day.

"I'm not going to be stupid like some of these other girls I see around me. I know I'm worth more than that and I plan on being somebody. A lot of boys, once they get what they want from you, they're through with you. Why would I want to be with somebody just to let them use me like that? My mama said, if all a boy wants is sex, then that's lust and not love. If a boy really loves you, then he'll wait until you're ready," I said.

"Well Tweety, to be honest with you... I mean...I was just testing you to see what you were gon say. Really, I'm not ready to have sex either. I'm glad you wanna wait til marriage and I respect yo decision. I never told any girl this before but, I'm a virgin too. I was hoping you wasn't one of those fast girls 'cause I really think I like you a lot. In fact, I know I like you. I love you. I mean, I love you even more now," he said.

I was so happy. Mikey was the perfect boyfriend. He was safe to be with and safe to love.

I didn't know he let his mama eavesdrop on the phone to prove a point to her.

CHAPTER TWENTY-ONE

"Something Is Wrong"

Sunday we had the grand opening of our new church. I saw Pastor Jacobs again. It had been a few years. I wondered if he had changed. I couldn't tell. He shook my hand, said God bless you, and walked off without another word. I wondered if this meant he had a change of heart.

Church was packed to the maximum with all the churches coming together. We had a nice time. Mikey and I stood outside in the parking lot and talked after service until it was time to go. There was no need for us to come inside the new church because the church was right on the street. All the cars were parked right as you walk outside, up and down the street. We were happy to finally be free to walk outside. We hung out more than we actually talked.

The next week our church took a trip to Pastor Jacobs' church. We were having a baptism service in a creek in the country. I was one of the baptism candidates. I'd become even more physically developed in the eighth grade with wider hips and a larger backside. I was five feet four inches and a hundred, twenty-eight pounds. I was physically fit due to gym, extra-curricular activities and especially softball exercise workouts, which included running laps around the large field. I looked grown.

When we got to the creek for baptism, we had to change in the woods. People were running from snakes and bugs which made me nervous. I wondered if alligators were in the dirty creek water. I couldn't believe we were going to be baptized in that dirty creek. Pastor Jacobs and Bishop Nichols were already in the water to perform the baptisms. We gathered around and prayed. We were in all white from head to toe. My head was covered with a long white head piece hanging down my back. The rocks were hurting my feet on the dirt road to the creek and I wished I brought my shoes. I had no idea we would be baptized under these conditions. I thought we were going to a lake. The congregation started singing, "Take Me to the Water to Be Baptized." We were standing on a bridge singing. I looked on the side of the creek and watched the baptism line forming.

Tameka, who I hadn't seen in a long time, came to be baptized. She acted stand-offish. I tried to talk to her. I wanted to know why she stopped talking to me and I wanted to explain that Mikey and I was now a couple. When I called her name she ignored me again and again. When I finally tapped her on the arm, she looked at her arm like it was poisoned and then she rolled her eyes at me and walked away. She was angry about me and Mikey talking. I was still hurt over her cold treatment towards me over all the years. I thought we were best friends forever.

I was in the fifth grade when they were together. We had grown up since then. She quit Mikey for another much older and experienced guy and then she left the church. I hadn't seen or talked to her in three years. I just wanted to explain how I felt. One of the girls told me she was going to get Mikey to quit me and get back together with her. I found out that she had been under the impression that Mikey and I started talking as soon as she left the church. I realized how Debbie's gossip turned her against me. Mikey and I were just friends all those years ago but when he told Debbie he didn't like her, I guess she assumed we were together possibly.

In hindsight, I could see why Debbie might have come to the assumption that Mikey and I were secretly going together due to the fact that Mikey and I were always at each other's throats until I spent the night with his sister. I told on Julia, his current girlfriend at the time because she was dating my cousin. That's when we made a pact to be civil towards one another, so we were suddenly being nice to one another and no one knew why. This is also when Mikey and Tameka got together. Debbie suggested to Tameka that Mikey and I were secretly going together behind her back the whole time she and Mikey were together. Debbie didn't know me as well as Tameka knew me. At that time, I had never considered the possibility of being with Mikey because he was way too old for me, and I would have never done that to Tameka. I wanted to tell her but she was being so cold, she never allowed me the opportunity to clear the air. I was hurt because I really cherished our friendship back then and would have given anything to keep our friendship. I also felt that Tameka should have known me better than to believe I would ever deceive her in any way.

At the baptism she talked about me and called me names and it all got back to me. I found myself angry with her. I noticed her trying to talk to Mikey when she thought I wasn't looking. I smiled when he walked off ignoring her. I knew this wasn't her last attempt. We were going to be there the whole day for service at Pastor Jacobs' church. I wasn't worried after Mikey pulled me aside and told me he would never leave me for her because I was ten times finer than her, I was more respectable than her, and he considered her used goods. He said her boyfriend got what he wanted from her and dumped her.

"Look at her. All she got is nice legs. But look at you. You got everything. And unlike her, you're respectable." Mikey said loud enough for everyone to hear.

I almost wanted to defend her because I never knew her to be disrespectable and I thought she was very pretty. I must not have known her as well as I thought.

I was nervous about getting in the water. Someone yelled there was a big water moccasin swimming on the other side of the creek. Mother Jordon had everybody start praying and the baptism continued. When my time came I got submerged completely in the water. I came out trying to get out as fast as possible. My eyes were closed. Pastor Jacobs and Bishop Nichols were lifting me up out of the water, but they weren't lifting me fast enough. I kicked my feet out trying to feel the ground and I missed it. They had to catch me when I fell back in the water again. I was embarrassed, but no one laughed when I got out of the water.

J Bug stared at me a whole lot. He and Erica were no longer together but I was with Mikey and very content. I felt like we would be together forever. I went back into the woods with the other women and changed clothes. I had on a water cap to keep my hair dry. I brushed my hair back into place and went to meet back up with Mikey. Tameka was standing beside Mikey tee heeing and talking. I overheard them talking before they realized I was walking up behind them.

"I can't believe you going with that lil girl!" Tameka said to Mikey, chortling.

"So! What's it to you?" Mikey snapped.

"Well, it's nothing to me..." she started.

"Alright then! Well you ain't got nothing to say about it then!" Mikey said.

Mikey walked away from her. I knew this wasn't the end of it. Couldn't she just get the message? It was obvious she was realizing the grass wasn't as green on the other side over the past three years after dumping Mikey. He was not the type of guy who would ever use a girl for sex and he had a way of making you feel special. He was also proving to be very loyal and trustworthy because I had confided quite a bit in him during our phone conversations. He told me he loved me every night and made me tell him I loved him every night as well. He obviously was no longer interested in Tameka. I was gaining more and more respect for Mikey.

We had a very nice time in church. We sang, shouted and listened to a lot of preaching. We heard a lot of singing as well. Our family had to sing and I also had to sing with the choir. I had to lead off two songs and I was nervous. Everybody had their own choirs from each of the three churches. Other groups were singing and some soloists sang. There were adult and children choirs so service ended late. They cooked a lot of food and fed us very well too. We got home from the three hour drive very late at night. We had school the next day. I also had softball practice after school.

At church a few nights later, Curly was acting weird. She was quiet and withdrawn. Her daddy was now one of our newest Pastors in church. I decided to abandon Mikey and go in the church to sit with Curly. She was staying inside all the time lately, which was very unusual.

I went to sit down next to Curly trying to make light conversation. Her eyes teared up the more I questioned her.

"Well Curly you don't have to sit in here all by yourself like you don't have any friends or anything. I'm your friend. What are you sitting around looking so sad for?" I asked.

"Naw Tweety, see, you just don't know. It's just...I just, well, I don't know. I just have a lot on my mind right now is all. I mean, you wouldn't understand if I tole you." Tears were running down Curly's face.

"Yes I will Curly. Try me. You know you can tell me," I assured her.

"See, I tole yo daddy 'bout it and I'm already scared he gon say something... I mean, Bruh' Ranch wouldn't do that would he? I mean, yo daddy seem real straight... I mean, I feel like I can trust him. See, you just don't know Tweety," Curly rambled on.

Curly started crying so I stood in front of her and leaned back against one of the chairs behind me to shield her face from being seen.

"Curly, what is it?" I asked.

"Man, you real blessed to have a daddy like you got. I wish Bruh' Ranch was my daddy. I mean, you just don't know...y'all real blessed. I'm for real. I mean, y'all is real real blessed," she said.

"Why do you say that?" I asked.

"I'm for real Tweety. I'd give anything to have a daddy like ya'll got. I just wish I could disappear somewhere. My old, low down, dirty daddy...he be coming in my room at night putting his nasty hands on me digging all up in my private parts and laying all on top of me, just like um just some kind of ole dog or something," she said.

"Curly! You're for real?" I said.

"Yeah, I mean you just don't know Tweety. I'm telling you, you just don't know. He treat me like I'm some kind of dog or something digging all up in me and stuff. He just make me sick. I mean he really make me sick Tweety. Girl, you just don't even know. I mean, I can't even tell you what all he be doing 'cause it just...I just be wanting to throw up and stuff just thinking 'bout him and what all he be putting me through," she said, as she cried harder.

"Curly, you're lying! I know your daddy isn't doing anything like that! Please tell me you're lying!" I said.

"Shoot, I wish I was lying. And then my mama...I mean, how I'm gon just tell her something like this right here?" she said.

"Curly, but your daddy's a pastor!" I said.

"Tweety just promise me you ain't gon say nothing 'bout this right here. I'm for real. See I knowed I shouldn've tole you. I knowed I shouldn've even said nothing. See, you gon say something," she said.

"I'm not gonna say anything. I promise. Why don't you tell Sister Nichols or Mother Jordon?" I asked.

"They the last ones I'd tell. I wouldn't tell them if my life depended on it. No way! I'm for real Tweety," she said.

"Why you say that?" I asked.

"Just don't tell nobody. Please don't tell nobody. Please just don't say nothing. Oh God, Tweety, Please, please, please don't say nothing 'bout this right here to nobody!" Curly begged as I grabbed tissue for her.

"I promise I won't say anything, but Curly, you gotta do something," I said.

"Don't worry. I got a plan. Show do. Something gon be done Tweety, so you ain't got to worry, okay? Alright?" she asked.

"Okay... If you sure," I said.

I felt horrible. I couldn't sleep tossing and turning, thinking about Curly. She told her cousin J Bug who in turn told Mikey. J Bug and Mikey snuck over there, climbed through the window and hid in Curley's closet all night with baseball bats. They planned to bust his head open when he came in her room to climb on top of her.

Mikey was just there to show his support and scared to death. He didn't know what he had got himself into when J Bug gave him a bat. Curly let them in her bedroom window and they stood in the closet half the night and slept under her bed the rest of the night until the buses ran again the next day. Her father didn't come into the room that night. Mikey was too scared to go along with it anymore so he didn't go back over there.

I was surprised Curly confided in my daddy about what was going on. All the children loved Daddy and looked up to him as a father figure. Daddy was kind and playful. He made all the children laugh. A lot of the children said they wished he was their daddy and told us how blessed we were. After Curly confided in my daddy, a lot of other people were also finding out. Too many people knew and somehow it got to Mother Jordon and then back to Curly's mother.

They had a meeting and confronted Curly's daddy. In their private meeting with Mother Jordon, Bishop Nichols and his wife, I couldn't understand why he remained a Pastor but he did. Curly told me he stopped touching her though. I was relieved for her. I couldn't understand how her own daddy would want to touch his own child.

****

At school the boy I liked last year named Bobby had become a good buddy. We studied together and helped each other with school work. Girls were still fighting over him, but I had a boyfriend and didn't need or want another one.

One of the girls brought a sexually explicit book to school everybody was talking about. I was curious about the book. I asked the girl for a turn to keep the book. She was giving everybody a week each to keep the book. I had about four or five people in front of me before it was my turn. I got more and more curious as they started sharing secrets, whispering and giggling constantly about the book. I had no idea what "sexually explicit" meant. I thought there would be a lot of kissing and touching with a little more detail than my Harlequin Romance books.

About three weeks later, I finally got a turn to keep the book from school. It was earlier than I expected. After practice, I went home. I was home alone again. Sonia was with Mama. Mama often picked up Sonia from school and brought her to Sister Nichols house while they prepared for the feasts. A new feast was beginning again.

I started reading the book totally shocked by the explicit content, language, and nude photographs. I covered my mouth and laughed at first. I started becoming aroused after a while. I became so aroused I balled up a shirt from my drawer and lay on top of it as I read the book. I began masturbating even though I had no idea what I was doing or what it was called. I just knew I felt aroused.

I pulled my door up in case someone came home. I lay on the bottom bunk bed and moved slowly on top of the shirt while I read. This was the first time I experienced an orgasm. After my orgasm, I continued to move trying to find the feeling again. I had been in my room for at least an hour. I rose to get up and turned colors when I realized Daddy was at the cracked door watching me. When I saw him, it looked like his pants were open, but I was not sure. Maybe he was about to have his shower.

I was extremely embarrassed as I wondered how long he had been standing in my door way. I expected he was going to say something to me, but he never did. I had done a very bad thing. I closed the book and made sure he was gone before I got up and threw the shirt in the dirty clothes basket. I wanted to become invisible. I vowed I would never do this again.

I worried since Daddy didn't say anything to me, that he was going to say something to Mama. I was worried she was going to talk to me. I wanted to hide the book in case she asked me what I was reading. I had never seen naked pictures with men and women on top of one another before. I had never seen a woman entirely naked showing pubic hair in such a sensual way. It made me curious about my body and what I looked like totally naked. I never paid attention to my naked body. I didn't see a complete picture of a man where it showed his genitals because every man was covered by a woman's body. I felt too ashamed to come out of my room the rest of the night, even to eat. I wanted to put off my scolding knowing Mama was going to talk to me about what Daddy saw me doing.

Sonia still slept with Mama and Daddy most of the time. We had the bunk bed in our room for Scootie and Sonia. I had my own bed near the window. We all still slept in the same room.

Mama applied for a three bedroom apartment, but was told it could be awhile before one would become available. Scootie and I both complained to Mama about having to share a room at our age.

Mama never said anything to me about what Daddy saw me doing. I was so sure he would tell on me.

I woke up in the middle of the night. Daddy was standing by my bed when I opened my eyes. He mumbled something about the time and looked at the alarm clock in my window and walked out the room. I thought I felt someone touching me but it must have been Daddy leaning over to see my clock. My cover was down so I pulled my cover up, turned over and went back to sleep.

Strangely enough, the next night I woke up and there was Daddy again. I opened my eyes and reached down to pull my covers up again. He was saying the same thing about seeing what time it was then he walked out. I lay there for a minute and blinked a few times trying to differentiate between reality and my dreams. I decided it was just a dream. I turned over and went back to sleep.

"Healing Roads Journal"

The greatest challenge about writing this book is the exposure it may bring. I'm disclosing a lot of my family and friends and some of them aren't ready to confront the issues presented in this book. Too often, family members are more concerned about protecting the "family image" than in supporting the recovery of the abused child. Certain people expressed concern over me revealing certain molesters. Their desire is for me to keep these people a secret. The word "Secret" can so easily be indicative of shame. I'm not ashamed of my life. It doesn't embarrass me that I was molested because I'm the victim who learned to do more than just survive the experience. I grew stronger and wiser. I don't hate any of my perpetrators; I've forgiven everyone. More importantly I've forgiven myself. I know God has given me courage to tell my story.

Find out why Tweety's nightmares
seemed to be real in
"Don't Touch Me" Volume II

What lessons will Tweety learn in
"The Healing Roads" Volume II

???

The Journey Continues...

CPSIA information can be obtained
at www.ICGtesting.com
Printed in the USA
FFOW03n0547080817
38583FF